DEI

L'ilui

Det. Jennifer Abramowitz
Elka Sima bas Chaim Levi

NYPD Special Victims Squad
and 9/11 First Responder

Ask Rabbi Jack

AS SEEN ON JEW IN THE CITY

RABBI JACK ABRAMOWITZ

FOREWORD BY RABBI GIL STUDENT
AFTERWORD BY ALLISON JOSEPHS

KODESH PRESS

Ask Rabbi Jack
by Jack Abramowitz

ISBN: 978-1-947857-46-9

Published & Distributed Exclusively by

Kodesh Press L.L.C.
New York, NY
www.kodeshpress.com

kodeshpress@gmail.com
sales@kodeshpress.com

Throughout my career in outreach the one issue that has constantly come up is how to help quench the spiritual curiosity of Jews. We are an inquisitive people who need to understand the world around us. Who created the world? Why do bad things happen to good people? Does G-d love me?

During my tenure as the International Director of NCSY, the largest Jewish youth movement in the world, we had to figure out an innovative way to get answers to our participants. There was only one man up for that challenge. With his encyclopedic knowledge and wonderful sense of humor, Rabbi Jack Abramowitz handled thousands of questions that came from all over the world to NCSY.com. Every answer was thoughtful and clear.

While Rabbi Abramowitz has fans all around the world, there was one young man who stood out. This individual had been sending all kinds of Bible questions to Rabbi Abramowitz and loved the answers. He mentioned that he would be in New Jersey for business and would love to take myself and Rabbi Abramowitz out to dinner.

As it turned out, this young man played for the Oakland Raiders and was in town to play the New York Giants. While everyone in the hotel lobby wanted his autograph, this young football star only wanted Rabbi Abramowitz's signature!

Rabbi Abramowitz is a Judaic treasure and I know that you will love his new book of Jewish answers to questions we all have. May the Almighty bless Rabbi Abramowitz with health and strength to continue educating us all for many years to come.

Rabbi Steven Burg
CEO, Aish HaTorah

OHR DAVID

Where Torah becomes a Living Experience.

Dean: Rabbi Yosef Granofsky

בס"ד

Rabbi Jack Abramowitz (a talmid and a friend) does not cease to surprise me. He completed a concise summary of the T"nach in a clear enjoyable way. Now he authored a new work, "Ask Rabbi Jack", dealing with real questions and real issues.

Although time constraints limited me for reviewing the entire book, the many parts I did read were inspiring. Even though we believe the Torah and our Torah lifestyle are absolutely true, we may not be able to explain many ideas and issues in a proper way. In this work, Rabbi Jack explains many of these difficult issues in a very clear and understandable way. In his uniquely humorous way he clarifies these ideas. Not afraid to address these issues and not afraid of being politically incorrect, he successfully makes these ideas understandable in a Torah true manner. Enjoyable to read and very enlightening, this book is a must for anyone involved in Jewish outreach and education. As a Torah educator for over 40 years, I see his book as an invaluable tool.

With Torah Blessings

Rabbi Yosef Granofsky

Rosh Yeshiva

Yeshiva Ohr David, Jerusalem

P.O.B 23049 Jerusalem, Israel 91230
Tel: 02-563-2826 Fax: 02-563-2846
E-Mail: info@ohrdavid.org
Website: www.ohrdavid.org

ת.ד. 23049, ירושלים 91230
טל: 02-563-2826 פקס: 02-563-2846
E-Mail: info@ohrdavid.org
Website: www.ohrdavid.org

USA OFFICE: 140-B Washington Ave Cedarhurst NY 11516 | Tel/Fax: 718-715-1800

Rabbi Jack Abramowitz has spent his entire professional career answering the questions that young people have about Judaism.

Truth to tell, older people have such questions too. But they seldom ask those questions, either because they think they know the answers, or because they are too embarrassed to ask, or because they assume that there are no answers.

In his new book, Ask Rabbi Jack, which is a collection of his previous writings fortified by significant new material, Rabbi Abramowitz demonstrates that there are sophisticated and well-reasoned answers, that one need not be embarrassed to ask them, and that many answers that are commonly adopted are inadequate and inaccurate.

He provides cogent and persuasive answers, guaranteed to satisfy to young and old alike. His answers are based upon traditional religious texts as well as contemporary academic sources. He does not shy away from provocative questions, but instead addresses them articulately with candor, sensitivity, and often a dose of good humor.

What I personally find most appealing in Rabbi Abramowitz's new book is the manner in which he confronts the climate of "identity politics" in which we now find ourselves. We are increasingly defined in terms of how we are identified culturally, religiously, racially, ethnically, or politically. This book provides the reader with the opportunity to sort out his or her own identity, arguing convincingly that one's Jewishness can and must be a major component to our identity. These days it is not only teenagers who struggle with the question "Who am I?" Mature adults struggle with that question as well.

Rabbi Jack, as he is known by his many admiring students and adherents, enables us to meaningfully define our Jewish identity. He helps us respond intelligently not only to the question "Who am I?", but also to the crucial question, "What does it mean for me to be a Jew in today's world?"

For this groundbreaking and comprehensive new book the entire Jewish community, left to right and in between, owes Rabbi Abramowitz its appreciation and gratitude.

Rabbi Dr. Tzvi Hersh Weinreb
Executive Vice President, Emeritus, Orthodox Union
Editor-in-Chief, Koren Talmud Bavli

Other books by Rabbi Jack Abramowitz

The Nach Yomi Companion vol. 1 – Neviim (Prophets)
The Nach Yomi Companion vol. 2 – Kesuvim (Writings)
The Shnayim Mikra Companion
The Taryag Companion
The Tzniyus Book
The God Book

Table of Contents

COVID-19

Foreword

Rabbi Gil Student

Rabbi Jack Abramowitz is a virtuoso of Torah teaching. He conveys Torah concepts that require years to master in language that is understandable and enjoyable. The last part—enjoyable—is important because Torah is supposed to be enjoyable. "The laws of God are right, rejoicing the heart" (Ps. 19:9). Not everyone feels that joy, particularly in school, because they lack the option to learn the subjects they want. Additionally, they may lack the textual skills that would make the study much easier. And some people do not find happiness in intellectual endeavors. It takes a master pedagogue like Rabbi Jack to make substantive Torah fun.

Rabbi Jack's previous books tackle the parts of Torah that are most difficult to make engaging. In various books, he guides students through most of the Bible, a list of all the Torah commandments, required dress codes and Medieval Jewish philosophy with confidence and ease. In his hands, Torah that from a lesser teacher would be boring comes alive. In those earlier books, Rabbi Jack speaks to his students. In this new book, Rabbi Jack engages in a dialogue, a question and answer. This takes the book in a dizzying tour of Torah topics, forcing Rabbi Jack to engage in topics across the gamut of Torah, requiring him to reveal his masterful command of so many subjects while still maintaining his sense of humor and his rare ability to speak directly to his readers.

I have a friend who spent one summer, during his years studying at a college-level yeshiva, serving as staff in a camp for adults with limited Jewish background. In the orientation, the rabbi in charge told the young staff members that if any attendee asked them a question on Jewish thought, they must respond, "I don't know, let's ask a rabbi." My friend asked the rabbi, "Won't they think that after over a decade of yeshiva, we don't know anything?" The rabbi replied, "They will be correct." The yeshiva curriculum has evolved in the subsequent decades but it still focuses mainly on textual skills and select topics. For good pedagogical and sociological reasons, much of the Torah remains outside the standard curriculum, waiting for the motivated student to find and study it. Too many people never take that initiative.

This book is not just for beginners, for outsiders trying to take a peek at the Torah. This book is for insiders, as well. It is perfect for the beginner and also for the yeshiva student with broad interests and the yeshiva graduate whose interests and questions have expanded since his youth. Rabbi Jack grounds the reader in traditional ideas and sources, couched in accessible language and arguments. At the Pesach Seder, we invite people in, "Let all who are hungry, come and eat." In all his writings and particularly this book, Rabbi Jack offers the same invitation to all those who are hungry for Torah, who come with questions about Jewish practice and belief, who wish to learn more about what Jews do and why. If they did not teach you this in yeshiva, you are not exempt from learning it. You must take the initiative, by studying on your own, asking questions to learned people, and finding teachers like Rabbi Jack to guide you in your studies of the vast and diverse subjects within the Torah.

Rav Betzalel Cohen, one of the two great Cohen brothers who served as senior religious judges in nineteenth century Vilna, in the introduction to his *Responsa Reishis Bikkurim*, argues that he can fulfill the mitzvah of teaching Torah by publishing his insights. When you write a Torah book and people then learn it, you are teaching them Torah. This view redeems the lonesome writers who sit behind computers all day, disseminating Torah through the written word rather than through the classroom.

Rav Moshe Feinstein (twentieth century, US; introduction to *Dibberos Moshe, Bava Metzi'a*) goes further. He says that we are obligated to teach

Torah to as many people as possible. If you can teach 100 people but only teach 50, you have not fulfilled your obligation. Therefore, if by publishing your Torah insights you reach more people, you are biblically obligated to publish them as part of the mitzvah to teach Torah. According to Rav Feinstein, a Torah scholar is obligated to publish his insights in a book in order to teach to his readers.

Rabbi Jack offers a unique voice of sophisticated but accessible Torah for a broad audience. I have not had the time yet to read carefully every page of this book so I cannot say that I agree with every phrasing and conclusion. However, I can say with confidence that Rabbi Jack's Torah teachings in this book will enhance your understanding of Judaism, engage you with traditional texts and opinions, challenge you to rethink your assumptions, and inspire you to learn even more. In my opinion, there is a desperate need for a book of this kind and Rabbi Jack fulfills a great mitzvah by publishing it for the thinking Jew of our day, as he expertly teaches both the novice acquiring his first knowledge of Judaism and the inquisitive yeshiva graduate expanding beyond the standard curriculum.

Gil Student
Elul 5780
Brooklyn, NY

Author's Introduction

The other day, my sister was giving me a good-natured hard time that I should have gone to medical school, the medical field generally being more lucrative than my chosen career path. While I had adequate grades in the sciences to pursue such a vocation, I had to inform my sister that I simply lacked sufficient passion for medicine. I'm a firm believer in the old adage that if you do what you love, you'll never work a day in your life, and in that I've been lucky. (Admittedly, both *Forbes* and *Psychology Today* call "do what you love" terrible advice, so I've been particularly lucky. Take your career and mental health guidance from them and not from me.)

The part of my career that I love best has always been answering questions. This started when I worked for NCSY, the youth division of the Orthodox Union. After regularly receiving umpteen unsolicited questions, largely but not exclusively from our teen constituents, I recommended that we formalize the service with a web page and a dedicated email address, and thus "Ask NCSY" was born.

Ask NCSY attracted tons of questions, many of which I later collected into a booklet for NCSY advisor training purposes. Two of my favorites were:

- "If a glob of dough is stuck to the ceiling, such as after a food fight, does it have to be removed before Pesach since a dog can't reach it?" (This person had a fundamental misunderstanding of the difference between "fit for a dog to eat" and a dog's ability to access it); and

• Am I allowed to lift weights at the gym if I make an angry face while doing it? (If you're not making an angry face, you're probably not doing it right!)

When I transitioned to other departments within the OU, I started receiving questions from an even broader population—literally global!—on an even greater array of questions. Many of these had nothing to do with my assigned areas of responsibility. When I asked my colleague who fielded the questions why she assigned them to me, she replied, "I like the way you answer them." Fair enough. It's good to be appreciated, I guess!

When I got involved with Jew in the City, my main responsibility was answering still more questions! The difference was that many of the questions I answered were to be shared publicly, on the Jew in the City website. Accordingly, these are longer and have a more formal style, citing more sources than I otherwise might include in a reply.

What's crucial to note is that I answer questions but I don't *poskin shailos*. That's not to say that I don't receive plenty of questions about unique or personal halachic issues; I do. But these I refer to appropriate authorities and I don't generally share them publicly, for fear that others might overapply halachic responses not appropriate for their own circumstances.

Also, these are *my* answers but I never claim that they are *the* answers. I've learned that no matter what one has to say, there will almost always be an outlier who differs. I once made a statement online that the *bracha* after eating rice is *borei nefashos*. While this is the (near?) universal position, I received some strong pushback from a reader who said that he recited *al hamichya*. If I could receive such impassioned opposition on what is truly the least offensive and least disputed statement in Judaism, you can bet that I get pushback when I actually express an opinion on a subject in which there is genuine debate!

I have tried to be intellectually honest in my replies and to let my research dictate my responses rather than cite sources that support my preconceived conclusions. On occasion, this has led to answers that are the exact opposite of what I expected. The more common result is that sometimes my replies favor the more stringent position, while other times they favor the more lenient. In both cases, I have experienced passionate pushback. In fact, two of the most spicy online debates ensued following my replies about secular music (for which some deemed me a libertine) and about Marie Kondo (for which others deemed me a fundamentalist). But as a certain *rav* told me when I was writing *The Tzniyus Book*, if half the people think you're too far to the right and the other half think you're too far to the left, that's a pretty decent indicator that you're in a good place.

I'd like to thank: my wife, Alana, AKA Morah Alana, who has indulged the hours every Sunday that I've invested in answering the questions that became the articles collected in this volume; our friend Channah Leah Siegel, who for years has suggested that I collect some of my Q&A into book form; Rabbi Alec Goldstein for his interest and assistance in bringing this work to light; Rabbi Gil Student, whose work I have long admired, for contributing the foreword; Rabbi Steven Burg, Rabbi Dr. Tzvi Hersh Weinreb and Rabbi Yosef Granofsky—role models, friends and mentors all—for their willingness to review and opine on the material collected herein; Allison Josephs and Sara Levine of Jew in the City for allowing me to partner with them in their *avodas hakodesh*; Daniel Adler and Rabbi Chaim Bronstein for their unwavering support. (Please backdate that last set of acknowledgments to the preface for *The God Book*, in which I neglected to acknowledge their contribution. Belated thanks!) Finally, I'd like to thank all those people, most of whose names I don't even know, whose questions over the years have pushed me to learn and grow, 'דאמר ר

.חנינא הרבה למדתי מרבותי ומחביירי יותר מרבותי ומתלמידי יותר מכולן

Rabbi Jack Abramowitz

18 Elul, 5780

P.S. – Look for more on the *Ask Rabbi Jack* YouTube channel!

Jews and Judaism

What is Judaism?

Q. I'm confused as to whether being Jewish is a religion, a race, a cultural identity or all three. If it's not a race, then how come Jewishness is inherited?

A. This is a tricky topic so let's define what things are.

A race is (presumably) a grouping of humans with shared biological distinctions. There are scientists, however, who assert that the concept of race is a construct. They maintain that there's only one race—the human race—and that any distinctions are only significant because we've decided that they are. (There's no inherent reason why skin color should be a more significant indicator or racial determinant than hair color or eye color.)

Ethnicity refers to shared cultural aspects that distinguish one group from another. Ethnic groups can share language, history, religion and/or ancestry, among other things that make them distinct from other cultures. Black vs. white is a matter of race; Spanish vs. Portuguese (for example) is a matter of ethnicity.

Religion, of course, is a belief system.

So where does Judaism fit into these categories?

Race, insofar as it exists at all, is a function of DNA. While there is a cluster of genes associated with being Jewish, non-Jewish people can possess those genes, and there are entire Jewish communities that don't have them (presumably because these communities became isolated before those haplotype markers entered the DNA). Finally, a person can't change his race but a person who isn't Jewish can become Jewish. So it's not looking good to define Judaism as a race.[1]

What about ethnicity? There is definitely such a thing as Jewish culture—imagine Yiddish theater, borscht-belt comedians, and bagels with cream cheese and lox. But these things do not truly define Jews as an ethnicity. In fact, these examples are more indicative of Ashkenazi Jewish culture, or even of American Jewish culture. The experiences of Iraqi Jews, Syrian Jews, Yemenite Jews, Hasidic Jews, and other populations are very different from one another. These groups are all Jewish but they lack commonalities in dress, food, and 2,000 years of language and history.

So, obviously, Judaism must be a religion, right? Ehhh… it's not that simple.

There's certainly a religion called Judaism but not everyone who calls himself Jewish observes that religion. First of all, there are many flavors of Judaism: Orthodox, Conservative, Reform, Reconstructionist, Humanistic, etc. Some of these will tell you that what others are doing is 100% against Judaism, yet they're all Jews. Additionally, many Jews are completely secular. They ascribe to no religious beliefs whatsoever and yet they're still Jewish. Finally, have you heard of Saint Teresa Benedicta of the Cross? How about Cardinal Jean-Marie Lustiger, Archbishop of Paris? Born Edith Stein and Aaron Lustiger, respectively, these are prominent Catholics who were born Jewish. (There is also the legend of Pope Andreas, but that tale is unconfirmed.) Such people are still considered Jewish by *halacha* and anti-Semites alike. So one can practice widely different forms of the religion, no religion or an altogether different religion and still be Jewish.

---

1. While Judaism may not be a race, it should be noted that anti-Semitic attacks are nevertheless a form of racism. In 2018, US Magistrate Mark Hornsby of Louisiana ruled in a case brought by Joshua Bonadona. Bonadona, a convert to Christianity, was turned down for a job because of his "Jewish blood." While the crime was motivated by anti-Semitism, this could not be considered a case of religious discrimination because Bonadona practiced Christianity. The Nazis also targeted Christians who had Jewish ancestry, such as Sister Edith Stein, as discussed elsewhere in this article. Despite being a practicing Catholic nun, Stein was sent to Auschwitz, where she died in the gas chamber, because of her Jewish ancestry. The reality is that haters don't care what the scientific classification of a race is and laws have to protect people from the harsh realities of hatred even if the perpetrators are acting out of ignorance.

So, if Judaism is not a race, nor an ethnicity, nor is it limited to religion, then what is it? Historically, the Jews were considered a nation, with a common history, religion and homeland. This is the way the Jews are described throughout the Bible. Consider Exodus 19:6: "You shall be to Me a kingdom of priests and a holy nation." This remained so even after the Jews were exiled from their land, as seen in Esther 3:8: "There is a certain nation scattered and dispersed among the nations in all the provinces of your kingdom…." (An exhaustive list of Biblical references to the Jews as a nation would take up *wayyyy* too much space.)

That the Jews were a nation would have been the accepted definition through the Middle Ages and even into modern times. Things started to change in the nineteenth century with the political ideology of nationalism. Previously, it was not taken for granted that a nation—such as the Jews—necessarily had to have its own land but the popular definitions changed. New assumptions, such as that that a nation had to have its own government, changed the way people viewed the Jews. (And let us not overlook the impact of nationalism on the modern Zionist movement, since it also assumed that a people needed a land.)

We might consider ourselves a nation but others might now have a different understanding of that term. So, if Jews are not a race, not an ethnicity, not just a religion and not a nation as others understand nations, then what the heck are we?

Again, let us turn to the Torah regarding the origins of the Jewish people:

"We are all the sons of one man…" (Genesis 42:11). "All the souls that were begat by Yaakov were 70 souls, and Yoseif was already in Egypt… And the children of Israel were fruitful; they increased abundantly and multiplied. They waxed exceeding mighty and the land was filled with them" (Exodus 1:5, 7).

The Jews—AKA "the Hebrews" and "the Israelites"—are also known as "the Children of Israel" (a phrase that occurs more than 600 times in Tanach), "Israel" being another name for our forefather Yaakov. We are very literally a family, a fact that is obvious from the following *halacha*:

A man is not permitted to marry his paternal grandfather's wife. This prohibition continues uninterrupted up one's paternal line so that even the wife of our forefather Yaakov would be prohibited to one of us (*Hilchos Ishus* 1:6).

This *halacha* only makes sense because we are literally one big family, not just a family in the metaphorical sense of the world. That Judaism is a familial relationship makes perfect sense. Many family members share common DNA markers but other people can marry into the family or be adopted (i.e., convert), carrying their own unique genetic material. Many of us share similar family customs but other branches of the family may develop their own practices. And we start out in the religion of our mothers and fathers but, even if some of our family members abandon it or go astray, they are still our brothers and sisters.

So if you ask me, Jews have aspects of race, ethnicity, and religion, but what we really are is a nation (in traditional terms), which is really just another way of saying that we're a big extended family.

Is Being Chosen Offensive?

Q. *My whole life, I've heard the Jews referred to as "the chosen people." It feels really offensive to think that we consider ourselves better than non-Jews. Isn't everyone created equal?*

A. Let's assume that you work in an office. The boss calls a meeting for all the sales staff to discuss things like quotas and commissions. You show up at that meeting and the boss says, "What are you doing here? This meeting is for sales staff and you're in accounting!" You reply, "Isn't everyone created equal?" The boss could then logically respond, "Of course they are. This meeting just has nothing to do with your job!"

It's sort of like that.

Let's look at the sources of the whole "chosen" thing.

God chose the descendants of Abraham (specifically through Isaac and Jacob) because he was the one who recognized God and reintroduced the idea of monotheism to a world that had fallen into idolatry. In Genesis 17:7, God tells Abraham, "I will establish My covenant between Me and you, and your descendants after you throughout their generations, as an everlasting covenant, to be a God for you and to your descendants after you."

Accordingly, God gives special attention to Abraham's descendants, as Moses details in Exodus chapter 4 when referring to the Exodus from Egypt: "Has any god performed miracles to take for himself a nation from the midst of another nation, with trials, signs and wonders, with war and a strong hand, with an outstretched arm and with great awesome deeds, like all that Hashem your God did for you in Egypt before your eyes?" (verse 34),—and the revelation from Sinai:—"Has a people ever heard God's voice speaking from the midst of the fire as you have heard and live?" (verse 33).

The idea of chosen-ness is stated explicitly in Deuteronomy 14:2: "You are a holy people to Hashem your God, and Hashem has chosen you to be a treasured people for Him from among all the nations on Earth." The prophet Isaiah revisits this idea numerous times—so many times, that he's probably the one who popularized the idea. For example, in chapter 41 of the book that bears his name, Isaiah quotes God as saying, "But you, Israel My servant, Jacob whom I have chosen, the descendants of Abraham, who loved Me, whom I grasped from the ends of the earth, from its nobles I called you and I said to you, 'You are My servant.' I chose you and I did not reject you" (verses 8-9).

So does this mean that some people are better than others? Or that God automatically likes some people better than others? Not at all! There are many other verses, like Numbers 27:16, which refers to God as "Hashem, the God of the spirits of all flesh"—meaning the God of all mankind, not just the Jews. Similarly, the Talmud (Sanhedrin 38a) discusses the question of why God created one man, from whom all mankind is descended. One of the answers given is so that no one should be able to claim descent from a superior ancestor.

There's another relevant Talmudic story, recounted on both Megillah 10b and Sanhedrin 39b. It is recorded in Exodus that the Jews sang a song of praise at the Red Sea to give thanks for their salvation. According to Talmudic exegesis, the angels also wanted to take this opportunity to sing God's praises but God did not permit them to do so. Rather, He chastised the angels, saying, "My children are drowning in the sea and you want to sing?" From this it is evident that the Egyptians (and other nations) are also God's children, about whom He also cares.

So if the Jews are indeed chosen, for what are they chosen? Well, for one thing, they were chosen to receive the Torah. Jews have 613 commandments (plus innumerable rabbinic enactments) rather than the seven laws commanded of all mankind. That sounds like we were chosen for responsibility.

Then there's Amos 3:2, which says, "Only you have I chosen from all the families of the earth, therefore I will punish you for all your sins." That sounds like the Jews were chosen for accountability.

Of course, Isaiah, who invokes the idea of chosen-ness so many times, also spells things out a little. "Behold My servant, I will support him; My chosen one, whom My soul desires; I have placed My spirit upon him, he will bring justice to the nations" (Isaiah 42:1). So the Jews are meant to be an example to the other nations, or as Isaiah puts it in verse 6 of this chapter, "a light unto the nations." This we have certainly done—just consider the religions that have incorporated the Jewish Bible into their own scriptures! (This idea of "a light unto the nations" is also the reason that Jews, unfair though it may seem, are always held to a higher standard than everybody else. That's why modern nation of Israel—a democratic country with women's rights and freedom of religion—is always accused of human rights violations by oppressive dictatorships.)

So being "chosen" doesn't mean inherent superiority. It means more responsibility, more accountability and an obligation to set an example. Being chosen means that Abraham's descendants (through Isaac and Jacob) are drafted for this role. Others can always get in on the action if they want to, through conversion to Judaism. If they do, they will be equally obligated in these duties. So, at the end of the day, "chosen" doesn't even mean "exclusive." It's merely the difference between being drafted and enlisting voluntarily.

Defining Orthodoxy

Q. What is the exact definition of an Orthodox Jew? I see that some men have peyos and others don't; some women wear pants and others don't. Where's the line?

A. To answer this question, we need a bit of a history lesson.

The word "Orthodox" doesn't appear in the Tanach, the Talmud or the *Shulchan Aruch*. In Jewish thought, there are simply Jews, and the Torah applies equally to all of them. This idea is expressed in numerous verses, including "There shall be one Torah for those who are born Jewish and for the converts who dwell among you" (Exodus 12:49) and "You shall have one law for yourselves..." (Leviticus 24:22), among others.

This doesn't mean that everyone was equally knowledgeable or observant. Even in Bible times, there were more observant people and less observant people—the prophets wouldn't have chastised them for Sabbath-violation, idolatry or acts of violence if such were not the case! Similarly, throughout the Talmud, we see that some people could be depended upon when it came to separating tithes or observing the laws of ritual purity, and others could not. There were always "frum" people and "not-so-frum" people, but they were all simply "Jews."

This changed in modern times with the introduction of Reform Judaism. (I'm going to have to oversimplify, and I don't claim that this is the entirety of the history, so please feel free to read up on it more if the subject interests you.) In brief, in early nineteenth-century Europe, Jews were becoming citizens for the first time, so they no longer lived in ghettos and they started dressing like their non-Jewish neighbors. (In short, they were assimilating.) After Napoleon was defeated, Jews started to lose their rights and were converting to Christianity in order to retain them. The more traditional element called upon the Jews to re-segregate themselves but a new movement sought to—follow me here—*reform* Judaism by "modernizing" it. This included holding services in the vernacular (and with mixed seating), introducing cantors and choirs, abolishing the second day of the various festivals, and other changes. (One surprising idea was the rejection of the yearning for the return of Israel as the

Jewish homeland, with Germany being seen as the "new Zion." Clearly, in retrospect, that idea did not work out and has since been reevaluated.)

Some felt that reform was necessary but that Reform Judaism's changes had gone too far too fast. Rabbi Zacharias Frankel, who considered himself a moderate between the traditionalists and the reformers, wrote that "the means (of change) must be applied with such care and discretion… that forward progress will be reached unnoticed, and seem inconsequential to the average spectator." In other words, change needed to be more *conservative*.

So, we have an offshoot calling themselves "Reform" and a reaction to that offshoot calling themselves "Conservative." Orthodoxy did not arise in response to those movements. Rather, it was the stream of Judaism that had always existed. "Orthodox" was the label placed upon the traditional Jews in order to differentiate them from the other streams. (After all, it wouldn't do to simply call them "the Jews," would it?)

Differences in theology notwithstanding—and there are some pretty significant ones—all streams of Judaism are ultimately one religion. When filling in a check box for religious affiliation, it would not be uncommon to see a dozen or more different Christian denominations listed separately, but one option for "Jewish." Similarly, people make lateral moves between different streams of Judaism all the time without converting.

This is because Judaism sees people as Jewish regardless of their level of religious affiliation. And, under Jewish law, the same Torah applies to everyone, though some may observe more and others may observe less. "Orthodox" is an artificial construct, invented simply as a convenience to differentiate the traditional Jews from the offshoots. There is no law of Orthodoxy, there's simply observing the Torah.

So, let's use your example. Bob and Sally both identify as Orthodox. Bob will only eat in restaurants with certain rabbinic supervisions, while Sally will eat a salad in places with no supervision whatsoever. Bob feels that Sally's actions are wrong. Sally either doesn't know any better, she disagrees, she just doesn't care. This is the way things have always been, since time immemorial: some people are more observant, others are less observant. Nowadays, however, we have the word "Orthodox" to quibble over. That label really doesn't matter so much.

Where's the line, you ask? Sabbath observance is generally the make-or-break determiner of observance. It has significance in Jewish law, such as defining eligibility to serve as a witness and to handle wine without concern. In terms of philosophy, Maimonides outlines thirteen "principles of faith" that Jews are expected to accept (God is One, He has no form, He gave the Torah, He rewards and punishes, etc.), though the details and parameters are beyond our scope right now.

In short, who is Orthodox? If you ask me, anyone who keeps Shabbos, self-identifies as Orthodox, and doesn't hold any beliefs that Maimonides' list would call heretical could qualify. If they dress differently than I do or eat in places I wouldn't, they may be less observant (or I may be overdoing things) but that's the way things have always been.

Zionism

Q. I have Orthodox friends who are very pro-Israel, but I have also read that some forms of Orthodoxy are vehemently anti-Zionist. I've heard of sects who consider the concepts of Zionism and Judaism to be two completely separate belief systems. What is the role (if any) of Zionism in an Orthodox interpretation of the Torah? Is Zionism simply a matter of individual beliefs and opinions?

A. Before I can answer why people are pro-Zionism or anti-Zionism we need to define what Zionism is. In its most basic form (and it is a very complex topic) I would say that Zionism is the idea that Jews can self-determine in the land of Israel before Moshiach (the Messiah) arrives.

The Talmud, based on several Bible verses, discusses what's called the *shalosh shevuos* (three oaths). The part that's relevant to our discussion is that one of these oaths is that we agree not to try and take back the land of Israel, in exchange for which the nations of the world will not oppress us with undue harshness. Based on this, some Chasidic sects take the position that there should be no Jewish state until Moshiach comes. (It must be noted, however, that these sects have large presences in Israel, which they recognize as the Holy Land. They have no objection to Jews living in Israel, they just think that there should not be Jewish rule until the Messianic era.)

The overwhelming majority of Orthodox Jews feel otherwise. (I don't have exact figures but, anecdotally, the turn-out for the annual Salute to Israel parade is hundreds of thousands and the Jewish counter-protest—the most extreme of the anti-Zionist group—is something like a dozen.) Why are so many Orthodox Jews Zionists? First of all, the "oath" only prohibits us from seizing the land by force. We didn't seize it; it was given to us by UN declaration. Nothing in the "oath" prevents us from accepting the land as a gift, or from using force to defend it once it's in our possession.

Secondly, the nations of the world did not honor their end of the bargain, which was not to oppress us too harshly. (The Holocaust ended just a few years before the State of Israel was established. Even before then, the Spanish Inquisition and the pogroms were certainly unnecessarily harsh!)

Even among "Zionist" Jews, there are different positions. Since you asked about the Orthodox, we're probably talking about religious Zionism, which sees the restoration of the Jewish homeland as the first step in the redemption process. The Bible promises that the arid deserts would bloom (see, for example, Isaiah chapter 35), which is exactly what happened when the Jews returned to Israel after World War II. But there's also political Zionism, cultural Zionism, and more.

So one relatively small faction of Orthodox Jews are anti-Zionist and they do have a religious rationale for their belief. Mainstream Orthodox Judaism, however, is definitely Zionist in one way or another, though they may disagree in the details and in their politics. To assume that all Orthodox Jews are in lockstep beyond that point is like assuming that all Americans who believe in democracy necessarily agree on healthcare, immigration and the economy.

Outdated Rituals

Q. *Someone told me that the mitzvos don't count anymore,—that all God wants is our goodness. Why else would the prophet Micah say, "What does God require of you? Only to do justly, love mercy, and walk humbly with thy God?" (Note that he says "only.") Also, I know there's something about circumcision of the heart instead of the flesh. Doesn't that mean it's all in our heart and that ritual is passé?*

A. Despite what some people might have you think, the *mitzvos* never go out of style. This point is made repeatedly in the Torah. Deuteronomy 29:28 says, "That which is revealed is for us and our children forever, to carry out all the words of this Torah." So we see that the Torah applies forever. Furthermore, no additions or deletions might be made; Deuteronomy 13:1 says, "All these things that I command to you, be careful to perform. Do not add to it or detract from it."

But couldn't God change His mind? No. Numbers 23:19 tells us, "God is not a person that he should lie, nor a human being that he should change his mind." So Micah could not mean that *mitzvos* no longer apply because (a) the Torah applies forever, (b) *mitzvos* may not be removed from the Torah and (c) God does not change His mind.

So what did Micah mean? I believe that Micah is addressing the what, rather than the how. This is similar to the famous story of Hillel and Shammai, as told in the Talmud, *Shabbos* 31a:

A non-Jew who wanted to convert to Judaism approached the great sage Shammai and said, "Accept me as a convert on the condition that you can teach me the entire Torah while I stand on one foot." Shammai drove the man away for being ridiculous and wasting his time. The man then approached Hillel with the same offer, "Accept me as a convert on the condition that you can teach me the entire Torah while I stand on one foot." Hillel accepted this condition and responded, "That which is hateful to you, do not do to others. That is the entirety of the Torah; the rest is all explanation—now go and study it!"

What Hillel—and Micah—are telling us is that God wants us to be good people. What the Torah tells us is *how* to be good people. It's like if I tell you, "All I want is for you to make me a tuna casserole." I could leave you to your own devices, but it makes a lot more sense for me to give you a recipe.

The same is true with the idea of "circumcising the heart." You don't cite a source for "circumcision of the heart instead of the flesh" and I don't know of a verse that suggests circumcision of the heart to the exclusion of the regular kind. The phrase appears in Deuteronomy twice, as well as in Jeremiah. The fact that the Torah tells us twice to "circumcise our hearts" (Deut. 10:16 and 30:6) should dispel any thought that it's instead of regular circumcision, which is in the selfsame Torah. In fact, verses like "Hashem your God will circumcise your hearts and the hearts of your descendants so that you may love Him with all your heart and with all your soul, and live" (Deut. 30:6) suggest to me that intention of circumcision of the heart is to enable us to better perform the *mitzvos*, not to obviate them! But no matter how you slice it (no pun intended), circumcision is one of the *mitzvos*, which we have already shown apply forever.

Changing Judaism

Q. *Why does Orthodox Judaism consider some changes—like Maimonides' approach, Kabbalah, or the Chasidic movement—as "kosher" but things like the Karaites' philosophy and other non-Orthodox movements throughout history as non-acceptable changes?*

A. Your question reminds me of something a great man once said: "Now the world don't move to the beat of just one drum. What might be right for you may not be right for some... It takes Diff'rent Strokes to move the world."

This is true in so many areas. Let's take something mundane, like copying and pasting on a PC. I might like to right click and then highlight "copy" and "paste." You might like to hit Control+C and Control+V. Someone else may like to point to the toolbar at the top of the screen and click on the scissor and clipboard icons. We each have our own reason for our preferences—it's more elegant, it's fewer steps, whatever—but at the end of the day, each way gets the job done.

Now let's apply this concept to a religious area. Jewish men are not allowed to shave off the hair at their temples (by which I mean the sides of the head, not the synagogue). These are called *payes* or "sidelocks."

Chasidic practice is to grow the *payes* long. Some curl them, some tuck them behind the ear—there are different styles. I, however, am a *misnagid* (non-*chasid*). I also have *payes* but you might not know it. I simply don't have the barber shave my sideburns. If he did, I wouldn't have *payes*.

Another example: there is a law that a Jewish man must separate the upper portion of his body from the lower portion of his body when reciting blessings or prayers. Chasidim do this with a special belt called a *gartel* that is designated to be worn during prayer. *Misnagdim* also follow this law, we just don't require a special belt for it. The belt we're already wearing—or for that matter the waistband of one's pants—accomplishes the same thing.

Someone might ask me why I don't have *payes* or wear a belt for prayer—but I do. They're just not as conspicuous as a Chasid's might be. We're doing the same thing, albeit in different ways. It's like he's right-clicking and I'm hitting Control+V.

Orthodox Judaism is a bigger tent than most people think. There's more than one way to look at things and more than one way to get things done. I was raised Reform but it never spoke to me. I was exposed to Chabad and, while I enjoyed it, their approach wasn't my flavor, either. When I was exposed to NCSY, that was more my style. Within NCSY, I gravitated towards the righter-wing ("black hat") element of a very mixed-bag advisory staff; others favored those with a more "modern" approach. I have never cared for Carlebach-style services (i.e., with copious amounts of song and dance); others love them. It takes Diff'rent Strokes to move the world.

The saying is that there are *shivim panim laTorah*—70 approaches to the Torah. I always say that 70 is a very large number, but it's also finite. You may be into *Chasidus*, someone else might be into Kabbalah, I might favor a more rationalistic approach—s'all good. But just because many things are inside the very big tent, that doesn't mean that everything is. Some things are decidedly on the outside.

You mention the Karaites. This movement dates back to the ninth century. It was preceded by such movements as the Sadducees and the Boethusians, which date back to the time of the Second Temple. What all these movements have in common is that they reject the Oral Law. According to Orthodoxy, acceptance of the Oral Law is an inherent religious belief. A movement that teaches otherwise cannot be accepted as just another approach. It's outside the tent.

Similarly, various "messianic" movements that teach that Jesus is the messiah. While there is certainly room for some debate regarding the identity of the messiah—this has been the case from Talmudic times right up through today—the Jesus-as-messiah ship has long since sailed. He doesn't fit the Biblical criteria for being the messiah and, besides, he died long ago. (There's no precedent in Judaism for a "second coming.") Additional ideas, such as that Jesus is God, a part of God, the son of God, or even a prophet, likewise have no basis in Jewish thought. The same is true of attributing a variety of unrelated Bible verses to the circumstances of Jesus' life. Bottom line, any movement that presents Jesus as the messiah is outside the tent. (This is not limited to Jesus. The same would be true of Shabbetai Tzvi, David Koresh, etc. Whether or not they were ever serious contenders for the job, they have all been eliminated from the running.)

Now, Maimonides and the Baal Shem Tov had innovative ideas that initially rocked the boat. Why did theirs ultimately get accepted? First of all, their approaches to various matters, while novel, still fit within the tent. Second of all, Marcel Duchamp.

I'm going to have to explain that, aren't I?

Marcel Duchamp was a modern artist. One of his works, *Prelude to a Broken Arm*, consists of a shovel hanging from the ceiling by a wire. He didn't even make the shovel, he just hung it from the ceiling! It's in the Museum of Modern Art in New York.

I first saw this when I was in college and it angered me. "I could do that!" I railed. I was working in a restaurant at the time and one of the waitresses was an art student. "Duchamp can do things like that," she explained, "because he has already established his credentials."

The light bulb went off. James Joyce could get away with *Finnegan's Wake* because he's James Joyce. The Beatles could get away with *Revolution Nine* because they're the Beatles. This I already knew. Similarly, I realized, Marcel Duchamp could get away with *Prelude to a Broken Arm* because he's Marcel Duchamp. I may not get this work of art but my lack of understanding doesn't delegitimize it. People who know far more about art than I ever will have accepted it.

You and I can express new ideas but they probably won't get much attention. We're not likely to spark any movements and our ideas are not likely to become accepted as religious approaches. But we're not Maimonides. When you're the author of the *Mishneh Torah* (the first code of Jewish law, predating the *Shulchan Aruch* by nearly 400 years), *Sefer HaMitzvos*, the Commentary on the Mishna and *Guide for the Perplexed*, your ideas are going to be heard. If these ideas are outside the box, people may become angry or confused. But being outside the box doesn't mean they're outside the tent. As long as they're in the tent—which Maimonides' ideas were—there's a very good chance they will ultimately be accepted.

"Old" vs. "New" Testaments

Q. *How do you respond when people claim that Judaism and the "Old Testament" are the vengeful part of the Bible and Christianity has a monopoly on love? As many times as you point out commandments like "love your neighbor as yourself," some people will still zero in on things like stoning a disobedient child.*

A. The "fun" thing about religion (he said sarcastically) is that both supporters and detractors can cherry-pick verses to "prove" that the religion means whatever they want it to mean. In our current political climate, this is most noticeable with Islam. There are plenty of Muslims who preach that Islam is a religion of peace, and they have the verses in Qur'an to support it. For example, Qur'an 3:199 says, "And indeed, among the People of the Book are those who believe in Allah and what was revealed to you and what was revealed to them, humbly submissive to Allah. They do not exchange the verses of Allah for a small price. Those will have their reward with their Lord. Indeed, Allah is swift in account." (In the Qur'an, "People of the Book" refers to non-Muslim monotheists, specifically Jews and Christians.)

Conversely, if you've seen ISIS beheadings and attacks around the world, you're probably aware that there are those who consider Islam to be a religion of hate; they, likewise have verses to support their position. For example, Qur'an 5:51 says, "O you who have believed, do not take the Jews and the Christians as allies. They are allies of one another and whoever is an ally to them among you, then he is one of them. Indeed, Allah does not guide the wrongdoing people." One could find many more verses to support either side of this debate.

But your question is about Judaism vis-à-vis Christianity. Is Judaism really the religion of vengeance and Christianity the religion of love? As with Islam, I can cherry-pick verses from both the "Old" and "New" Testaments to prove whatever I want.

It may surprise you to learn that Jesus said, "Do not think that I have come to send peace on earth. I did not come to send peace, but a sword. I am sent to set a man against his father, a daughter against her mother, and a daughter-in-law against her mother-in-law" (Matthew 10:34-35). That sounds pretty violent to me!

A funny story: At the time of the first Gulf War, I attended a clergy panel about whether or not we should participate in such a conflict. A colleague (a priest) said that we shouldn't, based on various New Testament verses. I challenged his sources with the aforementioned "I did not come to send peace, but a sword." He replied, "That's clearly a metaphor. Jesus didn't carry a sword; his disciples didn't carry swords...." I replied with a quote from John 18:10, "Then Simon Peter, who had a sword, drew it and struck the high priest's servant, cutting off his right ear."

Similarly, in the Parable of the Ten Minas, Jesus says, "I tell you that to everyone who has, more shall be given, but from the one who does not have, even what he does have shall be taken away. But these enemies of mine, who did not want me to reign over them, bring them here and slay them in my presence" (Luke 19:26-27). (There are those who will tell you that, as part of a parable, these aren't Jesus' own words but those of the character in his story. However, the character who says these words is the exemplar for Jesus himself.)

My point in doing this is not to bash Christianity. It is simply to illustrate that a Jew, a Muslim, a Christian, a Hindu, a Buddhist, a Wiccan, an atheist—you name it—can find verses to make their own belief system look good or someone else's look bad. Out of context, anything can be made to mean whatever you want it to mean. This is what's going on when people posit Judaism as the product of a God of vengeance. They are cherry-picking verses out of context to support their preconceived conclusions.

Another factor is that the text of the Torah doesn't give the complete story. For example, the Torah prohibits performing acts of labor on Shabbos, but it doesn't define what constitutes labor. You cite the case of the *ben sorer u'moreh* (stubborn and rebellious son), in Deuteronomy chapter 21. If the full details of a weekly mitzvah that affects everyone (i.e., Shabbos) are not provided in the text, it should not surprise you that the details of an obscure mitzvah like *ben sorer u'moreh* are not explicit. I provide just a few of the details in my book *The Shnayim Mikra Companion*:

> If a person has a thoroughly rotten son who absolutely will not toe the line, the parents may have him flogged in an attempt to rein him in. If he's completely incorrigible, he may even be put to death because his evil fate is inevitable. (To be eligible for this punishment, the boy must steal money from his father, use it to buy meat, which he must consume undercooked with a certain quantity of wine in front of his father's house with a circle of bad friends. There are a lot of other conditions, too. The Talmud in Sanhedrin 71a tells us that the case of the rebellious son never happened and was only included in the Torah for the lesson it imparts.)

Let's read that last line again: "The Talmud in Sanhedrin 71a tells us that the case of the rebellious son never happened and was only included in the Torah for the lesson it imparts." So, people get bent out of shape over a mitzvah that Jewish tradition tells us was never actually performed and was never intended to be performed. It seems an awfully hypothetical basis for drawing any "big picture" conclusions about Judaism!

The sheer volume of capital crimes makes a lot of people consider

Judaism to be violent. What they don't tell you are all the parameters necessary for someone to be executed. The person has to be warned not to do the thing he's about to do because it carries a potential death sentence, then he has to go ahead and do it anyway, in the presence of witnesses. He's tried before a court of 23 judges; it takes a simple majority (12 to 11) to acquit but it requires a supermajority (13 to 10) to convict. Judges who initially voted to convict can change their votes to acquit but those who voted to acquit cannot change their votes to convict. There are many other laws favoring the defense over the prosecution. Capital punishment was so uncommon that the Talmud (*Makkos* 7a) says if there was an execution more frequently than once every 70 years, it was a bloody court.

You cite the dictum to love our neighbors as we love ourselves (Leviticus 9:18). The Torah likewise prohibits favoring powerful people in court cases (Leviticus 19:15), taking something that a poor person needs as collateral for a loan (Deuteronomy 24:12), and oppressing widows and orphans (Exodus 22:21) or converts (Exodus 22:20)—even verbally. A skim of the 613 *mitzvos* will reveal hundreds that are clearly meant to protect the weaker members of society and only a handful that cry out for explanation. But even the seemingly troubling ones are far less troubling once one takes the time to look into them.

"But," I hear you ask, "if anyone can cherry-pick verses to make a religion appear as they wish, how do we know you're not doing the same thing?" Good question! And the answer is, because I don't want you to take my sample verses at face value. I encourage you to delve into the Torah, with all of its commentaries and codes of law, to get a big-picture view of things, including the things that require more explanation.

By familiarizing yourself with what the Torah says—and what it actually means—you will become well-equipped to respond to the troubling questions, whether they come from people misrepresenting Torah or from our own minds.

Lenient or Stringent?

Q. How can there be many "right" ways to live a Jewish life? There seems to be only one way, living within the parameters set by the Torah. And if there is

variation in the levels of observance within those parameters why is it acceptable
to choose anything other than the highest levels of observance?

That's an excellent question and there are a lot of different ways one could approach it, so I'm briefly going to hit a lot of different beats. Any one of these could potentially be fleshed out into a full discussion in its own right. For starters, the Torah tells us—regarding the Torah itself—that *lo baShamayim hi*, it is not in Heaven (Deuteronomy 30:12). This means that the Torah is no longer in God's metaphorical "hands." Rather, He has given it to us and it is our responsibility to interpret it. This principle was famously invoked in *Bava Metzia* 59b when a Heavenly voice took sides in a halachic debate. That's all well and good but the Torah is no longer in the Heavenly court's jurisdiction.

There are other verses and dicta that stress the idea that the Torah is subject to many different understandings. For example, Psalms 62:12 says, "One thing God has spoken; two things have I heard." The Talmud in *Sanhedrin* (34a) understands this to mean that a single verse can have multiple meanings and all of them can be correct.

Perhaps the most famous expression of this idea is the dictum that there are *shivim panim laTorah*, 70 facets to the Torah. This idea originates in the Midrash in *Bemidbar Rabbah* (13:16) and was popularized through its use by the Ibn Ezra, the Ramban, the *Zohar*, and others. Now let's try to see how this idea can explain different halachic practices.

Our lives are all different. Some people have stable home lives, others have dysfunctional family situations. Some people are financially secure, others barely make ends meet, if they do at all. Some people have good health and others are chronically ill. The variations are limitless. If life isn't "one size fits all," how can we expect the Torah to be so inflexible as to expect the same thing from all people all the time?

Let's examine an example: Let's say that a person in a particular community is a chronic offender in a certain religious matter and the local authorities want to censure him but there's a concern that doing so might drive this person farther away from Torah observance. Should they go ahead with the reprimand? I think we can agree that there are a lot of variables in this scenario. How big is the chronic offense? How are others being affected? How likely is the possibility that the chastised offender would actually leave Judaism altogether? If he did, would it be because he was sincerely discouraged in his religiosity or would this be a political move on his part, designed to get back at the religious authorities? So the question, "Should we punish a chronic offender if it might drive him farther away?" is one that doesn't have a "one size fits all" answer and automatically leaping for the most stringent approach could do more harm than good.

Having illustrated that the halachic process allows for shades of gray, let us now apply the concept to something more mundane than our previous example. Throughout the laws of *kashrus* you will observe that in various cases of doubt, our practice is often to act stringently but that sometimes, in cases that will cause a person a significant financial loss, one is permitted to act leniently. Does this mean that we can eat non-kosher food if it will cost us money to throw it out? Of course not! It means that in a gray area, it's better to act stringently but not everyone can afford the luxury of doing so. Not everyone can afford to throw away a chicken or a piece of meat and it's not fair to obligate everyone to do so just to uniformly abide by the highest standard.

These are just some obvious examples of why one might follow a lenient position but the underlying principles apply even without such obvious downsides. Sometimes we are lenient just to be intellectually consistent. I'll explain:

One of my favorite Talmudic dicta is that one who is always lenient is a wicked person, while one who is always stringent is a fool (*Chullin* 43b-44a). It's fairly easy to see why one who always looks for the shortcut should be considered wicked but why is always acting stringently considered foolish? Isn't that just the more pious way to act? Rashi explains why it's foolish by referring us to the Talmud in *Eruvin* (7a), as follows.

If a corpse's spine is complete, it conveys ritual impurity when one is under the same roof. There is a difference of opinion as to what renders a spine incomplete: missing one vertebra or missing two vertebrae. Whichever standard is used, the same rule for determining completeness also applies to rendering an animal non-kosher. Therefore, if an animal is missing only one vertebra, there are two possibilities: either it is still considered complete or it is considered incomplete. Each of these results in a stringency and a leniency:

- If a spine missing one vertebra is still considered complete, it can convey impurity (a stringency) but an animal can still be kosher (a leniency);
- If a spine missing one vertebra is considered incomplete, it will not convey impurity (a leniency) but such an animal can no longer be kosher (a stringency).

In this case, taking a stringent position across the board reveals the lack of an actual position because either opinion, when applied consistently, will lead to both a stringent outcome and a lenient outcome. That's not only okay, it's desirable. One should make an honest evaluation and apply the outcomes appropriately. As a colleague of mine once observed, it's easy to just act stringently all the time—it takes effort to figure out when one should be lenient.

I have heard some people lament what they perceive to be the failure of Orthodoxy to find and apply leniencies, followed by numerous examples of such shortcomings. While I concur with the premise that one should not always go straight for the stringencies just because they are the most expedient way to settle an issue, I simultaneously disagree with the assertion that one should necessarily look to apply every leniency simply because they are leniencies. An intellectually honest approach is to evaluate a situation and to reach a conclusion that is appropriate given all the facts at hand.

There a lot of reasons why some people may act stringently in an area while others act leniently. As with anything humans do, these reasons can be good and valid, or an over-application of principles that may not be appropriate in every scenario. Whether one acts leniently or stringently, it's important to act with thought in one's religious observance and not to have a kneejerk reaction. A well-rounded person will find that applying his principles consistently, he may have more leniencies or more stringencies but a person should never be all of one to the exclusion of the other. As the Talmud teaches, that would make us either wicked or foolish, neither or which is a particularly good thing.

NEW! The Orthodox View of Reform and Conservative Jews

Q. *How do Orthodox Jews deal with the Jews who are Conservative and Reform? I have seen observant Jews treat less observant Jews as pariahs. My grandchildren are being raised in a very closed community, where there is no recognition of other branches of Judaism. I am concerned that they will reject us. They have already begun to ask, "Are you Jewish? Why are you wearing pants?"*

A. "Orthodoxy" is just a name applied to the traditional Torah-observant lifestyle that existed prior to the formation of the Reform and Conservative movements in the nineteenth and early twentieth centuries. In the 18th, 17th, 16th, etc. centuries, going back as far as we can record such things, it would have just been called "Judaism." Orthodoxy isn't a brand and it has no universal organizational hierarchy. Anyone who observes the Torah the way our Sages understood it is by default "Orthodox." That makes Orthodoxy a pretty big tent—Ashkenazim, Sefardim, Yemenites, Yekkes, Litvish, Chasidim, "modern," etc.—can all be described as "Orthodox" even though they may observe Judaism in some very different ways.

So why is this important? Because it defines some important parameters. If someone starts a movement within Judaism and they decide that Shabbos should be observed on Thursday, we're going to fundamentally disagree with that because it goes against what the Torah says. So, while I could choose to attend a Satmar *minyan* or a Syrian *minyan* even though they are significantly different from my own Ashkenazi *minyan*, I could not advocate going to a "Thursdaytarian" *minyan* as a viable alternative. This is because they have placed themselves outside the halachic parameters as we understand them.

But what does this say about a Jew who chooses to observe "Thursdaytarianism," or who is born into it? Nothing. Because since time immemorial, all the way back to the Bible era, there have been those who observe the Torah, those who do not, and a huge spectrum of varying degrees of partial observance in between.

It is true that Orthodoxy cannot advise its adherents, "Go to any Jewish denomination you like; they're all the same" because we believe that any viable alternative must conform to the traditional understanding of *halacha* as defined by the Sages. Nevertheless, all Jews are equally Jewish, however observant they may or may not be.

Now, in your experience some observant Jews treat Reform Jews like pariahs? I don't doubt that, but do not mistake it for a matter of Orthodox theology. As noted, there are many varied communities that could be described as "Orthodox." Some of these are more sheltered and unfamiliar with outsiders but that is not a universal constant, nor is it a religious mandate of any kind.

As far as children, that's just the way children are. They're very black and white. Let's say that a child asks, "Why do we have that thing on our door and Billy's family doesn't?" A parent might then explain, "That's called a *mezuzah*, and we have it because we're Jewish; Billy's family isn't." This is all true but it has the unintended consequence that a younger child may then equate the presence of a *mezuzah* with a Jewish family and the absence of a *mezuzah* with a non-Jewish family. If grandma doesn't have one, she must not be Jewish. As children get older, they become more discriminating and learn that the world is not so black and white. This will happen naturally, with growth, so don't worry about the wearing pants thing.

Is every family doing an A+ job of raising their kids? Probably not. Is every community welcoming to strangers? Unfortunately, no. But these are human flaws that exist in all races and religions. They are not a part of some anti-other dogma that is inherent to Orthodoxy any more than they are to Reform or Conservative.

Judaism in Contemporary Society

Welfare and Kollel

Q. *I live in a city with a large Orthodox population and something perplexes me. Many of the families utilize Access cards—the equivalent of food stamps—because they have large families. Yet, they carry expensive purses and although modestly dressed, still do so with expense. I ask myself why must they utilize public assistance meant for the poor if they are making a religious choice to have many children and possibly live without an income or two incomes? Why can't those families go and work to support their families as I need to support mine?*

A. The answer is complicated in that there's no "one size fits all" that suits everyone. This family may have real hardships, the likes of which are not evident from observing them on the surface. That family may be receiving assistance from family members, so they have nicer clothes than they might otherwise be able to afford. Another family may have had parents unsuccessfully looking for work for months. (The economy is still bouncing back as I write this and many places are only hiring part-time to avoid having to give benefits.) Still another family may indeed be cheating the system. That's not cool, but I don't have any reason to believe that it's happening *en masse*.

The fact that people have large families for religious reasons is immaterial. Is that better, worse or the same as a single mother who has numerous children from different fathers? How or why one has children is really irrelevant: the issue is that they're here. So you really can't tell what's going on. I know a family (single mom) that gets government assistance and the woman of the house always looks like a million bucks. They work but their income is too little to survive on. She's mastered the art of thrift store shopping. We have a religious principle to judge others favorably. While I am sure there are many who take aid unnecessarily, I know of many, many cases where that is not the situation. Surface appearances, however, are often very misleading.

Now, there's one thing that you did not specifically ask, about which readers may be wondering, and that's about kollel. Kollel is when the man of the family studies Torah for a living. The yeshiva in which he is learning generally pays a stipend but it's not big money. The woman of the house often works in such cases but she may be pregnant and/or caring for small children, or the family may have a larger number of children, so she may not be able to work continuously or her income plus his stipend may not be sufficient for the size of the family. Accordingly, some people look down upon kollel students as "leeches on society." As is the case with generalizations, such characterization is too broad and unfair.

On the one hand, we have the concept of a "Yissachar-Zevulun" relationship. In ancient Israel, the Tribe of Zevulun (Zebulon) would engage in commerce and they supported the members of the Tribe of Yissachar (Issachar), who studied Torah full-time. The members of Zevulun shared the merit of the Torah study they supported. This is in part the model for the modern-day kollel: business people support those who engage in Torah study and earn merit through it.

But there is also an obligation to teach one's children a trade. In fact, one who does not teach his son a trade is considered as if he taught him to rob (Talmud, *Kiddushin* 30b). Similarly, the Talmud in *Shabbos* (118a) tells us that one should make his Shabbos like a weekday rather than accept charity. [Let's contextualize that last statement. That certainly does NOT mean to work on Shabbos! It means to eat two meals as one does on weekdays rather than the three meals one would normally eat on Shabbos.]

All of this addresses the one who may or may not be working. There is also an obligation to give others charity in a respectable fashion. Anonymity is preferred and we are meant to help people maintain their standard of living, not just help them squeak by. The highest level of charity, however, is helping someone to get a job and become self-sufficient. (Teaching a man to fish instead of giving him a fish, as the saying goes.)

So the kollel situation is multifaceted. It's necessary for our people in order to produce Torah scholars—we'd be in sorry shape without it!—but that's not to say that it's a choice for everyone. Some people do it for a year or two after marriage before entering the business world, while others do it long-term. By and large, however, most people do choose to pursue other forms of employment and those who learn in kollel are not so numerous as to drain a community's resources.

Rock and Roll

Q. As a frum baal teshuvah (returnee to observance) for over 30 years, I have continued listening to my favorite type of music, namely soft rock. I view this music as a gift from Above. Although I have given up many things (we don't have TV), these types of songs help me feel good and, so far as I am aware, have no bad effects. I typically play this music when alone, not in front of the kids. I have heard a lot about this, mostly negative, but these songs bring out the best in me, move me deeply, and help me to be more relaxed. When I think about giving this music up, I am ill at ease. Should I feel like I'm doing something wrong?

A. I may be biased in answering this because, this summer, I saw both The Who and Billy Joel in concert, a tidbit that may reveal my thoughts on the matter.

Defining "secular" music is tricky to begin with. Let's start with classical music. Many people think that listening to Beethoven is fine but listening to Wagner is reprehensible because he was an anti-Semite. I think that PR plays a larger role in that sentiment than most people credit: Hitler used Wagner as his "theme music," while the allies used Beethoven. (The famous notes of Beethoven's Fifth Symphony spell "V" for victory in Morse code: …_) *Lohengrin* and "Ode to Joy" are both the products of German composers; is one permitted and the other prohibited because we don't like one of the composers? Or because the music was favored by the wrong world leader? I don't believe this is a matter of *halacha* so much as one of personal preference. (A more current example would be the question of listening to Pink Floyd in light of Roger Waters' anti-Israel campaigns. It's not prohibited but it may make some people uncomfortable and boycotting Waters is certainly their prerogative.)

Let us assume that instrumentals are okay. Does it then matter when they were composed? Is something from 1850 okay but not something from 1965? I see no reason why that should be the case. Is a tune any less worthy because it was written by Lennon and McCartney? I wouldn't think so. So, here we have a nice guitar tune. If you start singing, "Yesterday, all my troubles seemed so far away..." is it suddenly prohibited? And here we have an elaborate piece with a string ensemble of violins, violas and cellos. Is it made non-kosher when I start singing "Eleanor Rigby picks up the rice in a church where a wedding has been...?" Personally, I don't see it.

Jewish music has long been known to incorporate secular music, from Mordechai Ben David setting the song *Yidden* to the tune of 1979 Eurovision winner *Dschingis Khan*, and Yossi Piamenta adapting Men at Work's "Down Under" as *Asher Bara*, to Shlock Rock's entire catalog. The *shul* I attend traditionally sings *Adon Olam* to the tune of Simon and Garfunkel's "Scarborough Fair" on the High Holidays.

One might wish to argue that, origins notwithstanding, certain genres might be unacceptable. Perhaps, but the aforementioned Yossi Piamenta used to tell the following story. He has a song whose words are "*mitzvah goreret mitzvah va-aveirah goreret aveirah*" (fulfilling one commandment leads to another, and committing one sin leads to another). These words come from the Mishna in *Avos* (4:2). While writing the song, he consulted a rabbi and asked whether it was permissible to set the words of a Mishna to a rock tune. The rabbi replied, "Permitted? It would be a mitzvah!" This is because it helps to disseminate the teaching of the Mishna and will perhaps interest listeners in learning more. In this rabbi's opinion, at least, rock music could be useful and harnessed for holy purposes.

Now, all this is just me talking. There are definitely other positions. Some people would never read a secular book let alone listen to secular music. That's fine. If someone feels that helps to elevate them spiritually, more power to them. But I think it's largely a personal decision rather than a mandate of Jewish law. A lot of us who were raised with our pop music are rather attached to it. As with you, it helps our moods. And *baalei teshuvah* (people who became religious later in life) are generally pretty dedicated. We gave up eating hundreds of non-kosher products and performing umpteen actions on Shabbos. We'd just rather not give up "Bohemian Rhapsody" if we don't really have to!

What we need to do is set our own boundaries of propriety. Are all books appropriate? No. Are all movies? No. The same is true for TV shows, magazines, web sites, and every other form of media and entertainment. I'm okay with the *Harry Potter* books but other people might not be. Similarly, the KISS song "Rock and Roll All Nite" might be within my comfort zone but "F— the Police" by NWA might not be. Songs that make the grade on my approved list might be a step too far for others and that's okay. Just like we choose whether to see G, PG, PG-13, or R films, we get to choose the parameters of our music. Some things will certainly fall within the realm of *halacha* (for example, I think we can all agree that pornography falls outside the bounds of Jewish law), but other things will be up to the reader/viewer/listener's discretion. How much profanity and violence can you tolerate in a movie before you decide it's not for you, or for your kids? Everyone's tolerance level is going to be different.

You might be groovin' to Metallica. Something far more innocuous, like The Mamas and the Papas, might be offensive to another person's sensibilities. But in my opinion, we get to decide. If, as you say, it brings out the best in you, then I think it's a good thing. If it has the opposite effect, it would be a bad thing.

I'm Just Wrong About Rock Music

Q. *I'm confused by your answer to a reader's question about rock music. The halacha strictly forbids songs known as shirei agavim—explicit love songs. This is first mentioned in the Gaonic literature, quoted in Rambam, and codified in Shulchan Aruch. I think a large portion of love songs, especially those from the last 40 years, fall into this category.*

A. Thanks for the pushback. In the comments, I mention that the *Shaar HaTziyun* prohibits singing *shirei agavim* to infants; this is a very narrow prohibition indeed! Most of the traditional sources forbid *shirei agavim*, which can either be understood as songs of lust or songs with explicit lyrics. The *Magen Avrohom* objects to music used in other religions' services. As I understand it, The Beatles' songs do not fall into either of these categories and, from a halachic standpoint, would be permitted.

Most objections to various genres of music are hashkafic or kabbalistic in nature. That's very nice for those who wish to embrace them, but it's not something that one can impose on the community as obligatory.

It's odd that you say it's explicit in the *Shulchan Aruch* since the *Shulchan Aruch* prohibits *all* music because of the *Churban* (destruction of the Temple).

I'm not ruling that one *must* listen to secular music and I don't think it's your place to rule that others may not. Also, what's appropriate for someone raised in an observant home may not necessarily be obligatory for a *baal teshuvah* to embrace. Their situation in life is not the same as yours, so your mileage may vary. Of course, when one has a question in a matter of practical *halacha*, one should always ask their own rabbi and not follow the differing opinions of strangers on the Internet.

Davening on Airplanes

Q. *On a recent flight, after dealing with hours of a cancellation, a reschedule and then a delay, I finally boarded the plane. As we awaited our much-anticipated departure, one young Jewish guy stood up and began to daven mincha. The captain announced that the flight attendants should do their final checks and prepare for take-off but, even after the flight attendant asked him twice, he didn't sit down. Is it worth making such a chillul Hashem (desecration of God's name) and keeping an entire plane of strangers waiting just so you can stand for the last three paragraphs of mincha? Would it be appropriate in this case to daven while seated?*

A. Talking about *halacha* can be tricky because virtually any halachic statement one could make has a dissenting viewpoint. For example, the common practice is to recite the *bracha* of *shehakol* on Pringles potato crisps, which are made from reconstituted potatoes. I happen to say the *bracha* of *ho'adoma* on Pringles. What's important (and germane for our discussion) is (a) I know that I'm following a minority opinion and (b) my acting counter to the majority doesn't inconvenience anyone else. That having been said, most authorities—perhaps surprisingly—rule against behaving as your fellow passenger did.

Relevant *halachos* go back all the way to the Mishna, long before airplanes. *Brachos* 4:5 tells us that one who is riding on a donkey must dismount to daven. If he is unable to do so, he should turn his face towards Jerusalem. If he cannot do that, he should direct his intentions towards the site of the Temple. Mishna 4:6 continues that one who is riding on a boat, in a wagon, or on a raft—all of whom would be unable to stand—should daven seated, directing their intentions towards the Temple. The same would apply in modern times to cars, buses, trains and planes. So, right off the bat, one should daven seated on a plane just out of safety concerns. We haven't yet discussed the inconvenience to others.

Davening on a plane can inconvenience others in a number of ways. In your case, it delayed take-off. Sometimes it blocks the aisles, keeping others from reaching the lavatories or preventing flight attendants from getting through with the food-service carts. When there's a *minyan* (a quorum of 10 men davening), it's even worse. Aside from the physical obstacle posed by a *minyan*, the noise made by a *minyan* bothers other passengers, who may be trying to read, sleep, talk, or watch the movie. This can be exacerbated when the *shaliach tzibbur* (prayer leader) needs to raise his voice so that the rest of the *minyan* can hear him over the sound of jet engines.

You rightly posit that standing to daven and forming a *minyan* on a plane run the risk of creating a *chillul Hashem*. In such a case, it would be preferable to daven individually in one's seat. Talking strict *halacha*, Rav Moshe Feinstein ruled that it is permitted to daven seated on a plane if standing presents difficulty. (It is actually preferable if standing inconveniences others.) One should rise just before the parts in *Shemoneh Esrei* where one would normally bow (*Igros Moshe* OC 4:20).

Rav Shmuel Wosner says to be sure to sit when the fasten seatbelt sign is lit, and to avoid davening in large groups. If it is not possible to say

Shemoneh Esrei standing near one's seat, it should be recited sitting. Rav Shlomo Zalman Auerbach says to daven seated, not in the aisles where it will inconvenience others. He was also against *minyanim* on airplanes, because they bother others (*Halichos Shlomo*). Rav Ovadia Yosef davened by himself on airplanes out of consideration for other passengers.

To my knowledge, Rav Pinchas Scheinberg was the only authority of standing who advocated davening with a *minyan* on an airplane as opposed to individually in one's seat. However, even Rav Scheinberg indicated that this must be done in a way that doesn't disturb other passengers. That's not to say that there aren't positions that say otherwise. Those who form *minyanim* on planes may well have authorities whose opinions they are following. I suspect, however, that most people who do so are acting out of ignorance, from an assumption that one is "supposed to" form a *minyan* in the air just as we do on the ground. For many, being informed of the rulings of Rav Moshe Feinstein and the other Torah giants will be sufficient. Many others, for right or wrong, are just going to be stuck in their ways.

Gun Rights

Q. What does Judaism say about gun rights?

A. Before we get into it, I'd like to preface by saying that, whatever we determine the Torah's position to be, it does not necessarily mandate a political position for us. For example, the Torah permits slavery and polygamy, which were the societal norms at the time in which it was given. Not only does this not obligate us to practice these things, I know of no religious authority who would advocate for making these practices legal in contemporary society. Man is permitted to outlaw that which the Torah permits.

Conversely, the Torah does not permit us to drive on the Sabbath, nor to eat non-kosher foods. Nevertheless, I know of no religious authority who maintains that we have the right or the obligation to impose these moral values as secular law. The Torah's rules are for us to follow, not for us to impose on others.

Accordingly, even if I conclude that the Torah permits unfettered gun ownership, I can still advocate for restrictions. Similarly, if I conclude that the Torah prohibits gun ownership, that would only be a moral guideline for my own behavior; it doesn't mean that I have the right or the responsibility to expect it of others. Our conclusions here are not intended as political mandates either way.

With that in mind, I have observed that sometimes people's religious interpretations are informed by their political views, rather than the other way around. This leads people to perform some incredible mental gymnastics, presenting the point of some religious dictum as the opposite of what it really means. I'm going to try my best to avoid that.

Quite a few years ago, I read a piece in which I think the writer fell victim to that urge and read the sources through the prism of his preconceptions. He presented the prohibition against owning a vicious dog (*Bava Kamma* 79a) as ironclad proof that gun ownership is prohibited, overlooking a significant difference between the two cases: a dangerous dog is a living creature that has a mind of its own. A violent dog is capable of attacking innocent victims without any human catalyst; a gun can be misused but it can't misuse itself. (I know that, for some, this observation might be uncomfortably close to the pro-gun slogan "guns don't kill people; people kill people" but the Ramban comments on Genesis 4:23 that swords don't choose to kill people and they bear no responsibility for their actions, so the idea has precedent.) Accordingly, the law about a dangerous dog may be important for our discussion but that author's conclusion might be a little premature.

Let's start with a verse in the Torah. As we discussed recently, Deuteronomy 22:8 obligates us to install a fence on the kind of flat roof that people use, such as those on modern apartment buildings; this is to prevent the possibility of innocent people falling. The Torah's operative phrase "so there should not be blood on your house" is the basis of a general halachic rule against allowing any hazardous condition to remain unchecked (*Bava Kamma* 15b). This general prohibition would include the aforementioned ban against owning a vicious dog, though there are mitigating circumstances that would permit it, such as if the dog is kept on a chain (*Choshen Mishpat* 409:3). From here we see that something dangerous might be permitted if reasonable precautions are taken. Additionally, the Gemara tells us (*Bava Kamma* 83a) that one can have a guard dog in a city that's close to the nation's border (i.e., an area in potential danger), so what's prohibited in one place because it poses a hazard might be permitted in another out of necessity.

Similar to this, I think, is the case of a certain type of spiked sandal that the Talmud (*Shabbos* 60a) tells us may not be worn on Shabbos. The Gemara explains that, during a period of persecution, a group of fugitive Jews hid in a cave where they were permitted to enter but not to leave for fear that the enemy might find them. One of these fugitives accidentally strapped his sandals on backwards, which made his incoming footprints look like outgoing footprints. This created a panic during which the people hiding in the cave pressed together, impaling one another on their spiky shoes. The Gemara tells us that they inflicted more damage on one another than the enemy caused. This led to the ban on spiked sandals. But why were they prohibited only on Shabbos? If they're so dangerous, shouldn't they be prohibited on weekdays as well? The answer is that on Shabbos, people gather together in large crowds, so such shoes present a danger on that day. This is not the case on weekdays, so spiked sandals do not present as large a threat. We see again that "danger" is contextual and not absolute.

In terms of practical *halacha*, the *Shulchan Aruch* (*Orach Chaim* 151:6) writes that some authorities prohibit entering a *shul* carrying one's weapons. Some later authorities, such as the *Tzitz Eliezer*, differentiate between exposed and concealed weapons, permitting a holstered weapon or even a gun whose bullets have been removed, thereby negating its status as a weapon. And the restriction doesn't apply at all to a soldier, a police officer or a security guard who needs his (or her) weapon for the protection of others.

While weapons appear to be generally permitted, it should be noted that the Talmud (*Avodah Zarah* 15b) specifically prohibits the sale of weapons to people whom we have reason to believe may use them for nefarious purposes. This seems analogous to our modern background checks and waiting periods.

In conclusion, I would like to point out that, while owning weapons might be permitted in *halacha*, it's not a badge of pride. The Mishna in tractate *Shabbos* (6:4) prohibits a person going out on Shabbos carrying weapons. Rabbi Eliezer suggests that it should be permitted because a man's weapons are ornaments for him, but the Sages shoot down that idea, saying that having to carry weapons is disgraceful. To support their assertion, the Sages cite Isaiah 2:4, "They will beat their swords into plowshares and their spears into pruning hooks; nation will not lift sword against nation and they will not make war any longer."

Weapons are not ornaments, nor are they toys; they're a necessary evil and it's sad that we have to rely upon them. The extent to which they are permitted largely depends on the safeguards that one implements and whether a particular situation is more dangerous with or without them. As with most things, the Torah position reflects the "middle path" of moderation. Therefore, using Torah sources to support either extreme is probably inaccurate and potentially disingenuous.

Corporal Punishment

Q. I heard that hitting kids in schools is still legal in 19 states and that some of the most insular schools in the Orthodox world still hit kids and justify it with a verse from Proverbs. Is that really what it means?

A. For the benefit of those who may not know, the verse in question is Proverbs 13:24. Readers are probably familiar with it, or at least with a famous variation of it: "One who spares the rod hates his son but one who loves him chastises him early."

This verse is the source of the popular expression "spare the rod and spoil the child." The question was, are people taking this verse too literally? How do the classical commentators explain it? Disappointingly, though perhaps not surprisingly, most of the commentators understand that it isn't a metaphor, it literally refers to disciplining one's child. But that still doesn't mean that one should strike one's child with a stick. In fact, it very much doesn't.

You see, the Torah was written to be understood by the audience that received it. It speaks about loading donkeys, oxen treading grain, and women delivering babies on birthing stools—things to which most of us cannot relate. It doesn't talk about DNA or black holes or flatscreen TVs because these are concepts that would have been incomprehensible to the original recipients. Similarly, if King Solomon (the author of Proverbs) wanted to discuss disciplining children, he was going to use corporal punishment as his illustration because time-outs didn't exist, and I suspect that neither did grounding or docking allowances.

This is not just wishful thinking on my part; let's examine the sources.

First of all, striking another person is seriously frowned upon in Judaism. Deuteronomy 25:3 tells us that someone sentenced to the penalty of lashes may not be struck more than the designated amount (a maximum of forty lashes). First the Torah tells us that "the wicked one deserves lashes" (25:2), but then we are told that we may not exceed the court-imposed amount because if we do, "your brother will be degraded." The *Sifrei*, quoted by Rashi on 25:3, demonstrates that before the punishment is administered, the offender is considered "wicked." After he has paid his penalty, he is once again called "your brother" and it is forbidden to strike him. If we're not allowed to strike a convicted criminal more than absolutely necessary, it should go without saying that we may not strike someone who was not so sentenced by the courts—not even if their behavior bothers us!

Striking someone outside of the context of court-ordered whiplashes is actually considered evil. In Exodus 2:13, Moshe asks "the wicked one," "Why will you strike your friend?'" The Talmud in *Sanhedrin* (58b) points out that the person is called wicked just for raising his hand, even though he has not yet delivered a blow.

The Talmud in *Moed Katan* (17a) prohibits a parent spanking an older child, based on the principle that we may not do something that will cause others to sin (*lifnei iver*). The child might respond by cursing the parent or striking back—both serious sins—and the parent would be responsible for provoking that reaction. The Ritva (13th century) says that "older child" isn't exhaustive. For sure one may not strike a child above the age of bar or bas mitzvah but, additionally, one may not even strike a younger child who is likely to retaliate in words or deeds. Rav Shlomo Wolbe (20th century) suggested that the cut-off for spanking would be age three.

Rav Wolbe's position is not a mere concession to modern parenting. *Peleh Yoetz* (1824) says that even in the case of a young child, if the parents know that his nature is not to accept authority, they should discipline him using calm, soft tones.

True, the Rambam writes that a teacher may strike a student (*Hilchos Talmud Torah* 2:2), but that very same *halacha* specifies that he may not use a whip or a rod, but only a "small strap." (So much for "rod" literalists!) And how big is a "small strap?" The Talmud in *Bava Basra* (21a) says no larger than a shoelace.

More about the Rambam's supposed license for teachers to strike students:

- Rav Moshe Feinstein wrote that a teacher may not even have a stick to frighten or intimidate his students—more bad news for "rod" enthusiasts! (*Igros Moshe Yoreh Deah* IV, 30:4);

- Rav Avrohom Pam called the Rambam's statement an example of "*halacha v'ein morin kein*" ("such may be the law but we don't teach it that way"). In other words, while there may be textual support for corporal punishment, it does not reflect our practice and we shouldn't justify it;

- Rav Yaakov Weinberg said outright that "rod" means "discipline" but not necessarily a literal rod. He continued that if a misbehaving child would behave based on a stern look, then spanking him would be considered an act of cruelty. Not only that, if providing positive reinforcement would do the trick, then even the stern look would be considered cruel. In other words, the gentlest form of effective discipline should always be employed—anything beyond that is to be discouraged, if not condemned;

- There is also the concept of *dina d'malchusa dina*—"the law of the land is the law" (*Bava Basra* 54b). If a civil law does not violate the Torah, we are obligated to obey it. Accordingly, we must pay our taxes and wear our seatbelts, just like everybody else! (Perhaps more so because we have a *halacha* that obligates us.) Since there is no Torah mandate to use corporal punishment, we are certainly obligated to observe civil laws in this matter.

We see that the Rambam—the one real source that might justify corporal punishment—is extremely limited, even by the Rambam himself! Aside from his limitation of a "small strap," we see elsewhere that the Rambam forbids striking any innocent person, even a child (*Hilchos Choveil u'Mazik* 5:1). He also writes that when one feels the need to discipline his children or others, he should never do so from a place of anger. Rather, he should feign anger but remain inwardly calm (*Hilchos Deios* 2:3).

So, yes. "Spare the rod" literally means that we do our children a disservice if we permit them to run rampant. As King Solomon wrote, one who loves his children is quick to correct their behavior. But the "rod" part is literary license. Even if that meant a literal rod in King Solomon's day (and I don't know that it did), it ultimately means an appropriate form of correction in each generation. But whatever the case may be, harsher-than-necessary means are considered cruel and should therefore be avoided.

Marijuana

Q. What is the Torah view of marijuana use? Is there a difference between medical and recreational use?

A. This past summer, my wife and I vacationed in Utah. One of the places we visited was the Brigham Young University Museum of Paleontology. When planning the trip, my wife asked me, "Do Mormons even believe in dinosaurs?" I said, "I don't know; let's find out!" I Googled the question and was taken to a page on the Latter-day Saints website that did not take a position, saying instead that "there have been no revelations on this question." "Why can't we do that sometimes?" I quipped, only half-joking.

This is one of those areas where I wish we could do that because, whatever I answer, some people are going to vehemently disagree. I have some personal thoughts on the subject based on my own understanding of

current medical thought but I'm going to limit my remarks to what I have
seen in the name of recognized Torah authorities and not indulge my own
speculations on the matter.

Genesis 1:29 tells us that "God said, 'I have given you every seed
that produces herbs on the face of the earth, and every tree that has seed-
producing fruit—it shall be food for you." Unlike insects, fish, birds and
mammals, every plant is inherently kosher. But, being Genesis chapter 1,
this is literally the beginning of the story, not the end.

Deuteronomy 4:15 cautions us, "zealously guard your souls," which is
understood as an obligation to protect our lives and our health. Accordingly,
it would be prohibited to ingest any substance that is detrimental to one's
health.

Discussion of marijuana in particular didn't come about until modern
times, though that doesn't stop people from looking for references or
precedent in earlier texts. For example, it has been suggested that the
kaneh bosem—one of the ingredients in the Temple incense as listed in
Exodus 30:23—is an etymological root for the word "cannabis." Tempting
as this may be, I think it's a linguistic coincidence and nothing more. *Kaneh
bosem* is traditionally translated as "fragrant cane," and Rashi explains the
term to preclude species of cane that are not fragrant. Rashi's explanation
of the term seems far more reasonable, and not just because Rashi's the
one who said it.

On the other hand, the *Shulchan Aruch* (*Orach Chaim* 264:1)
certainly appears to mean cannabis when it lists *kanabos* as a material
that may be used for the wicks of Shabbos candles. This is not surprising,
given that hemp has long been recognized as a useful textile, and using it
as a wick says nothing about the permissibility of smoking it. (It should
be noted that the *Mishnah Brurah* and other *poskim* recommend against
lighting with hemp if other options are available, so if anyone did want
to infer something about marijuana from the *Shulchan Aruch*, it would
immediately be mitigated by later authorities.)

The foremost discussion of the permissibility of sparking up comes
from Rav Moshe Feinstein, in a *teshuvah* (responsum) that is cited by
literally everyone who addresses this topic. In *Igros Moshe* (*Yoreh De'ah* III,

35), Rav Moshe lays out half a dozen reasons why smoking marijuana is prohibited. Among these are that marijuana is harmful to both mind and body, in violation of the aforementioned Deuteronomy 4:15; smoking pot causes "the munchies," which leads to gluttony, which is a separate prohibition (based on Deuteronomy 21:18); marijuana lowers our inhibitions, which leads to a violation of the prohibition against following our hearts and eyes (Numbers 15:39); lighting up violates the obligation to be holy (Leviticus 19:1) as Ramban understands it, causing one to act reprehensibly in ways that are not overtly prohibited. (Rav Moshe has several other rationales that I have not included here. One of these is the concept of *dina d'malchusa dina*—that we are obligated to obey the law of the land. If marijuana is illegal where you live, that's it, end of discussion; if it's legal where you live, then *dina d'malchusa* doesn't enter into the equation.)

There are those who would argue that the reasons cited by Rav Moshe in his *teshuvah* are based on faulty or repudiated science and should therefore no longer apply. They insist that science has determined that rolling a blunt is less harmful than alcohol and is not addictive. To that, I have two responses:

First, it's not so clear that marijuana is as harmless as people like to say it is. Rabbi Yair Hoffman cites a number of medical professionals who are concerned about "acute and chronic risks, a lack of evidence for efficacy (and) the absence of data on appropriate dosing." Additionally, the majority of proponents of marijuana are potential users, not medical professionals. Regarding this, Rabbi Hoffman quotes Sharon Levy, assistant professor of pediatrics at Harvard Medical School and chair of the American Academy of Pediatrics committee on substance abuse, in the *Washington Post* that "simply acceding to patient demands for a treatment on the basis of popular advocacy, without comprehensive knowledge of an agent, does not adhere to the ethical standards of medical practice."

Second, I once heard a lecture from Rabbi Dr. Moshe Tendler, a professor of biology, noted expert on medical ethics, and a son-in-law of Rav Moshe Feinstein. While discussing Rav Moshe's responsum on cigarettes, Rabbi Tendler extrapolated what Rav Moshe might have said given information that became available since his passing. But, Rabbi Tendler cautioned, Rav Moshe said what he said and we can't act on hypotheses. If Rav Moshe's own son-in-law, an expert in the field, hesitates to "update" Rav Moshe's responsa based on subsequent data, laypeople should certainly think twice before "second guessing" responsa literature as published.

So it seems that respected authorities have prohibited recreational marijuana use and I do not know of authorities who have yet permitted it. But what about medical use?

You may be aware that Judaism takes the sanctity of life very seriously. In fact, one who closes the eyes of a dying person is considered a full-fledged murderer for ending the patient's life by mere moments (Talmud *Shabbos* 151b). Nevertheless, Rav Eliezer Yehuda Waldenberg ruled (*Tzitz Eliezer*, 13, 87) that heavy doses of morphine could be administered if necessary for pain relief despite the fact that doing so might actually shorten the life of the patient. This is because the intention of the treatment is not to hasten the patient's death but merely to relieve his pain. That being the case, it should go without saying that medical marijuana, whose side effects are far less drastic than death, should be permitted when necessary and properly prescribed.

In fact, in what was initially seen as a bold move, the Orthodox Union certified a number of medical marijuana products as kosher. Now, given our initial statement from Genesis that all plants are inherently kosher, you might wonder why this is necessary. The OU explains that "the OU certified kosher marijuana product comes in three forms: pills, oils and vapor. While the cannabis plant is inherently kosher, the final product may contain kosher-sensitive ingredients such as alcohol, gelatin and oil." Accordingly, it is appropriate to seek out kosher-certified alternatives. (This is all the more so in the case of marijuana "edibles.")

Bottom line, if someone needs medical marijuana as a legitimate form of treatment, it's no different than any other prescription medication. But when it comes to recreational use, one would be hard-pressed to find an authority who has permitted it.

Is the Torah Racist?

Q. *I've heard people claim there are racist sources in the Torah and Talmud. Can you clarify? Do Orthodox Jews who are racist have sources to back up their hate?*

A. In my opinion, no. There is no Torah basis to justify hatred based on race. Throughout Tanach (the Jewish Bible), people fight about all sorts of things—battles over land, over theology, over the crown, over women. Some of these fights are just, others are misguided or outright wrong, but in no place do we see people fight over the color of one's complexion, nor does the Torah ever declare people of skin color A superior to people of skin color B.

There are, however, some things that people may use to justify as supporting a racist agenda. These can often be found on anti-Semitic web sites that exist to "prove" that Judaism is racist, misogynistic or (believe it or not) pro-pedophilia. They do this by taking sound bites out of context. (This is like when a movie review calls a film "a spectacular failure." The film then excerpts this review as: "...spectacular..."—*The Times.*)

I have seen on these anti-Semitic sites that Maimonides calls black people somewhere between monkeys and humans. I looked up this supposed source and, sure enough, he doesn't say that at all. What he says is that a person is not wholly human without God since he is missing an essential spiritual component. People to whom this applies, he says, include the Turks in the north, the Ethiopians in the south, and people in his own country (*Guide for the Perplexed* III, 51). Clearly Maimonides is making a statement about theology, not race.

Here's something else that looks horrible at first glance: Rashi on Genesis 12:11 cites a Midrash that calls the Egyptians "black and ugly." That seems pretty straightforward until one looks more closely.

Compare this with Song of Songs 1:5, in which the woman says, "I am black but beautiful." If she's black but beautiful, clearly she's an exception. Therefore, under normal circumstances, black must equal ugly, right? Not so fast! Context matters, remember? The very next verse continues: "Don't stare at me for being blackened by the sun. My brothers were angry with me and they made me tend the vineyards...." Now it is clear that we're not talking about race but about overexposure, which we all know can wreak havoc through sun damage.

You might still argue that Rashi on Genesis 12:11 is talking about race but consider this: the Jews and the Egyptians were racially identical. If you don't believe me, check out Exodus 2:19, in which Jethro's daughters say, "An Egyptian man rescued us from the hand of the shepherds; he also drew water for us and watered the flocks." If the Jews were white and the Egyptians black, how could Jethro's daughters mistake Moses for an Egyptian?

What about the "curse of Ham" (by which we mean Noah's son of that name, not the non-kosher meat)? This was an excuse used in Civil War times (not by Jews, by the way) to justify slavery as God's will by pointing to the curse given by Noah in Genesis chapter 9. There we are told how Noah planted a vineyard, got drunk, and was naked in his tent. His son Ham saw and told his brothers, Shem and Japheth. They took a blanket, looked away, and covered their father. When Noah sobered up, he "knew what his son had done to him." (Sodomy? Castration? Mockery? General indifference? The text doesn't specify.) In any event, Noah cursed Ham's son Canaan that his descendants would be slaves to the descendants of the other brothers.

I have several problems here. First of all, a curse is not a command. If Noah cursed Canaan that his sons would be slaves, as soon as it happened, the curse would be fulfilled. That's not justification to keep doing it. It's similar to God's prophecy to Abraham that his descendants would be slaves in a foreign land. If so, why were the Egyptians punished for fulfilling God's word? Two reasons: (1) God said the Jews would be enslaved; Egypt didn't have to be the ones to do it and (2) even if God wanted them to do it, they overdid it, treating the Jews far more harshly than would have been necessary to fulfill the prophecy. Similarly, a plantation owner had no responsibility to fulfill Noah's curse but he does have a responsibility to do the right thing.

My other problem with the "curse of Ham" is that the African races are indeed descended from Noah's son Ham—through his son Cush. Canaan is the ancestor of—follow me here—the Canaanite nations. Enslaving the descendants of Cush does not fulfill the curse against Canaan. To do that, you would need to find yourself a Hittite or a Jebusite.

There is one incident that is apparently race-based. Numbers 12:1 says, "Miriam and Aaron spoke against Moses regarding the Ethiopian woman he had married, for he had married an Ethiopian woman." Now, Midrashically there is a whole different understanding of this incident (Miriam and Aaron complained that Moses was ignoring his conjugal duties, etc.) but the simple reading of the Torah is: Moses married a black woman, his siblings complained, and God punished them for it. My takeaway from this is (1) Moses was not a racist, since he married a black woman and (2) if anyone complains about such a thing, God says, "Don't be a hater."

Upon inspection, it becomes clear that, not only does the Torah not support racism, it's against it. Genesis 1:27 tells us that man was created in the image of God. The Talmud (*Sanhedrin* 38b) tells us that God created only one man, from whom all are descended, so that no one could claim superior ancestry.

The Midrash (*Sifra Kedoshim* 4) records a debate between Rabbi Akiva and Ben Azzai as to the seminal message of the Torah. Rabbi Akiva proposed, "Love your neighbor as yourself" (Leviticus 19:18). The problem is that one can split hairs, considering one person to be his "neighbor" but not another. Ben Azzai therefore counters with "This is the book of the generations of Adam; in the day that God created man, in the likeness of God He made him" (Genesis 5:1). This seemingly mundane verse is actually quite profound; it tells us both that all men are brothers and that we are all created in God's image.

When it comes to racism, the bottom line may be found in the words of the *Midrash Tanchuma*: "If you hate any person, you hate God, Who created man in His image." So don't be a hater.

When to Call the Authorities

Q. *On one hand the Torah tells us we're not supposed to speak lashon hara (evil speech), on the other hand, the Torah commands us to not stand idly by our neighbor's blood. If we think someone is dangerous, how do we know when to remain silent and when to speak up?*

A. This is an excellent question and God no doubt anticipated that there would be such a tension: fear of gossiping preventing people from speaking up when there is danger. The Torah itself ends the verse about prohibiting evil speech with the commandment to not stand idly by your neighbor's blood. It's similar to another point of tension in the Torah. "Honor your parents" is followed by "keep Shabbos." *Kibud av v'eim* (like not speaking *lashon hara*) is important, but not at the expense of breaking Shabbos. Let's take a look at how these laws interact practically, beginning with *lashon hara*.

The Torah tells us, "Do not go about as a talebearer among your people" (Leviticus 19:16). This is the source of a prohibition we call *lashon hara*, which literally means "evil speech" but refers specifically to gossip. The laws of *lashon hara* are many and there's no way we could possibly cover them all, so I'll just hit a few high points. (There are many fine books available that will cover the topic in greater detail.) In short, we are not permitted to say anything about another person that is derogatory (even if it will not cause him injury) or that may cause him injury (even if it is not derogatory).

An example of derogatory but not harmful: "Mary's dress is ugly." Nothing bad will happen to Mary because you shared this opinion but it's just not nice. An example of harmful but not derogatory: "John voted for candidate X" (when said to someone who hates candidate X with a passion). It's an objective statement of fact, perhaps something John himself shares freely in other circumstances, but it negatively colors this person's impression of John.

There are other forms of speech that are similarly prohibited. For example, one may not overly praise a person, especially in front of his enemy, as this will cause other people to react by putting him down. Similarly, one may not make a vague statement that could be taken two ways. The classic example of this is telling someone who is looking for a meal, "Try the Smiths—they always have a pot on the stove!" This could be taken to mean that the Smiths are hospitable and are always ready to receive guests, or it could mean that the Smiths are gluttons, always eating. (If a nebulous statement is made in front of three people, the assumption is that the speaker assumes it will get back to the subject and therefore we assume that the positive sense was intended and it is permitted.)

There are a lot of ways that people try to justify *lashon hara*: "I'd say it to his face," "It's just a joke," and the most popular defense, "But it's true!" None of these permits *lashon hara*. "But it's true!" is a particularly weak argument since *lashon hara* is by definition true. If it weren't true, it would be called *motzi shem ra*—literally, "spreading a bad name." In English, we would call this slander, as opposed to *lashon hara*, which is gossip.

However, there are some situations where we are not just permitted but are obligated to speak negatively of others. Usually (if not always), this is done in the defense of innocent victims and, as you say, is based on the second half of that same verse, "…do not stand idly by the blood of your neighbor." If Bill is a kleptomaniac, do I have the right to share this information with Tony if there's no conceivable chance Bill will ever get near Tony's stuff? No. But if Tony is thinking of inviting Bill to stay for the weekend, I have the responsibility to tell Tony, in order to protect him from loss.

There are many situations where this principle could come into play. The most common is when being asked about a person for a job reference or for a *shidduch* (a prospective match). We don't have free rein to go around badmouthing people, but there may be pieces of information that a potential boss or spouse needs to have in order to make an informed decision. You know that Bob forged his MBA diploma using PhotoShop? If you're his reference, you must disclose that to the interviewer. You're aware that Susie has a husband and six kids in another state? Her fiancé deserves to know that.

There are, however, conditions to sharing the negative that must be met:

1. You have to know that the information you're disclosing is true; you may not embellish or exaggerate;

2. Sharing the information has to be the only way to protect the endangered party, or to accomplish some other necessary constructive purpose;

3. The speaker's intention must sincerely be to protect the endangered party or to accomplish the constructive goal. (If one is sharing information about a person he doesn't like, it can be really hard to be objective about this!);

4. The consequences of sharing the information cannot cause undue harm to the subject (and certainly not to anyone else!). If reporting that Joe took home a ball point pen from work will get him fired, the consequences are not commensurate with the offense and one might not be permitted to disclose that information.

Of course, there's harm and then there's harm. "Joe took home a ball point pen from work" is very different from "Joe is hiding in the alley with a machete, waiting to chop your head off." The immediacy of the latter is clearly much more urgent. If you feel that a situation is truly dangerous, appropriate steps must be taken. That doesn't necessarily make it easy.

Let's take religion out of it for a minute and use the strictly hypothetical example of someone questioning whether or not they should call Child Protective Services on a friend or neighbor. On the one hand, you're hesitant to call—it will destroy your relationship, you're afraid someone's kids might get taken away unnecessarily, etc. On the other hand, you feel compelled to call—if you don't and something bad happens, you'll never forgive yourself! You'll note how this scenario is a dilemma even before we add anyone's religious sensibilities into the equation!

If you had a calling-CPS dilemma, you might describe the situation to a friend who's a social worker and ask for guidance. They're the expert and you value their insight into the matter. Similarly, if you have a non-urgent disclosure dilemma involving the laws of *lashon hara*, the best course of action is to ask an expert—in this case a rabbi. There are times when we may or must disclose negative information but, when we're involved, we're not always the best judges of those situations.

However, as we said earlier, saving someone in imminent danger always takes priority. In a case of clear and present danger, appropriate protective action must be taken immediately. To save a life, we drive on Shabbos, we eat on Yom Kippur, and we don't hesitate to reveal negative information. If your friend's babysitter is a convicted sex offender, say something. Your neighbor's daughter has been set up with a known date rapist? Share that information. This is even true in spiritual matters. For example, if your cousin's new spiritual advisor is secretly a missionary, tell him.

Speaking out to save someone from danger doesn't conflict with the laws of *lashon hara* any more than it does with the laws of Shabbos. Usually, we don't drive on Shabbos; sometimes we must. Similarly, we usually keep negative information to ourselves but sometimes we must reveal it. Just as we learn when to call an ambulance (for a heart attack, not for a splinter), we have to use good judgment to evaluate when to keep quiet, when to speak up, and when to ask for guidance.

Committing Fraud

Q. *Isn't being honest and ethical part of a religious Jewish life? Sometimes I read about Orthodox Jews committing fraud. What does Judaism forbid, and why are people such hypocrites?*

A. No doubt this question was motivated by last month's news in which seven "ultra-Orthodox" Jewish couples were arrested in a raid amid allegations of welfare fraud. Before answering your question, I'd like to mention that just a few weeks earlier, sixty-eight people were arrested in a welfare fraud raid in Pennsylvania. Why was the arrest of 14 people national news but not the arrest of 68? Largely because the 68 didn't include any "ultra-Orthodox" Jews (AKA "*chareidim*"). People take a certain amount of glee when Jews, particularly *chareidim*, are caught up in such scandals. Anti-Semites love it because it substantiates their feelings about Jews, money and conspiracies. Even some Jews love it because they think the *chareidim* consider themselves better than everyone else, so they enjoy seeing them "put in their place." Unfortunately, it's more than just the offenders who suffer from such stories. Many modern Orthodox Jews think that all ultra-Orthodox Jews are up to such things, many secular Jews assume it about all Orthodox Jews (including the modern Orthodox), many non-Jews assume it about all Jews (including secular Jews), etc. It's a huge *chillul Hashem* (desecration of God's Name) and it doesn't do anybody any good.

Now as to your question, of course Jews are obligated in honesty and ethics! The Torah is replete with commandments making this clear. Many types of theft are prohibited, including robbing someone with stealth, such as by breaking into their house in the dead of night, and robbery by force, such as mugging someone in an alley. (In *halacha*, robbery by stealth is called *geneiva* and robbery by force is called *gezeila*.)

We are also commanded explicitly to be honest in business transactions. Leviticus 19:35 tells us, "You shall not commit injustices using weights, measure or volumes." We are specifically prohibited to cheat others by shorting them in anything that is measured, whether it's a bolt of cloth or a pound of cole slaw. If it's sold by length, weight or volume, we are responsible to see that our customers get what they paid for. To do otherwise is called *avel bamishpat*, a perversion of justice. That's pretty strong terminology for a petty, passive offense that the customer might not even notice. The language of the verse likens the merchant to a judge because this is actually a very serious matter.

The very next verse (Leviticus 19:36) continues this theme by adding, "Proper scales, proper weights, proper dry measures and proper liquid measures you shall have; I am Hashem your God, Who brought you out of the land of Egypt." This is an obligation for all merchants to ensure that the tools of their trade are accurate. If we have unreliable implements, it's a foregone conclusion that someone's going to get cheated, even if only accidentally. An example of this mitzvah in action is that it is prohibited for a merchant to have weights made of a material that will naturally erode and get lighter.

The Talmud (*Bava Metzia* 61b) explains the end of this verse: "I am Hashem your God, Who brought you out of the land of Egypt." God knows every minute detail of all creation. He knew everyone's parentage in Egypt so that during the plague of the first-born He could punish those of Egyptian paternity but not those of Jewish paternity. Similarly, God knows which merchants have crooked weights and He will pay them back for that as well.

It doesn't stop there. Not only are we required to have honest tools, it is prohibited even to possess dishonest measures. Deuteronomy 25:13 enjoins us, "You shall not have large and small weights in your pouch." Even if one doesn't plan to cheat his customers, merely having access to dishonest weights can tempt someone into such misdeeds. Accordingly, such potential stumbling blocks must be discarded.

Some people wrongly think that Jews are permitted to rob non-Jews or to cheat them in business. There are even anti-Semitic web sites that quote Talmudic dicta out of context or completely fabricate such things in order to make it appear that this is the case. This is completely inaccurate. Judaism believes that all mankind is obligated in the seven universal (Noachide) laws, one of which prohibits theft in all its forms. Jews and non-Jews have reciprocity when it comes to *mitzvos*, just like states recognize one another's drivers' licenses. Accordingly, any mitzvah in which non-Jews are obligated, we must treat them the same as we do other Jews. This includes honesty in business transactions.

(An example of a case where Jews may treat non-Jews differently is interest. Jews may not charge one another interest; we may not agree to pay interest to other Jews, or even to serve as a witness for interest-bearing transactions! Non-Jews, however, are not commanded to avoid interest. Nevertheless, non-Jews have a level playing field in this matter because not only may they be charged interest *by* Jews, they may charge interest *to* Jews! Neither party has an inherent advantage in this matter.)

These are just some of the Torah's many examples of honesty in business. The general rule is "Keep yourselves far from a false matter" (Exodus 23:7).

Now for your second question, about people being hypocrites. I hesitate to label people hypocrites so quickly. If a "green" activist condemns SUVs but flies across the country in a private jet, using more fuel in one shot than a soccer mom uses in a year (true story), I think that's hypocrisy. On the other hand, when a particular political figure, a former secretary of education, advocated for virtues and called for limiting our vices, many called him a hypocrite because his own vice was gambling. I hesitate to call him a hypocrite because gambling wasn't on the list of things he condemned. (Apparently he either didn't consider gambling a vice or he specifically omitted it from his book because including it would have made him a hypocrite!)

So are the Orthodox welfare cheats hypocrites? I don't know; did they ever speak out against the evils of defrauding the government? If so, they're hypocrites. If not, they're just flawed.

Koheles (Ecclesiastes) 7:20 tells us that there's no person in the world so righteous that he only does good and never sins. It's natural for people to be tempted—that's why we're not allowed to hold onto any inaccurate business tools we may have! But just because someone stumbles in one area, that doesn't mean they're insincere in other areas. None of us are perfect and we all do things we know we shouldn't (though perhaps not as spectacularly criminal as in this case). None of us can truly judge the entirety of another person based on one lapse, no matter how huge.

The malfeasance itself is to be condemned in no uncertain terms. It was gratifying to see that the Lakewood Vaad (rabbinical council) quickly issued a statement that stated unequivocally "[t]here is no such thing as 'justified' theft" and "there is never any excuse for dishonesty in any form."

The Torah demands honesty and we cannot justify criminal behavior when it occurs. Nevertheless, we can condemn the behavior without presuming to know what's in the hearts and minds of the perpetrators. None of us deserve to be judged by our flaws alone.

Tikkun Olam

Q. *Growing up as a secular Jew, I heard a lot about the concept of "tikkun olam" but Orthodox people don't really talk about it. What does it really mean and is it a Torah value?*

A. It's definitely a Torah value, but there's a reason it hasn't been bandied about in Orthodoxy as much as in some other streams of Judaism. For starters, to quote Inigo Montoya in *The Princess Bride*, "You keep using that word. I do not think it means what you think it means."

Let's start with translating the phrase. *Tikkun olam* literally means "repairing the world." But what does it mean to repair the world?

Historically, this has nothing to do with building houses for hurricane victims, bringing clean water to African villages or fighting global climate change. (That's not to say that those aren't worthy endeavors, just that it's not to what *tikkun olam* traditionally refers!) Originally, *tikkun olam* had to do with divorce.

The phrase first appears in the Mishna, in the fourth chapter of tractate *Gittin*, which deals with divorce. In Mishna 4:2, we are told that, originally, a man could send a bill of divorce to his wife in another city and, before she received it, convene a *beis din* (court) to cancel it. Rabban Gamliel prohibited this because of *tikkun ha'olam*, repairing the world. The Mishna continues with another example: Originally, a man writing a bill of divorce could use one of his several names or one of his wife's several names. This could throw things into confusion, so Rabban Gamliel instituted that the divorce document specify "The man so-and-so—and any other name by which he is known—and the woman so-and-so—and any other name by which she is known…," again because of *tikkun ha'olam*.

The Bartinuro (a commentary on the Mishna) explains the meaning of *tikkun ha'olam* in each case. In the first scenario, the messenger (who is already *en route*) doesn't know that the man has canceled the divorce. He delivers the document, the woman thinks she's divorced when she isn't, and gets remarried. That's bad. In the second situation, there would be repercussions for the children of the woman's second marriage. Their parentage would be called into question because people would think that their mother wasn't divorced from Joe, not realizing that he also goes by Mike.

This chapter of the Mishna continues with many other examples of *tikkun olam*, most of which have to do with divorce or freeing slaves. (The Torah version of slavery hasn't been practiced for millennia and even when it was current, it was very different from what we think of when we use the term, but such is beyond our scope.) For example, Mishna 4:5 discusses the case of a man who is half-slave and half-free (because he was freed by one of his two masters). Such a person can't marry a freewoman (because he's half-slave) and he can't marry a slave-girl (because he's half-free). We therefore compel his owner to free him because of *tikkun ha'olam*. (In this case, "building the world" literally as the reason to do this is so that he can marry and reproduce in order to populate the world.)

There are a few examples of *tikkun olam* in this chapter that do not involve divorce or freeing slaves. For example, in Mishna 4:6, we are told not to pay exorbitant ransoms for captives or for religious articles because of *tikkun ha'olam*. There, the issue is that we don't want to provide a financial inducement that would encourage hostiles to take captives or steal religious items in order to sell them back to us.

We can see how all of these are examples of *tikkun olam* in that they improve society—women can remarry, children's parentage is blemish-free, slaves can marry and we don't have marauders constantly scooping up people or Torah scrolls in order to make a quick buck. So how did the phrase come to refer to cleaning up after a flood or feeding shut-ins?

Grammatically, this is what we call metonymy. This is a figure of speech in which a thing is called by another thing's name because of some attribute they share. For example, if I say "Frankenstein," most people will think of Frankenstein's monster rather than Dr. Victor Frankenstein. The monster is known by his creator's name because of metonymy.

Similarly, I believe that *tikkun olam* has become closely identified with building houses and other public-works projects because *tikkun*, literally meaning "to build or to repair," conjures images of such physical activities.

Now, as to your anecdotal experience that secular Jews have a greater emphasis on *tikkun olam*. That may be so, but it may also be a question of mere percentages. I'll explain. Orthodoxy has a lot of ritual practice—Shabbos, davening, Torah-study, etc. We also have what we would traditionally call *gemilus chasadim*—acts of kindness—that people now popularly refer to as *tikkun olam*. Other streams of Judaism may have less emphasis on ritual—secular Jews may have no ritual practice at all!—with the result that *tikkun olam* activities may represent a greater percentage of their work. (Some organizations specialize to the extent that a particular activity may be all they do.) So Orthodox Jews also engage in *gemilus chasadim* (*tikkun olam*) as one out of a perhaps dozen Jewish things they do. For others, it may be one out of six Jewish things, or one of three Jewish things or the only Jewish thing! We all do it, it's just a question of what else is on the docket. Orthodox Jews don't value it less, it merely has to compete with more other interests.

So, even if the name is a misnomer, we all engage in acts of *tikkun olam*. (While that name has been popularized throughout all streams of Judaism, in certain more traditional circles it probably still suggests facilitating divorces and freeing slaves. In such circles, they would probably refer to building houses as *gemilus chasadim*.) It's important for everyone to engage in *tikkun olam* but it's also important for us to remember the One Who put mankind on earth and commanded us to work it and to protect it (Genesis 2:15). In the *Aleinu* prayer, we express our hope *l'takein olam b'malchus Sha-dai*—"to establish the world under the dominion of the Almighty." We should build the world as much as possible but we should not focus on *what* we're doing to the exclusion of *why* we're doing it.

Anti-Semitism

Q. I know anti-Semitism is an age-old problem and there are Torah sources for this, such as Eisav soneh l'Yaakov (Esau hates Jacob). At the same time, I think we should still try our best to be exemplary people and explain our customs to those who are curious because they can seem weird from the outside and can be beautiful when explained. But I see some of my co-religionists just giving up. They say, "They'll hate us anyway. Why bother trying to be better or explain what our customs are about?" So who is right? Can we win over some people who have negative feelings about us even if our sources say that we will always be hated?

A. For starters, let's examine your source text. You may recall that Yitzchak thought Eisav (Esau) was meant to be his successor but God told Rivka that it was really supposed to be Yaakov (Jacob). She contrived a plan to get Eisav out of the way for the day so that Yitzchak would bless Yaakov instead. When Yitzchak became aware of the ruse, he realized that Yaakov was in fact his true successor and he ratified the blessing. Nevertheless, Eisav felt that Yaakov had stolen the blessing from him so he swore to kill his brother. Yaakov ran away to stay with Lavan, with whom he lived for 20 years. Genesis 33:4 describes the reunion of Yaakov and his Eisav, saying "Eisav ran toward him and embraced him; he fell upon his neck and kissed him, and they wept."

In the Torah, the word *vayishakehu* (he kissed him) has a series of small dots over its letters, which is a sign that the word holds deeper significance. Rashi on this verse cites a Midrashic difference of opinion as to Eisav's sincerity in kissing Yaakov. One opinion is that of Rabbi Shimon bar Yochai, who says that Eisav hated Yaakov through and through but, at this particular moment, he was overcome with compassion and kissed his brother sincerely. The first part of Rabbi Shimon's statement in Hebrew is "*Halacha hi b'yadua she'Eisav soneh l'Yaakov.*" But what does that even mean?

"*Halacha hi b'yadua*" is an unusual phrase that occurs nowhere else in rabbinic literature. The popular understanding is that it means "It is a well-known law that Eisav hates Yaakov" but "law" in this context wouldn't mean that non-Jews are commanded to hate Jews. Rather, it's like the law of gravity. A better translation would be, "It's an established fact that Eisav hates Yaakov." But even that may not be quite accurate.

While the version cited by Rashi says "*halacha*" (it is a law), that may be a scribal error. Other manuscripts say, "*haloh.*" This would be translated as, "Behold, it is well-known that Eisav hates Yaakov." This is certainly less emphatic than calling it a universal constant!

But whether it says "*halacha*" or "*haloh,*" to whom is it meant to refer? From context, it would appear to mean one thing: Eisav (the person) hates Yaakov (the person), no more and no less. Neither the Talmud nor the Midrash extends this concept any further. And while Rashi cites the *Sifri*, consider the version of the statement that appears in the Midrash Tanchuma (*Shemos* 27). There, discussing brothers generally, it notes that Eisav hated Yaakov but also that Cain hated Abel, Yishmael hated Yitzchak and Yoseif's brothers hated him. (This is contrasted with Moshe and Aharon, who loved one another.) Sometimes a Yaakov and an Eisav is just a Yaakov and an Eisav.

The first person to extend the parameters of this dictum seems to be the Abarbanel (15th century), who expanded it to mean that the Romans and their inheritors (who are Eisav's heirs) hate the Jews (who are Yaakov's heirs). This is a reasonable understanding of what Rabbi Shimon might have meant. Given that he lived under the Roman occupation, "Eisav" could easily be a code for "Rome." And consider the Midrash cited by Rashi on Genesis 25:23 that the "two nations" (or, based on the Torah's spelling, two great leaders) in Rivka's womb refers to the Roman emperor Antoninus and Rabbi Yehuda HaNasi, the compiler of the Mishna (*Avodah Zarah* 11a).

The idea that this dictum applies to all non-Jews doesn't appear to have taken hold until the 19th century. (I would be remiss if I neglected to acknowledge that Rav Moshe Feinstein, *ztz"l*—my usual go-to among contemporary halachic authorities—did cite this source in this manner, in *Igros Moshe* CM 2:77.)

So, we have the following possible understandings: (1) Behold, Eisav hates Yaakov; (2) it is a natural law that Eisav hates Yaakov; (3) it is a natural law that the Romans hate the Jews; and (4) it is a natural law that all non-Jews generally hate Jews. Only this last understanding requires addressing under the parameters of your question. (And even according to this worst-case understanding, nobody says that absolutely *every* non-Jew is an anti-Semite. Even in Nazi Germany, there were non-Jews who risked their lives to save Jews.)

So why do we have anti-Semitism? Religious philosophers over the centuries have proposed a number of reasons. The Netziv (19th century) said that anti-Semitism serves to remind Jews that we are eternally distinct from other nations and that God is ultimately the only One upon Whom we can rely. Rabbi Avigdor Miller (20th century) wrote that part of our test as Jews is always to be a minority surrounded by a hostile majority. He adds that our success as a people is not *despite* the oppression we have faced, it's *because* we cling to God in the face of our adversities.

However you understand *Eisav soneh l'Yaakov* and whatever you consider the purpose served by anti-Semitism to be, the fact remains that God directed us to serve as a "light to the nations" (Isaiah 42:6, 49:6, 60:3, *et al.*). God has no reason to make us spin our wheels in vain. If He told us to do this, I am confident that He hasn't given us a Sisyphean task that can never be accomplished.

Abortion

Q. Is Judaism pro-life, pro-choice or some combination?

A. Sometimes I'll be asked to field a question and I'll decline on the basis that "no good can come of that." I almost went that route on this question because there are obviously strong feelings on both sides of the political spectrum and, whatever I say, someone's going to be really upset about it. It is, however, an important issue so I decided to address it with a couple of caveats, namely: (1) what I say here is strictly apolitical—I in no way mean to imply who anyone should vote for and any political implications that readers may draw from my words are completely their own doing; (2) this is just the tip of a really big iceberg. We examine the basic sources but there is a lot of contemporary responsa literature on the subject not covered here; and (3) there is by no means enough information here for anyone to draw any conclusions for practical application. If one has a real-life situation that needs addressing, an authority must be consulted.

That having been said, Jewish law and tradition do not fit comfortably into either the "pro-life" or "pro-choice" camps. Rather, it's a gray area with a foot in each camp. The Torah does not permit abortion on demand but there are situations in which abortion would be permitted, or even required.

The Torah not only prohibits abortion for Jews, it is universally prohibited under the seven Noahide laws under the general category of murder. God commanded Noah, "*Shofeich dam ha'adam ba'adam damo yishafeich*," generally translated as, "Whoever sheds man's blood, by man shall his blood be shed" (Genesis 9:6), meaning that one is executed for murder. The Talmud in *Sanhedrin* (57b) gives an equally-valid alternate interpretation: "Whoever sheds the blood of a person inside a person [*ha'adam ba'adam*], his blood shall be shed." "A person inside a person" means a fetus. This reading informs us that abortion is considered murder.

While abortion may be considered a form of murder, it's not exactly the same as "regular" murder. Consider the case in *parshas Mishpatim* (Exodus 21:22-23). There, we are told the case of two men who are fighting and a pregnant bystander is injured. If the woman miscarries, the one who injured her must pay a fine but if she dies, it is a capital crime. We see a difference here between killing the mother—which is manslaughter—and killing the fetus, which is a lesser offense.

This brings us to the concept that a fetus is not an independent entity but rather it is a limb of its mother (*Bava Kamma* 78b). This certainly makes aborting easier to permit when it's necessary than if abortion is the same as outright murder but it still doesn't facilitate abortion on demand. Go to your rabbi (or your doctor) and ask for permission to have a healthy arm or leg chopped off because it's your body and your choice. I suspect that you won't get the green light.

Perhaps a lesser concern (but still potentially an important issue, theologically-speaking) is that abortion goes against the obligation to procreate. The Talmud in *Yevamos* (63b) says that Moshiach won't come until all the souls that are waiting to be born have been born (based on Isaiah 57:16), so intentional refusal to procreate holds up the redemption. Additionally, one who refuses to procreate is likened to a murderer (based on the juxtaposition of these concepts in Genesis 9:6-7) and is responsible for diminishing God's glory in this world, since man is in the image of God (based on the juxtaposition of concepts in Genesis 1:27-28). Of course, these particular objections also apply to birth control in general, which is much more lenient than abortion, so let's leave them aside.

So far, all this sounds like arguments for the pro-life side. Now let's hear the pro-choice part.

Generally speaking, one is permitted to violate any mitzvah in order to save a human life, including "big" ones like violating Shabbos and even eating on Yom Kippur. The exceptions to this principle are murder, idolatry and sexual immorality (i.e., adultery and incest). Based on this, one might think that abortion should always be prohibited as a form of murder, regardless of the circumstances. However, the Mishna in *Ohalos* (7:6) teaches us that one is permitted to abort when the pregnancy poses a danger to the mother. It does note, though, that once the baby has mostly emerged, this is no longer the case.

The Talmud (*Sanhedrin* 72b) explains the distinction. The fetus endangering the mother is treated like a *rodeif* (pursuer). A *rodeif* is a person who pursues an innocent in order to kill them. Bystanders are obligated to kill a *rodeif* if this is necessary to save the innocent victim. This obligates doctors (and expectant mothers) to do what is necessary to save the mother's life when endangered. But the analogy only goes so far because the fetus is not literally a *rodeif*. Once the baby is considered born, its life is as valuable as the mother's. At this point, it's the circumstances that are considered to be endangering the woman's life and not any conscious action on the part of the born baby, who is an independent person. Since we may not commit murder to save a life, such abortions may not be performed.

It must be noted that it's not only physical dangers that can permit (or require) an abortion; the same can be true of mental and emotional disorders. There are women who simply cannot carry a baby to term without risking their mental or emotional health; this may be the situation in cases of pregnancy caused by rape or incest. In such cases, abortion may be permitted (or required).

Most authorities do not recognize the baby's potential "quality of life" as a factor to warrant abortion. Accordingly, things like Down syndrome and Tay Sachs are not generally seen as reasons to abort, though the impact of bearing the child on the mother's mental health may be a consideration in some cases. (I reiterate that in any question of practical application, an authority must be consulted!)

So, getting back to the question of pro-life vs. pro-choice, there are certainly Orthodox Jews on both sides of the aisle. Those who are pro-life believe that abortion is tantamount to murder and, falling under the rubric of the seven Noahide laws, universally binding. Those who are pro-choice recognize that there are times when an abortion may be permitted or even required, and they see the need to protect that option even though many other people will pursue abortions that are not permissible under Jewish law.

The bottom line is that the position of *halacha* on this matter is more "pro-life" than the American political left but also more "pro-choice" than the American political right. Perhaps not being too committed to either extreme is a wise approach. After all, the Rambam tells us (*Hilchos Deios*

1:7) that the path of moderation is the "path of God" referred to in Genesis 18:19, "I have known him so that he will command his children and his descendants after him to keep the path of God." This is seen as a source of blessing as the verse continues, "so that God will bring upon Abraham all that He promised him."

Sexual Molestation

Q. I once spoke to an Orthodox Jew who told me that he didn't have to report sexual abuse because there's no source prohibiting it in the Torah. How are we to understand that it is wrong according to Judaism?

A. Wow. There is so much wrong with that that I don't even know where to begin.

Just because something isn't overtly named in the form of "Thou shalt not," that doesn't mean that it's necessarily permitted. The Torah doesn't say anything about light bulbs, cars or computers but I suspect the Orthodox Jew in your question would concede that the Torah has rules about the use of such devices on Shabbos. Similarly, if I were to stab that person in the shoulder with a knife, I suspect that he would argue that doing so is prohibited despite the lack of any overt Biblical injunction against it.

Driving on Shabbos is Biblically prohibited. Stabbing someone in the shoulder is Biblically prohibited. Molestation is Biblically prohibited. You just have to know where to look.

Before we look at the legal portions of the Torah, let's look at Biblical precedent that occurs in the narrative portions of the text, of which there are two.

The first, and more famous, is the rape of Jacob's daughter Dinah by Shechem in Genesis chapter 34. Her brothers Shimon and Levi not only executed the offender, they led a massacre against the entire city for refusing to bring him to justice. Their father, Jacob, objected to their actions—not because it was unjust but because he was afraid of the reaction that other inhabitants of the land would have. Shimon and Levi replied, "Should we let our sister be treated like a prostitute?" You will notice that they get the last word on the subject.

The other incident is when King David's daughter Tamar was raped by her half-brother Amnon in II Samuel chapter 13. In this instance, Amnon was killed by Tamar's full brother, Avshalom. This drove a wedge between David and Avshalom (later reconciled, subsequently estranged for other reasons). But this was strictly a familial matter—it would be a big strain on relations in any family if one of the kids were to kill another regardless of the provocation. But again, none of the objections include any suggestion that Amnon didn't deserve what he got.

In truth, rape and seduction are both prohibited (Deuteronomy 22:29 and Exodus 22:15-16, respectively). For that matter, so is any extramarital sexual congress even if consensual (Deuteronomy 23:18). Not only that, so is extramarital romantic activity that doesn't include actual sex (Leviticus 18:6). So the assertion that molestation is somehow not prohibited by one or more of these is downright bizarre.

I have seen on anti-Semitic web sites the claim that Judaism permits the sexual molestation of children because the Talmud discusses the legal ramifications of sex with children above and below different ages. None of this makes any sense because discussing the legal ramifications does not suggest in any way that the action is permitted. It only reflects the punishments should such a thing occur. It's disheartening enough to see such canards on explicitly anti-Semitic websites; do well-meaning but ignorant Jews really need to give them additional fodder?

Another point to consider: Leviticus 19:16 prohibits standing idly by when another person is in danger. Even if sexual abuse were not explicitly prohibited—and it is—reporting it would still fall under the rubric of saving the endangered.

Not only that, there is a legal principle of *dina d'malchusa dina*, that "the law of the land is the law" (*Nedarim* 28a, *Gittin* 10b, *Bava Kamma* 113a and *Bava Basra* 54b-55a). Secular governments can't compel us to do things that the Torah prohibits but they can oblige us in areas not proscribed by the Torah. You have to pay your taxes because secular law requires it. You can't drive 95 and speed through red lights because secular law prohibits it. And if the Torah didn't prohibit molestation—which, again, I assure you it does—it would still be religiously prohibited because we are bound by the principle of *dina d'malchusa dina*.

The assertion that sexual abuse of any kind is not explicitly prohibited by the Torah is both fallacious and dangerous. It's prohibited by precedent, by numerous overt Torah prohibitions and obliquely by other prohibitions. Even if none of this were the case, the Torah would require that one refrain by dint of secular law.

There's no area that isn't covered by Torah—"Turn it over and turn it over, for everything is in it" (*Avos* 5:22)—but some things are easier to find than others. Sometimes, things are staring us in the face and, for whatever reason, someone chooses not to see them.

Marie Kondo's Cleaning Philosophy

Q. Does the animism of Marie Kondo's popular KonMari method present any problems for observant Jews?

A. Let's skip to the bottom line: you would be best served asking this of your own Orthodox rabbi, not a stranger on the Internet. Now let's take the scenic route.

Let's start with what animism is. Animism is a religious belief that even inanimate things have spiritual essences, so even rocks, trees and locations are in a sense "alive." If you ask me, this belief is not consistent with Jewish theology.

Is cleaning guru Marie Kondo an animist? Apparently. She used to work in a Shinto shrine and Shinto includes animism, which she brings to her work. In her own words, "The first thing I do when I visit a client's home is to greet their house. I kneel formally in the centre [*sic*] of the house and address the house in my mind…. I ask for help in creating a space where the family can enjoy a happier life…."

A review of Kondo's 2014 book says that Kondo tries to be "considerate of [objects'] wishes—to be folded neatly, to be stored without strain, to have a 'home' within your home, to be touched gently and lovingly, to be allowed to rest after a long day's work."

So Kondo wants us to think about how socks feel and to thank books

The more you clean out, more positively

before discarding them. I can't speak for you but this is not consistent with Jewish religious philosophy as I understand it. (Before you leap to "so the *challah* shouldn't be embarrassed," I have written elsewhere not to take that so literally. That's a moral lesson after the fact, not the actual reason we cover the *challah* at Kiddush.)

Can one use Kondo's cleaning methods without embracing her animism? I dunno. Maybe? It probably depends who you ask.

The issue at hand lies in *Bemidbar* (Numbers) 15:39, a verse familiar from Shema: *v'lo sasuru acharei l'vavchem v'acharei eineichem asher atem zonim achareihem*, "so you won't stray after your hearts and your eyes, which can lead you astray." The idea of not chasing after our hearts is not to pursue philosophies that are antithetical to Torah. This is because doing so confuses a person's mind with potentially heretical ideas. If an idea that is not consistent with Torah—such as "What if such-and-such person is really God?"—should happen to pop into a person's head, one is not supposed to pursue it. The appropriate course of action is to shut it down and focus one's attention on Torah.

Such a dilemma can arise in a lot of places. One area, perhaps surprisingly to some, is yoga. As many people are into yoga a form of exercise *cum* meditation, many may not realize that yoga is a spiritual practice with its roots in Hinduism. The yoga poses, called "asanas," are part of a greater philosophical school that is meant to include such things as abstention and liberation. When people say that whites doing yoga is cultural appropriation, they're not wrong. Trying to extricate yoga from its Hindu roots is like claiming that the "Kabbalah" studied by celebrities is unrelated to Judaism. Watered down though it may be, the Kabbalah (or the yoga) is still a product of its origins.

Am I saying you can't do yoga? Absolutely not! But for what it's worth, Rabbi Menachem Mendel Schneerson, the seventh Lubavitcher Rebbe, *did* say that—twice. In 1978, he wrote regarding "certain Oriental [*sic*] movements, such as transcendental meditation, yoga, guru and the like... inasmuch as these movements involve certain rites and rituals, they have been rightly regarded by rabbinic authorities as cults bordering on, and in some respects actual, idolatry." I'm not saying that such is necessarily the only position but it's definitely a not-unprecedented position.

There are actually a lot of areas where such an issue can arise. I once got into a knock-down, drag-out argument with a friend of my wife over *The Secret*. If you're not familiar with it, it's a book that popularizes "the law of attraction." If you're not familiar with *that*, it's the idea of "ask, believe and receive," i.e., since people and thoughts are both made of energy, a person can channel that energy to get the universe to give them stuff. This does not happen to agree with my understanding of how God, prayer or the universe operates. I don't see it as compatible with Jewish philosophy and I told her as much, which she did not appreciate. (For the record, I'm pretty open-minded. You can read and believe whatever you like and it's none of my business. But if you're going to sit at my table and extol the virtues of a certain philosophy with which I disagree, there's going to reach a point where I will express a dissenting opinion.)

More areas where this can question can arise include, but are not limited to, martial arts, Freemasonry, *Harry Potter*, alternative medicine, etc., etc., etc. You're very likely to find different tolerance levels for these and other things based on underlying philosophies that may or may not actually be present in a given situation. And I can't tell you which of these are okay and which aren't. I have my own opinions but it's not my place to decide for you, so ask your own Torah authority for guidance.

In the 19th century, Rabbi Samson Raphael Hirsch expressed the philosophy of *Torah im derech eretz*—Torah combined with the way of the world. The Mishna in *Avos* (2:2) uses this phrase to refer to Torah study combined with a profession. The concept was expanded by the Maharal (16th century) to include knowledge of the natural sciences and by Rav Hirsch, later still, to include broader secular learning as well as knowledge of the greater societies in which our Jewish communities reside. But this is limited to scientific and cultural literacy; it does not include embracing philosophies that may be antithetical to Torah.

The Midrash in *Eicha Rabbah* (2:13) says, "If someone tells you that there is wisdom among the nations of the world, believe it." (This is based Obadiah 1:8, which refers to the wise men of Edom.) However, the Midrash continues, "If someone tells you that there is Torah among the nations of the world, do not believe it." (This is based on Lamentations 2:9, which refers to exile among other nations, where there is no Torah.) Scientific knowledge—like vaccinations—should be accepted regardless of the source. But what about acupuncture? Aromatherapy? Crystal healing? I don't know. There's a line drawn somewhere but everyone's line may be in a different place. Practices based in other religions' philosophies are problematic and extricating practices from their philosophies of origin may be tricky (if it can be done at all!). It's for exactly this kind of thing that one should have a good religious figure to whom to turn for guidance.

DNA Testing

Q. Can DNA prove Jewish identity?

A. There are a couple of things to consider when examining such a question. The first thing to understand is that the Torah's methodologies do not necessarily line-up with our modern assumptions. I'll explain.

When I was a kid, I heard someone opine that "obviously" the Torah was written by humans because it lists the bat among the unclean species of birds and an all-knowing God would know that bats aren't birds.

The problem with this person's conclusion was that it was based on the assumption that all systems divide wildlife the way he does: mammals, birds, fish, reptiles, etc. In fact, the Torah does not use this classification system. Rather, the Torah uses "beasts, flying things, sea creatures, creeping things, etc." So a cow is a beast, a bat is a flying thing, a whale is a sea creature and a mouse is a creeping thing, irrespective of the fact that we would classify them all as mammals. Our current assumptions about what's "obvious" is not the only way of looking at the world.

The next thing to consider is that not everything can be proved using science. Some things require eyewitness testimony or an unbroken tradition. Let's consider the case of *tzaraas*, a type of spiritual skin affliction in people or mold in a house. If something is afflicted with *tzaraas*, there are rules about to what it transmits impurity, but these rules only take effect once a *kohein* declares the blemish to in fact be *tzaraas*. This is different from medical science in which a house with mumps or measles can spread infection regardless of whether a doctor has pronounced a quarantine. So spiritual matters can differ from purely temporal experiences.

Similarly, someone may have committed a crime, and we may know it for a fact, but it may not be actionable in *halacha* without proper testimony. The idea of "proof" in the absence of a tradition or eyewitness testimony may or may not be relevant in a variety of cases, including such questions as: "Can we eat this locust?" "Should we use this blue dye in our *tzitzis*?" "Does this food contain non-kosher ingredients?" "Did this milk come from a cow?" "Is this person a *kohein*?" "Is this person Jewish?" and "Can this woman remarry?" Sometimes, proving something with science is an acceptable standard and other times it isn't. (Opinions as to where the line falls may vary.)

The DNA question actually dates back to the 1950's, when blood tests were first being used to determine paternity. Rav Bentzion Chai Uzziel, the Sephardic Chief Rabbi of Israel, ruled that blood tests are not acceptable for this purpose, while Rav Shlomo Zalman Auerbach permitted them. (The question is rooted in a Talmudic discussion in *Niddah* 30a; Rav Uzziel had a very straightforward interpretation, while Rav Auerbach was more liberal in his approach.)

Rav Ovadia Yosef later addressed a case in which a young woman had a baby outside of marriage. A certain man claimed to be the father, which the woman denied. The man wanted a DNA test to prove his claim but the woman refused. The *beis din* hearing the case initially told the woman that her refusal to allow the test would be taken as an admission that the man's claim was correct. (Otherwise, why should she refuse the test?) Rav Ovadia interceded, saying that paternity is not considered provable under halachic principles so we cannot coerce someone with DNA, which would be considered inconclusive.

The Talmud in *Bava Basra* 58a records a story in which a paternity case was resolved based on the actions of one of the man's putative sons rather than on scientific evidence. The Rashash says that this was done in this way so as not to determine conclusively that the mother's other sons were actually illegitimate. He cites the commentaries to Mishna *Eduyos* 8:7 that *mamzeirus* (illegitimacy) should not be publicized.

This is similar to our example of *tzaraas* not being infectious until diagnosed; perhaps the other sons are illegitimate but the halachic problem does not arise until someone is actually known to be a *mamzer* and we have no obligation to go looking for trouble. In fact, it's probably preferable if we don't! Arguably, this is part of the reason why blood tests were not embraced to prove paternity: because if *halacha* accepted them as conclusive, they would also prove illegitimacy, which we're not supposed to do.

Rav Kook made an interesting observation regarding *halacha* and science. The *halacha* is that if a doctor says that a certain sick person may not fast on Yom Kippur and the patient says that he wants to fast, we listen to the doctor. Conversely, if the doctor says that the sick person may fast but the patient is convinced that doing so will be dangerous, we listen to the patient. We see from this that scientific information is useful in *halacha* but it's not the last word. The doctor's opinion does not automatically trump the patient's. Rather, it's taken into consideration among other factors.

In any event, genetic testing would be of limited use in actually determining one's Jewishness. A person might have Jewish ancestry but not be halachically Jewish. A full-fledged convert might have no Jewish genetic material at all. And what about sperm and ova from Jewish donors that might be brought to term in a non-Jewish woman's womb?

So, for a variety of reasons, DNA testing is not considered a halachic "slam dunk." Rather, it is just one more thing to be taken into account when rendering a decision. It carries more weight for things that might require a lower standard of proof, such as identifying a deceased's remains to allow his widow to remarry and Israel's Law of Return, than it does for, say, allowing someone to marry in or to serve as a *kohein*. But DNA is not a legal trump card, because if we used it to include those who have a tradition of being on the outside, it could also be used to exclude those who have a tradition of being on the inside. While DNA might be useful in reaching a conclusion, such a test is therefore not accepted as a sole determinant in *halacha*.

It's Not Easy Being Green

Q. As observant Jews, what is our responsibility to the environment?

A. Our responsibility to the environment does not vary based on whether we are observant Jews, non-observant Jews or non-Jews; we all have the same responsibility. This is because the way in which we interact with the environment is based on the directives given to Adam, who is the ancestor of us all.

Genesis 2:15 tells us, "And the Lord God took the man and put him in the garden of Eden to work it and to protect it." This sounds like an obligation rather than a privilege but the very next verse says, "And the Lord God commanded the man, saying 'Of every tree of the garden you may eat freely...'" so we see that the garden was actually intended for our use. (The verse after that excludes the fruit of the Tree of Knowledge so we also see that there are some restrictions.)

From these parameters, it is easy enough to derive that we are permitted to use the environment but not to abuse it. This is a lesson that we see reinforced through various *mitzvos*. For example, Leviticus 22:28 prohibits slaughtering an animal and its offspring on the same day. You'll note that we are allowed to slaughter animals for food, we are even allowed to slaughter both the animal and its young, we're just not allowed to do so on the same day. This is to sensitize us to the fact that, while we may destroy aspects of nature for our needs (food, clothing, shelter, etc.), doing so is still destructive and we must do so with restraint.

Along these lines, consider the story of Rabbi Yehuda, which we discuss elsewhere in a different context. The Talmud (*Bava Metzia* 85a) tells us that Rabbi Yehuda once saw a calf being led to the slaughter. The calf ran to him and sought shelter by sticking its head under the rabbi's cloak. "What do you want from me?" he asked the calf. "This is why you were created!" Because of his lack of sympathy towards the calf's plight, Rabbi Yehuda was afflicted for 13 years, until he demonstrated that he had mastered compassion for animals.

You will note that slaughtering the calf was a permitted act and Rabbi Yehuda isn't criticized for allowing it to proceed, he was only punished for being insensitive about it. He rightly stated that this was the reason for the calf's creation, but he had become jaded to that reality, rather than recognizing the loss of the calf's life as a solemn byproduct of man's necessities. His story serves as a lesson to us.

For this reason, while we are allowed to hunt for food—and even for skins or fur if necessary—hunting for sport is strongly frowned upon. In his writings, Rabbi Yechezkel Landau (d. 1793), known as the *Noda b'Yehuda,* criticized recreational hunting. He points out that our Biblical exemplars include plenty of shepherds but no hunters. The only hunters we see are Nimrod and Esau—hardly characters we consider role models! While it may not be explicitly prohibited, the *Noda b'Yehuda* concludes that hunting for sport is unseemly because it is an expression of wanton cruelty. (You know how I said above that we may use nature but not abuse it? According to the *Noda b'Yehuda* and others, hunting for sport would fall into the category of "abuse.")

Probably the mitzvah most people would think of in response to your question is the one we call *bal tashchis*—"not to destroy." Deuteronomy 20:19 prohibits cutting down fruit-bearing trees as part of a siege. This is part of a greater principle that we should not casually destroy useful things. Yes, burning down an orchard might dishearten the enemy but we have to look at the big picture. We need to recognize the value of what God has given us and not ruin it in our short-sightedness. But again, the principle of "use but not abuse" applies. Accordingly, one may cut down fruit trees for constructive purposes, such as for lumber or to benefit an overcrowded grove.

I think this nicely encapsulates our responsibility to the environment: use but don't abuse. Eating animals? Go ahead, but don't endanger a species. Fossil fuels? As necessary. Some people need an SUV and others don't, so let's not ban them but maybe we don't need to take a Humvee to the corner store for a loaf of bread. Air conditioning? Yes, mankind survived for millennia without it but I'm afraid you're going to have to pry this innovation from my cold (from air conditioning) dead hands. Keep in mind that it's all about making a cost-benefit analysis, and our personal analyses may not all be identical.

Psalms 115:16 says, "The heavens belong to Hashem but He gave the Earth to mankind." You might think that we can do whatever we like with a gift but sometimes there are strings attached. Consider that nothing belongs to a person more than his own body. We are obviously allowed to use our bodies, which definitely causes wear and tear, but we are simultaneously obligated to protect our bodies and not permitted to abuse them. If we are limited in how we use our own bodies, which only affects ourselves, I think it's just common sense that we should exercise restraint in how we use our natural resources, which affects everyone, including future generations.

Wearing Fur

Q. *Fur is being banned in NYC. This obviously affects all the Hasidic Jews who wear fur hats. What's the Torah opinion on fur?*

A. Let me clarify the matter for those not in the know. As of this writing, the sale of fur is being considered for a ban in New York City; wearing fur is not being banned. The proposal impacts thousands of people who work for hundreds of businesses, many of which have been around for generations. That's putting out of work a lot of people who have never known any profession beyond the fur trade.

Incidental to that, some Hasidic sects will be affected by this ban because of the custom for the men to wear fur hats known as streimels. Some legislators are pushing for a "religious exemption" to allow streimels to continue to be available. Some people say that a religious exemption is unnecessary because wearing a streimel is not a religious obligation. Still other people opine that a religious exemption would be dangerous because excepting the *chasidim* from the ban would foment anti-Semitism. But let's address the halachic question rather than the political ones.

I recently addressed our obligations toward the environment. There, I pointed out the directives that God gave Adam (and through him, all mankind):

Genesis 2:15 tells us, "And the Lord God took the man and put him in the garden of Eden to work it and to protect it." This sounds like an obligation rather than a privilege but the very next verse says, "And the Lord God commanded the man, saying 'Of every tree of the garden you may eat freely…'" so we see that the garden was actually intended for our use.

From these directives, we see that we are permitted to use the environment but not to abuse it. This includes killing animals for food, skins, and presumably fur, though hunting for sport is frowned upon. The particular issue at hand is called *tzaar baalei chaim*—causing needless suffering to living things.

There is ostensibly a difference between meat production and fur production in how the animals are treated. Animals for food are typically slaughtered—in Jewish law, we strive to do so in the most humane way possible—but the methods used in fur trapping are often perceived to be somewhat gorier and/or more painful. Whether or not that is an accurate assessment, it's not necessarily *tzaar baalei chaim* because one is not hurting the animal gratuitously; it's being done for some human need.

Similarly, there are those who object that fur is simply unnecessary. This is not a halachic parameter, as the same can be said about meat. Some object to killing animals for meat as unnecessary given our modern food and nutrition options but doing so is unambiguously permitted by the Torah. God gave permission to Noah for his descendants to eat meat, saying, "The fear and awe of you (i.e., mankind) shall be upon every beast of the earth, every bird of the air, everything with which the ground swarms, and all the fish of the sea; they are delivered into your hand. Every living thing shall be food for you, just like the vegetation I have given you" (Genesis 9:2-3). Later, regarding kosher meat, the Torah explicitly permits one to slaughter meat "as much as your soul desires" (Deuteronomy 12:21), not restricted by one's dietary requirements *per se*.

God told Adam that mankind was to "have dominion over the fish of the sea, the birds of the air, and every living thing that crawls on the earth" (Genesis 1:28). These things were given to us to use as we deem necessary. That doesn't give us the right to cause any more pain to an animal than necessary but it does permit us to cause animals a certain degree of pain if it serves some human purpose. This purpose doesn't have to be necessary for survival. It can be for luxuries.

If one's moral compass steers them away from meat, leather or fur because they feel they don't truly need these things and they oppose causing any pain at all to an animal, that's a wonderful thing. But if others feel differently, *halacha* does permit these things despite the obvious downside in terms of animal suffering.

Suicide

Q. I know that suicide is technically prohibited in the Torah, but what about people with mental illness like Robin Williams, who suffered from bi-polar disorder? Is all suicide prohibited equally? How do we reconcile the Torah's prohibition of suicide with our modern understanding of mental health?

A. Please note: the following is not intended to be relied upon for matters of Jewish law. For questions of practical application, please consult your local Orthodox rabbi.

As a consequence of Robin Williams' high-profile suicide, many people have been asking about suicide in Jewish law. To put it plainly, it's complicated.

First off, suicide is definitely prohibited but there are occasionally mitigating circumstances. The Torah tells us, "I will hold you responsible for the blood of your own lives" (Genesis 9:5). This law was stated to Noah rather than to Moses, meaning that it applies to all mankind, not just to Jews.

There is an important distinction that must be made. You will note— at least if you read the original Hebrew—that the Torah never says "Thou shalt not kill." It says, "Thou shalt not murder." There are times when one may, or even must, kill another person. In battle. Executing a criminal. In self-defense or the defense of another. These acts are killing but they are not murder. Similarly, there may be cases in which killing one's self is not "self-murder."

Offhand, I can think of three suicides in Tanach (the Jewish Bible), and four people who considered death preferable to life and even prayed to die. As we will see, there is at least one circumstance that justifies suicide, though I would stop short of saying that it's ever the recommended course of action.

Our first Biblical suicide was Samson. People misunderstand who Samson was. He was a commando. His mission was to harass the occupying Philistines as a loose cannon, giving the Jews plausible deniability. At one point, his own people even tried to arrest him and hand him over to the Philistine authorities (the original "PA"). Ultimately, Samson was captured, shaved (robbing him of his great strength), blinded, set to slave labor, and made an object of derision. Life was pretty much over for Samson. He prayed to God to restore his strength so that he could take out the Philistines even though this meant that he would also perish in the attempt. We see that this was permissible since God granted Samson's request. While this act certainly resulted in Samson's own death, I hesitate to consider it suicide *per se*. I think it is better indicative of the ability a person has to risk his own life for the greater good, be it a fighter pilot running a "suicide mission" or a firefighter saving victims at the cost of his own life. (Please don't liken Samson to a suicide bomber. Remember, killing may sometimes be necessary but murder is never permitted. So-called "suicide bombers" intentionally kill innocent people indiscriminately. That's murder.)

The second Biblical suicide I'd like to discuss is Achitofel in the book of II Samuel. Achitofel was an advisor to King David who rebelled and joined the coup of David's son Avshalom. When Avshalom stopped taking Achitofel's advice, Achitofel knew that it was inevitable that David would be restored to the throne. Therefore, he pre-emptively took his own life. Our understanding of Achitofel's actions is this: David would execute Achitofel as a traitor. Those executed for treason had their property confiscated by the authorities, against whom they had rebelled. By committing suicide, Achitofel beat David to the punch, enabling his sons to retain their father's estate. While that was certainly considerate of Achitofel, it is not a permitted rationale for committing suicide.

Our final Biblical suicide was King Saul. Saul was utterly defeated by the Philistines. He was on the verge of being captured. His options were either a quick death now or torture followed by death at the hands of the Philistines. Saul asked his armor-bearer to finish him off but the request was rightly refused, so Saul did it himself. He is not criticized for this as his death was inevitable and his motivation was merely to avoid the pain of torture. (Please note that the armor-bearer was correct in refusing to kill Saul. Not only that, in II Samuel chapter 1, a man claims to have found Saul mortally wounded and finished him off. He is executed for this. The threat of torture might justify killing oneself but it does not justify killing another.)

Now let's briefly look at four who prayed to die:

The first, surprisingly, is Moses. In Exodus 32:32, he asks God to forgive the Jews. "If not," he says, then "please erase me from Your book, which You have written." While people generally assume that Moses meant that God should remove him from the Torah, the Talmud (*Rosh Hashana* 16b) suggests that Moses is referring to the "Book of Life." In other words, "forgive the nation or give me death!"

The second is probably the most familiar. After delivering his prophecy to Nineveh—which he did not want to do—the prophet Jonah became a beachcomber. He lived under a gourd plant that provided him with shade. When the plant withered and the sun beat down upon his head, Jonah was distressed and prayed to die. God said to Jonah, "You're despondent because of a tree that you didn't even plant. Shouldn't I be concerned about a big city like Nineveh, which is full of people who need guidance?"

The third case, Job, is a little different in that he was actually being encouraged by others. Originally, Job had everything—family, wealth, prestige, health—and then he lost it all. Things got so bleak that his friends advised him to "curse God and die." Job initially accepted everything that happened to him until he finally snapped and accused God of being unfair. God then put things into context for Job and ultimately replaced everything that he had lost.

The fourth person who prayed to die was Elijah, in I Kings chapter 19; things got better for him, too.

These situations are similar in that they were all born of despair. What we see in these three cases is that things do get better. Had any of these people perished at their low points, they would not have been around to see the improvements. Even Job, who lost his children, ultimately had another reason to live.

Now, as far as mental illness, that is not a justification *per se*, but it is certainly a mitigating factor. To blame a clinically-depressed person for their state of mind is like blaming a diabetic for his state of insulin. "Just suck it up" is an unreasonable expectation; people must be given the help they need. If the unthinkable should happen, the assumption is that the person was not in control of his actions and therefore not responsible. (Traditionally, a suicide is not buried in a Jewish cemetery but nowadays we generally assume that the deceased was the victim of a mental illness and we permit it.) God, of course, knows for sure who is and who isn't in control of their actions.

So, wrapping it all up, suicide is prohibited by the Torah for Jews and non-Jews alike. There are rare cases where suicide might be justifiable, such as to avoid torture. However, assisting a suicide, even in such a case, is still considered murder. In the case of mental illness, suicide is not "justified," but the person in question is presumed not to have been in a proper state of mind and therefore not responsible for their actions.

NEW! Torah vs. Science

Q. How are we supposed to believe Judaism when it contradicts scientific truths like evolution and the Big Bang?

A. Chlorophyll wasn't discovered until the nineteenth century but that scientific discovery didn't bother anyone. We still believe that God makes the plants grow; chlorophyll just tells us *how* He does it. Similarly, other scientific discoveries may enlighten us as to how God runs the world. For some reason, however, some people are bothered because they perceive there to be contradictions between Torah traditions and various scientific discoveries.

When we perceive an apparent contradiction between Torah and science, we have three possible solutions: we can assume that the Torah is "wrong" (God forbid), we can assume that science is wrong, or we can assume that Torah and science somehow agree in a way that we don't yet understand. I favor that third option, which turns out to be true more often than one might think.

Let's take fossils. When people started digging up the fossilized remains of dinosaurs and cavemen, Judaism wasn't particularly bothered. We never resorted to claims like they were from creatures that "missed Noah's ark" or that they were "put there by the devil" in order to trick us. Rather, they actually supported Jewish tradition—assuming, of course, that one was familiar enough with Jewish tradition to recognize it.

The Midrash Rabbah (Genesis 3:7) cites Rabbi Yehuda the son of Rabbi Simon on the phrase "And it was evening." From the fact that God didn't say "let there be evening," we can see that time existed before the world. Based on this, Rabbi Abahu says that God creating multiple worlds, ultimately destroying them and building more advanced worlds on their remains.

This sounds a lot like the various strata representing various geologic ages. So much so, in fact, that when the skeleton of a mammoth was unearthed in Siberia in 1807, Rav Yisroel Lipschutz, the *Tiferes Yisroel*, basically said, "So what?" He wrote in *Derush Ohr HaChaim*, "It is clear that everything the kabbalists have told us for hundreds of years, that the world had existed and been destroyed, then it was reestablished four more times, each time in a more perfect state than before, now in our time it has become clear in truth and righteousness. Would you believe, my brothers, that this wonderful secret is clearly stated in the beginning of our holy Torah?"

Similarly, consider carbon dating and other methods of estimating the age of the world and the universe. The standard objection is along the lines of, "The Torah says the world is 6,000 years old but this rock carbon dates at millions of years! And if the universe were only 6,000 years old, the light from the stars—which are millions of light years away—wouldn't have had time to reach Earth yet!"

These are valid scientific observations but, once again, our tradition provided a response even before the question arose. The Talmud in *Chullin* (60a) tells us that everything was created in its final, adult form. Was Adam created as a newborn, lying at the base of the Sapling of Knowledge? Of course not! Adam was like a 30-year-old man on the day of his creation and, had you cut down the Tree of Knowledge on the day of its creation, there would have been hundreds of rings in its trunk. Similarly, if you carbon dated a rock during the first week of creation, it would have demonstrated the properties of a mature rock. And the stars? They were created with their light already reaching Earth; Adam could see starlight at night.

Even the Big Bang is alluded to in rabbinic literature. The Ramban (Nachmanides), in his commentary on Genesis 1:1, describes how God didn't create each individual object in the universe out of nothingness. Rather, he created a small amount of primordial matter, called *hyle* in Greek. This proto-matter was full of potential energy and it was from this that God created everything in the universe. That's a pretty good description of the Big Bang for the thirteenth century!

In short, the more we know about Torah, the less such "contradictions" raised by scientific discoveries bother us because they often agree with our traditions more than people think.

I know that, so far, I sound like a fundamentalist, downplaying science in order to make it fit Talmud or Midrash. Sometimes, however, we have to re-evaluate what we thought a piece of Torah meant in light of newly-established facts. We see this even in the Talmud itself.

A debate is recorded in tractate *Pesachim* (94b). There, the Jewish Sages say that the sun travels under the sky by day and behind the sky by night. The secular scholars say that the sun travels under the sky by day and under the Earth by night. Rebbi (Rav Yehuda HaNasi) sides with the secular scholars saying that their position simply makes more sense. We now know, of course, that Rebbi and the secular scholars were correct—at night, the sun is on the other side of the earth, not on the far side of the sky.

This flexibility is important when discussing whether the universe is 6,000 or 13 billion years old. (Ultimately, I would recommend reading *Genesis and the Big Bang* by Dr. Gerald Schroeder, which describes how both accounts can be describing the same event from different perspectives. It's far more compelling than anything I have to say on the subject, but I'm not a physicist so I have to take my own approach.)

In Maimonides' day, science believed that the universe always existed; Jewish tradition was "anti-science" because we believe that the universe had been created. In *Moreh Nevuchim* (2:25), the Rambam writes that the reason we reject the idea of an eternal universe is not because of the Torah's creation account. Yes, the Rambam says, the Torah describes the creation of the universe, but it contains far more descriptions of God as a corporeal Being. We have no problem saying that terms like "hand of God," "throne of God," etc. are allegorical. Similarly, if the eternity of the universe were absolutely proven, we could easily write off the creation account by considering it a metaphor. However, there is a major difference between the two cases: the incorporeality of God has been proven, which necessitates understanding verses to the contrary as metaphors. The eternity of the universe has not been proven and we do not abandon the literal understanding of Biblical verses in order to accommodate a theory.

It's noteworthy that the Rambam says that he would be willing to relegate the creation account to the realm of allegory if the eternity of the universe were absolutely proven. It's a good thing he didn't leap to accommodate scientific thought because it turned out to be wrong! Nowadays, we all agree that the universe was created—we just quibble about how long ago. (To paraphrase a line apocryphally attributed to Winston Churchill, George Bernard Shaw and others, we've established what it is, now we're just haggling over the details.) If, given sufficient proof, the Rambam would accept that the universe always existed, it seems a small leap that he could accept a 13-billion-year-old universe if compelling enough proof were provided.

It's important to recognize that scientific "fact" changes as science advances. How many planets are in the solar system? Today we say eight but when I was in school it was nine—and none of them were destroyed in the interim! A mere century earlier, the correct answer would have been 12, including such bodies as Ceres, Pallas, Juno and Vesta (but not Pluto, which had not yet been discovered). A millennium before that, the answer was seven—and two of those were the sun and the moon! As per the Rambam, we are flexible when it comes to indisputable fact but the sad reality is that "facts" change with alarming regularity.

So don't get too troubled over how old a rock is or the fact that there are dinosaur bones in the museum. *How* God did something is not as important as recognizing *that* God did it. We've established what it is, now we're just quibbling over details.

Jewish History

Rivka's Age

Q. Rivka got engaged at three years old? How are we supposed to understand this?

A. I'm gratified that you said "engaged" rather than married because that's a huge difference.

The idea that Rivka was three is not the only opinion, but it's been popularized because it's the one cited by Rashi on Genesis 25:20, and everyone learns Rashi. It's based on calculations that make a number of assumptions, including that Yitzchak was 37 at the time of the *akeidah*—which is in turn based on the assumption that Sarah died during the *akeidah*—and that Rivka was born at the same time. None of this is explicit in the text. They are all Midrashim and they all have to be literal history to yield the result that Rivka was three. There are other opinions, such as that Yitzchak was 13 at the *akeidah* (see Ibn Ezra 22:4), which will yield very different results.

Even according to the most literal understanding of all this, that doesn't mean that Yitzchak consummated the marriage at that time. Rashi on 25:26, based on *Pirkei d'Rabbi Eliezer*, suggests that they waited ten years, at which point she would have reached the age of majority.

But, as noted, all of this is based on Midrashim, and Midrashim can be tricky things. Rabbeinu Avraham ben HaRambam explains in detail how some midrashim (and *aggados*) are intended literally, while others are intended for other purposes, such as to impart moral lessons. We don't always know which are which. Taking every Midrash as literal would not only be improper, it would be foolish when one considers that many Midrashim contradict one another! For example, one Midrash says that Iyov (Job) was an advisor to Pharaoh, while another says he was a fictional character in a parable written by Moshe. You can't have it both ways.

Most of us learn Midrashim as children. They capture our interest and shed light on the text of Chumash. All too often, however, we fail to revisit them as adults and to consider what deeper messages they might be trying to convey.

For example, I don't believe that the arm of Pharaoh's daughter magically stretched like that of Plastic Man in order to retrieve the basket containing baby Moshe. To me, that appears to be a message that if we attempt to perform a task that seems beyond us, God will offer us assistance. (It should be noted that Rashi on Exodus 2:5 indicates that, for grammatical reasons, the stretching arm can't be the simple meaning of the verse and is clearly homiletical wordplay.)

I also don't believe that we cover *challah* on Shabbos because bread is capable of being embarrassed. That's clearly a homiletical interpretation of the *halacha*, designed to impart the moral lesson that, if we're concerned with the "feelings" of inanimate objects, how much more careful we must be not to shame one another.

So what lesson do I derive from the assertion that Rivka was three? "Three years old" is an age with very specific halachic ramifications throughout the Talmud. A girl who was converted, freed from captivity or redeemed from indentured servitude until the age of three is like she was never non-Jewish, taken captive or indentured at all. The Midrash discusses the depravity of Rivka's homeland. By saying that she was three years old when she married Yitzchak, it employs recognizable halachic terminology to convey that she was unsullied by the environment of her birth.

As noted, Midrashim can and do contradict one another. The *Sifri* says that Rivka was 14 when she married Yitzchak. This is the position accepted by the *Seder Olam*, whose entire *raison d'etre* is to create a chronology of events. Sure, 14 is still pretty young by our standards but I think we can not be appalled if that was a marriageable age 4,000 years ago. Since we can't take both Midrashim literally, I choose to believe that this opinion more closely represents the literal history of things.

The Golden Calf

Q. I just don't understand the story of the golden calf. How could a people who had just seen open miracles so quickly turn to idolatry?

A. We draw a lot of conclusions about people based on the words they use. For example, if someone commonly refers to God as "Hashem," we might make certain assumptions about his background. If someone calls God "the Lord" or "HaKadosh Baruch Hu," we might make different assumptions. While all these terms refer to the same Being, the choice of Name employed suggests—rightly or wrongly—that a person has a particular mindset.

Similarly, if we hear a person say, "I have to pray," most people, even Jews, might picture congregants on their knees with their eyes closed and hands clasped. If he were to say, "I have to meditate," we might envision someone seated in the lotus position, trying to clear his mind. And if he says, "I have to daven," we might think of Jews with curly sidelocks and black coats swaying back and forth. All of these terms could be used to describe the same experience of communing with God but because of the cultural assumptions we make, we pigeonhole worship into segments. We associate the way people talk to God rightly or wrongly with the nomenclature used.

When we hear about the golden calf, we automatically make certain assumptions. This is because we culturally associate such things with idolatry. But this is not necessarily what was going on with the Jews in the wilderness! We assume they thought a statue of a cow was somehow divine but that may just be a logical leap on our part.

If you were raised in India, China or Saudi Arabia, you would no doubt have a different "default" idea of how one talks to God than you do if you're from North America or Europe. If you had no instruction and were left to your own devices, you would probably just emulate what you had seen all around you. Similarly, someone raised in ancient Egypt had a very different idea from us about how to pray. Left without guidance, the Jews did the only thing they knew how to do, based upon the culture in which they were raised. We assume it was idolatry but that wasn't necessarily the case.

The *Kuzari* explains that everyone at the time of the Exodus worshiped tangible objects. There were surely people who believed in a non-corporeal God (or "gods"), but even they required some physical object upon which to focus their attention. In this, the Jews were no different from the society in which they were raised. For example, after their departure from Egypt, the Jews focused their attention on the pillars of cloud and fire that led them by day and by night. They knew these things weren't God, they were just concrete phenomena towards which they could direct their thoughts.

So Moshe ascended Mount Sinai and the Jews were waiting for him to return with the *luchos*, which would serve as another physical manifestation of God's greatness upon which they could focus. But Moshe was gone for forty days and there was some confusion as to the count so the people got anxious. Out of frustration, they demanded some other physical object upon which they could focus. This may have been misguided but it was intended to serve as part of their service to God. Their error was in fashioning an idol (which God had prohibited) and ascribing holiness to it. The Jews did not intend to reject God through their actions, but they did reject some of His *mitzvos* by trying to take the law into their own hands.

The *Kuzari* compares the actions of the Jews who served the calf to those of a patient who injures or even kills himself by self-medicating when a doctor could have saved him by administering proper dosages. The calf didn't feel like a grievous sin to them—and it was certainly not their intention to worship idols! They were merely grasping on to a mode of worship that was as familiar to them as a shul is to us. (The *Kuzari* also contextualizes that only 3,000 of the 600,000 men who left Egypt worshiped the calf. That's 1 in every 200. The other 199 out of 200 did not stumble in this area.)

It should be noted that even the Temple, holy as it was, was a concession to the way people were used to praying. The Rambam in his *Guide for the Perplexed* discusses how the Temple is really a kind of religious "half-way house." People were used to temples with priests and sacrifices so God gave them that, albeit in a very limited fashion.

There was only one Temple, in Jerusalem. Sacrifices could not be offered elsewhere. One couldn't train to be a priest; he had to be born into it. And there were a dozen different types of ritual impurity, ranging from bodily emissions to unclean carcasses, any of which would keep a person from being able to visit the Temple for a period of time. God gave us a Temple but He seriously limited the extent to which we could interact with it.

Contrast this with synagogues. Synagogues are everywhere. If they don't happen to be found in a particular locale, that's not by design; synagogues could potentially be built in any city, state or country. One can attend the synagogue at any time, ritual purity or impurity notwithstanding. As much as God limited our use of the Temple, that's how unlimited our ability to attend *shul* is. (And make no mistake: while we tend to think of synagogues as replacements for an absent Temple, that's not entirely true; there were synagogues in Temple times as well. There was even a synagogue as part of the Temple complex, so the two modes of service were always in operation at the same time.)

As we have seen, the way we worship and the way we understand different forms of worship is very much a factor of the times and places in which we are raised. Make no mistake, the Jews who worshiped the golden calf were definitely in the wrong but as much as we look at the incident and scream "Idolatry!" such was not their intention. They were victims of an extremely misguided attempt to get closer to God by emulating the only kind of service they had ever seen. Was it bad? Yes. But upon reflection, it was perhaps not so inconceivable after all.

The Lost Tribes of Israel

Q. *I'm wondering if there is more information about the ten lost Tribes? Which Tribe would Ashkenazi Jews come from?*

Answering your question requires a refresher course in Biblical history. There were actually 13 Tribes. Eleven of these were named for 11 of Jacob's sons, whose descendants constituted the populations of these Tribes. As per lyrics from the musical *Joseph and the Amazing Technicolor Dreamcoat* (which is easier to recite than looking them up in their actual order of birth), "Reuben was the oldest of the children of Israel, with Simeon and Levi the next in line. Naftali and Issachar, with Asher and Dan. Zebulon and Gad brought the total to nine. (Jacob! Jacob and sons!) Benjamin and Judah, which leaves only one...."

Jacob may have had only one more son, Joseph, but there were two more Tribes: Ephraim and Menashe. These were named for Joseph's sons (Jacob's grandsons), each of whom was the progenitor of his own Tribe. A firstborn son normally receives a double portion but Reuben forfeited this when he disrupted his father's marital arrangements (in Genesis 35). Jacob then gave the double portion to Joseph, who was the firstborn of his mother, Rachel.

So, here we have 13 Tribes: Reuben, Simeon, Levi, Naftali, Issachar, Asher, Dan, Zebulon, Gad, Benjamin, Judah, Ephraim and Menashe. However, we only ever count 12 of them. Typically, this is done by omitting Levi. This is because the Tribe of Levi did not have a territory in Israel. Their job was to work in the Temple and they were supported by various tithes and offerings, as is explicit in Deuteronomy 18:1-2. Sometimes, however, Levi is included in the count. When this is the case, the Tribes of Ephraim and Menashe are typically combined into a single unit comprising all the descendants of Joseph. (These are the most common ways but there are others. For example, I Chronicles 27 includes Levi, Ephraim, and Menashe *twice* because Menashe had territory on both sides of the Jordan with different leaders! Nevertheless, the count of 12 Tribes is maintained by omitting Gad and Asher.)[2]

So, while we always speak of 12 Tribes, there were actually 13. As noted, Levi didn't have any territory of their own; they lived in various cities throughout the 12 territories though they were largely concentrated near Jerusalem because that's where the Temple was.

---

2. I have made an observation that the numbers 12 and 13 are often fungible in this way. (a) How many months are in the Hebrew year? Twelve. A leap year has 13 but instead of a unique month, we get an extra month of Adar, so 13 is still 12. (b) The name "Shemoneh Esrei" means 18 but there are 19 blessings in that prayer; one was added later to the middle section of 12 blessings, so 13 is considered 12, at least as far as the name of the prayer is concerned. (c) What's the age of majority in Jewish law? Either 12 or 13, depending on if one is a girl or a boy. The significance of this phenomenon, however, eludes me.

After King Solomon died, his son Rehoboam was approached by the people demanding tax relief. He decided to show them who was boss by refusing their demand. This backfired because ten of the 12 Tribes holding territory seceded and formed their own country. (This included Reuben, Simeon, Naftali, Issachar, Asher, Dan, Zebulon, Gad, Ephraim and Menashe.) The new, northern kingdom made up of these ten Tribes took the name Israel. The southern Kingdom—which included Levi, Benjamin and Judah—retained the Davidic dynasty, as well as the Temple in Jerusalem. They took the name Judah. (This all happened around 797 BCE, as described in I Kings 12.) The two kingdoms were initially at war. They eventually became allies but they never reunited.[3]

The northern kingdom of the ten Tribes was "lost" when they were conquered by Assyria. This didn't happen all at once; it occurred in waves. The Tribes on the other side of the Jordan—Reuben, Gad and half of Menashe—were the first to go, around 566 BCE, as detailed in I Chronicles 5. Zebulon and Naftali were exiled by Assyria around 562 BCE, as described in II Kings 15. The rest of the northern kingdom was exiled around 548 BCE, as seen in II Kings 17. The *modus operandi* of Assyria was to relocate conquered peoples, mixing the populations in foreign lands to preclude the likelihood of uprising and rebellion. This was how the ten Tribes got "lost." (It was also how we ended up with the quasi-Jewish "Samaritans" who created so much trouble in the second Temple period.)

God has foretold through His prophets that the lost Tribes would eventually be restored and the nation reunited. For example, in Ezekiel 37, God has that prophet write the names of the two kingdoms on two boards,

---

3. Readers who are more familiar with the books of the early Prophets may be aware that the Tribe of Shimon did not have one contiguous territory. Rather, they had cities scattered throughout the territory of Yehuda. The question therefore arises as to how, exactly, they seceded with the rest of the ten Tribes. Rashi on I Chronicles 4:31 suggests that the residents of Shimon were forced out of Yehuda's territory during the reign of King David, long before the schism that divided the nation. On the other hand, Tosfos Yom Tov infers from Mishna *Sotah* 8:1 that Shimon only broke away from Yehuda politically; they remained in the same location geographically. (I find this latter position more difficult to understand given Tanach's description of the blockades established by King Rechavam to keep the two nations separated physically.)

which He miraculously merges into a single board. This is also the theme of the song *U'vau Ha'Ovdim*, whose words come from Isaiah 27:13, "It will come to pass on that day that a great shofar will be blown and those who were lost in the land of Assyria will come, and those who were dispersed in the land of Egypt, and they shall worship Hashem on the holy mountain in Jerusalem." "Those who were lost in the land of Assyria" refers to the ten Tribes of the northern kingdom, while "those who were dispersed in the land of Egypt" refers to the southern kingdom of Judah, which was conquered by Nebuchadnezzar around 432 BCE, the survivors escaping to Egypt (II Kings 24-25).

Okay, so all the Tribes were lost except for Benjamin, Judah and Levi, right? Actually, it's not that simple. Imagine if the entire population of the United States were exiled except for one small section: the Eastern seaboard. That means that Minnesota, Arizona, North Dakota and Ohio are all gone. Now think about the cities that remained. Don't you think that a lot of people from Minnesota, Arizona, North Dakota and Ohio might have been visiting New York, Boston, Florida and the District of Columbia when the exile occurred? Similarly, Jerusalem was where the Temple stood. Not only is it reasonable to assume that representatives of all 13 Tribes were in Jerusalem (or elsewhere in Judah) when the ten Tribes were "lost," it would be unreasonable to expect otherwise! (See *Metzudas David* on I Kings 12:23, who backs me up on this, albeit in a different context.)

Unfortunately, our genealogical records took quite a beating in exile and we lost reliable family histories with the result that, for the most part, we no longer know our Tribes. Accordingly, Jews now come in three "flavors": *kohanim* (priests) and Leviim (Levites—both from the Tribe of Levi), and Yisroelim (Israelites—i.e., everybody else). Any other differentiation of population, such as Ashkenazi, Sefardi, Yemenite, Yekke, Chasidishe, etc., is the result of further migrations that occurred over the centuries since the Romans destroyed the second Temple in 70 CE. But all of those populations contain descendants of all the types of Jews— *kohanim* and Leviim descended from Levi, and Yisroelim—largely but probably not exclusively descended from Judah and Benjamin.

Over the years, many outrageous claims have been made in attempts to identify various groups as descendants of the lost Tribes. "The British are descended from the lost Tribes," "Native Americans are descended from the lost Tribes," "the Japanese are descended from the lost Tribes," etc. There is scant evidence to support these theories. ("The British get their name from the *brit*"—i.e., the covenant. Uh... no.)

That's not to say that there have never been more credible claims. In the ninth century, the Jews of Babylonia, Tunisia and the Iberian Peninsula were visited by Eldad haDani (Eldad from the Tribe of Dan), a traveler who claimed to come from a Jewish community in East Africa populated by the descendants of Dan, Asher, Gad and Naftali. ("What do you mean we were lost? We thought *you* were lost!") There is a difference of opinion as to how legitimate he may or may not have been.

Even nowadays there are such claims that should be taken seriously. Many believe that the Bene Israel of Ethiopia (formerly referred to as "Falashas") are descended from the Tribe of Dan and that the Bene Menashe of India are, as their name implies, descended from Menashe. These claims had enough halachic credence that Israeli chief rabbis recognized the populations in question as being of Jewish descent.

So that's the long and short on the "lost" Tribes. God has told us that they would eventually be restored and that may already be a work in progress. In the messianic era, everyone's Tribal affiliation will be clarified prophetically. (This last point is made by Maimonides in *Hilchos Melachim* 12:3; see there for the Rambam's Biblical sources.)

The Golem

Q. Did the Maharal really build a golem?

A. While I believe in the afterlife and souls and the miracles that are described in Tanach, I'm a real skeptic when it comes to things like magic, ghosts, demons, dybbuks and golems.

Whether the Maharal created a golem or not, he didn't create the idea. The Maharal of Prague lived in the 16th century, but the idea of a golem can be traced to the Talmud. In tractate *Sanhedrin* (65b), Rava created a golem, whom he sent to Rav Zeira. When Rav Zeira spoke to the stranger, he realized that it was an artificial man and returned him to dust.

Since the Talmud discusses golems, you might ask how I can be skeptical about them. The reality is that there are a lot of things in the Talmud that many don't take at face value, including such things as sorcery and *sheidim* (demons). This is because of the view espoused by the Rambam that such things don't actually exist. (In *Hilchos Avodas Kochavim* 11:16, the Rambam writes that there's no such thing as sorcery, saying that those who believe in magic are foolish. He writes that *sheidim* don't exist; see, e.g., *Peirush HaMishnayos* on *Avodah Zarah* 4:7 among other places.)

The logical question is: if such things don't exist, why does the Talmud discuss them as if they do? There are several approaches. Some people believe that these things used to exist but don't anymore. (I don't subscribe to this approach because, according to Maimonides, these things never existed. According to his opinion, even the "magic" worked by the Egyptian sorcerers in the time of Moses was really just sleight of hand.)

Some feel that the Sages of the Talmud just believed what the people of their times believed. (This seems reasonable enough but, while I am a confirmed skeptic, I'm not that big a cynic.)

The approach that I favor is that when the Talmud discusses such things, it is using coded language and it's our responsibility to uncover the deeper meaning. I'll give you an example:

The Talmud in *Bava Basra* (73b) tells a series of stories about the great sage Rabbah bar Bar Channah. In one of these tales, he claims to have seen a frog the size of the fort in Hagronia, which was the size of sixty houses. Along came a snake and swallowed the frog. Then along came a raven and swallowed the snake. The raven then landed on a tree. Rabbah's point? Imagine how strong that tree was! (Rav Papa bar Shmuel claimed to be an eyewitness to the event.)

Did this really happen? Was Rabbah telling tall tales? Or is something else going on here?

Our understanding is that the Rabbah bar Bar Channah tales are allegories with moral lessons. The meaning of this particular tale is as follows:

The giant frog represents the mighty Greek empire. It was swallowed by a snake, representing the Roman empire that succeeded it. This was swallowed by a raven, representing the Islamic caliphates. The raven landed on a tree that must be super-strong to support all that; the tree represents the Torah, which has endured all of those empires. Rav Papa bar Shmuel says that he was an eyewitness to this because all of our souls were present when the Torah was given at Sinai—that's what gives us the strength to keep on going despite all these empires conquering one another (and in the process, us).

So why does the Talmud say things in such an obscure manner? Maybe they're not so obscure to those in the know. In a famous incident, a Czarist official told a local rabbi that the outlandish stories of the Talmud couldn't possibly be true. The rabbi responded by saying, "Let's say that the Czar signed a decree against the Jews of my city. A poet might say, 'a single drop of ink washed away a thousand people.' That would not only be true, it would be quite eloquently put. It's just not literal. Someone living 100 years from now might read that and say it's ridiculous. But the fault is not in the text, it's in the reader's understanding of it."

Similarly, many such tales in the Talmud are full of hidden meanings and truths. Rather than glossing over them as fables and superstitions, we should try to discern those inner meanings and truths.

So, getting back to the Maharal, did he really build a golem? Some people believe so; some don't. We don't have a time machine, so we'll never be able to prove our beliefs to those who believe otherwise. But assuming that he did not actually do so, why would such a belief arise? To answer that, I'll share one more story:

The Chofetz Chaim was once called upon to serve as a witness in a court case. The judge asked his credentials and the lawyer responded by recounting tales of the rabbi's legendary piety—what we might call "rebbe stories." Hearing these praises, the judge asked the lawyer, "Do you really believe all that?" The lawyer responded, "No, your honor, I don't. But they don't tell such stories about you and me."

There's a certain truth in stories even if they're not literal history. We all know that young George Washington never chopped down a cherry tree, but the story persists because it underscores Washington's well-deserved reputation for honesty. Similarly, the Maharal may never have built a golem but the legend might have legs because of the way it reinforces the way in which that great man protected his community from both internal and external threats.

Then again, for all we know, maybe he did...

Who Wrote the *Zohar*?

Q. *I heard that the Kabbalah was written by Rabbi Shimon Bar Yochai. Is that the only opinion or are there other approaches?*

A. Thanks for your question. Bar Yochai isn't credited with writing "the Kabbalah"—Kabbalah is the entire corpus of Jewish mysticism—he's credited with writing the *Zohar*, which is the preeminent work of kabbalah. Before we get into that, let's talk about Rabbi Shimon.

According to the Talmud (33b-34a), the Roman occupiers didn't take too kindly to some criticisms that Rabbi Shimon had made, so they sought to execute him. Not wanting to be executed, Rabbi Shimon and his son ran away. Originally, they hid in the study hall but that was a pretty logical place to look for them, so they relocated to a cave. God made a miracle and provided them with a carob tree and a spring of water. In order to preserve their clothes, they would disrobe, bury themselves in sand up to their necks and spend their days immersed in intense Torah study. After 12 years, the prophet Elijah informed them that the emperor had died and the decree against them had been annulled.

Rabbi Shimon and his son emerged from the cave but they were so full of spiritual energy that every place they looked was immediately burned, with the result that they had to return to the cave for another twelve months. The Gemara then relates some things that Rabbi Shimon did when he returned to the world. At the end of the story, he encounters the one who had informed on him to the authorities. When Rabbi Shimon expressed surprise (or perhaps dismay) that this person was still alive, that informer "turned into a pile of bones."

Presumably, it was during his time in the cave that Rabbi Shimon—

who lived in the second century CE—composed the *Zohar*. At least such is the traditional attribution. There are those who believe that it was authored by Moses de Leon (13th century, Spain), who passed it off under Rabbi Shimon's name as a "pious fraud."

The bulk of claims against Rabbi Shimon's authorship boil down to anachronisms of various types. Anachronisms are not the kiss of death that detractors like to think. The Talmud was authored by Ravina and Rav Ashi but you'll find later insertions that were made by the Gaonim. Even the Bible has at least one anachronism! (Shir HaShirim 3:9 contains the Greek word *apirion*, which was a kind of seat that was carried by bearers. Greek was unknown in Israel in the time of Solomon, who composed the Shir HaShirim, so it must be a fraud, right? Not so fast! We know that King Solomon's writings were edited by his descendant King Chizkiyahu—see, for example, Proverbs 25:1. Greek may have been unknown in Israel in Solomon's day but this certainly wasn't the case in Chizkiyahu's lifetime!) Even if Rabbi Shimon was the primary author of the *Zohar*, the difficult, esoteric nature of the material and the oral transmission (at least initially) is a combination crying out for insertions by later transmitters until the work's ultimate fixed form in writing. (It is believed that the *Zohar* was a "living document" in this manner for about 300 years after its initial composition.)

In preparing this response to your question, I went online to try to get a few specific examples of anachronisms in the *Zohar* and I found a whole laundry list of "proofs" that the work couldn't have been written by Rabbi Shimon. It far exceeded my knowledge of the *Zohar* and my ability to respond. Rather than cherry pick a few easy examples, I forwarded the list to my friend and colleague Rabbi Yochanan Bechhofer, who is far more well-versed in the *Zohar* than you, I, or the person who compiled that list of proofs. He was able to respond to each one, rapid-fire and in great depth. Following are just a few of the "proofs" against the *Zohar* and a snippet of his reply to each. (I have labeled the so-called proofs "Point" and the responses "Counter-Point." I have also phrased the information in my own words, so my apologies for any damage caused to Rabbi Bechhofer's thorough responses.)

Point: A great person visited Moses de Leon to learn the history of the *Zohar* and was told by de Leon's wife that he had made it up.

Counter-Point: The story is incredibly garbled (and is apocryphal to begin with). The great rabbi was Rav Yitzchak d'Min Akko, an associate of the Ramban. When he traveled to Spain, he met someone who told him in the name of someone else that he heard that de Leon's wife said something to that effect. It was a big game of telephone, which Rav Yitzchak discounted because of the unlikelihood that de Leon could have composed a work anywhere near the magnitude of the *Zohar*.

Point: de Leon, lacking a clear sense of history, describes Rabbi Shimon as conversing with people who lived long after his death.

Counter-Point: There are many people across the generations who share the same names. Even in the Talmud, it's not always clear who a speaker is. There's more than one Hillel, more than one Rabban Gamliel… The same name is not always the same speaker.

Point: The book includes terms that were not coined until much later.

Counter-Point: No, the book contains terms that weren't *recorded* until much later. That isn't proof that the terms didn't exist.

Point: The book includes ideas copied from the *Kuzari*, which came much later.

Counter-Point: The *Zohar* never quotes the *Kuzari*. If it has ideas in common, that could just be because they're authentic concepts in Jewish philosophy.

Point: The book includes the Rambam's ideas about physics.

Counter-Point: No, the *Zohar* includes *Aristotle's* ideas about physics, which were later repeated by the Rambam. Aristotle lived long before Rabbi Shimon bar Yochai.

Point: The book mentions putting on two pairs of *tefillin*, a practice that only dates to the 12th century.

Counter-Point: Actually, no. We may call the two types of *tefillin* "Rashi" *tefillin* and "Rabbeinu Tam" *tefillin* but that's because of their famous debate about the order of the sections in *tefillin*. The two types of *tefillin* go back to time immemorial—neither Rashi nor Rabbeinu Tam introduced a new type of *tefillin*.

Point: The book includes misquotes from the Talmud, which wasn't even written in Rabbi Shimon's day.

Counter-Point: No, they weren't yet *written down* in Rabbi Shimon's day, but the Talmud represents ancient wisdom that was transmitted orally over the course of many centuries. Many works of rabbinic literature include the same ideas in slightly (or vastly) different words. (Rabbi Bechhofer gives the example of *Pirkei Avos*, *Avos d'Rabbi Nosson* and *Pirkei d'Rabbi Eliezer*.)

Point: The Talmud and Midrash are unaware of the *Zohar*.

Counter-Point: Again, failure to mention it by name is not proof of its nonexistence. (Whenever someone tries to "prove" to me that something didn't exist because the Torah never mentions it, I say, "The Torah also never mentions Avraham using the facilities but I assume that he did.") Rabbi Bechhofer uses the example that the Talmud discusses learning the mystical topics of the creation account and of God's "chariot" but it never says where that information can be found. Those things are in the *Zohar*, which was kept hidden and was only revealed orally and secretly.

There are other things that go against de Leon being the author, such as the fact that the *Zohar* openly contradicts some ideas that de Leon wrote in books that we know he authored.

Most important, however, is the fact that the *Zohar* has been universally accepted by the Torah world. Passing one's own writing off as a famous person's work is often attempted and rarely successful. It didn't work for Clifford Irving's "autobiography" of Howard Hughes and it didn't work for the "Hitler diaries." The Pseudepigrapha is a whole corpus of books attributed to various Biblical personages but they didn't sneak their way into the canon because the experts can tell the difference. Conversely, from the *Sefer HaChinuch* to the *Federalist Papers*, it's always a phenomenon when an anonymous work is accepted as a masterpiece. When it happens, it's because the truth shines through. If de Leon did write the *Zohar*, then he lucked into extremely advanced, deep, and esoteric Torah truths far beyond his level.

Our tradition is that Rabbi Shimon authored the *Zohar*. The Rambam lists 13 principles of faith and believing that isn't one of them, so if you want to follow the opinion of the academics, such is your prerogative. What's important is that the *Zohar* has been accepted as authentic by the Torah world, including our greatest scholars who are in the best position to evaluate its authenticity. Even if one chooses to be cynical about the *Zohar*'s provenance, one shouldn't be dismissive of its contents.

Men, Women,
Appearance and Deportment

Tattoos

Q. I know under Jewish law it is forbidden to get a tattoo but why is this?

A. Tattooing is specifically prohibited by the Torah (Leviticus 19:28), so the reason, ultimately, is because God said not to. Our job is to try to understand the underlying rationale and the lessons we can derive from this mitzvah.

My understanding of this mitzvah is that it is based on the idea that we are not our bodies. We are our souls; our bodies are just vehicles that God gave us to get around. And, just like when you borrow a car, you have to take care of the loaner vehicle.

When you borrow a car, you fill the tires, change the oil, fill up the tank. Maybe the car gets a ding here and there, but that's normal wear and tear. You don't give the car back and tell the owner, "Thanks for the use of your car—I had flames painted on it!"

Similarly, we have to take care of our bodies with proper diet and exercise. Sometimes parts of us get damaged and need work or even replacement. But that's no excuse to take bodies that are ultimately not ours and to mark them up with graffiti.

As popular as tattooing is in our society, there's still plenty of tattoo regret. Tattoo removal is a big business. It's expensive and painful and it never looks the same as a never-tattooed patch. Also, there isn't an adult who doesn't look back at pictures from their youth and think, "What was I thinking?" If our judgment regarding fashion and hairstyles seems dubious 20 years later, why should our judgment when it comes to skin art be any better?

Jewish Burial with Tattoos

Q. *Is it true that a person with tattoos can't be buried in a Jewish cemetery?*

A. That Jews with tattoos cannot be buried in a Jewish cemetery is a persistent myth, right up there with "Jews don't believe in Hell." And, like "Jews don't believe in Hell," it occasionally finds its way into pop culture, which only reinforces the misinformation and exacerbates the problem. But it has no basis in fact.

There is a strong hypothesis about how the "Jews with tattoos" myth got started. In theory, it was a myth perpetuated by parents of previous generations as a scare tactic to keep their younger generations from getting tattooed. That such a tactic would be employed specifically in the case of tattoos makes sense because tattoos are by definition permanent. It's easier for one who has strayed to come back from a period of Sabbath-desecration or cheeseburger-eating without a permanent reminder of his time outside the community than it would be for one who has marked himself indelibly. Coming back after a lapse in observance with a tattoo would potentially create social problems, from embarrassment at the *mikvah* to difficulties in matchmaking. So it makes sense that earlier parents would try to spare their children from all the baggage that comes with an irrevocable decision they might later regret.

Objectively speaking, tattooing is no worse than any other violation of Torah law, it's just more visible. And we have *teshuvah* (repentance), which wipes the spiritual slate clean if not the epidermis. So if one does go astray and get tattooed, they can still rejoin the community with all rights and privileges, including burial in a Jewish cemetery. The problem with perpetuating a myth to the contrary is that generations grew up believing it and never had occasion to discover that it's simply not true.

I've been talking about people who were raised in observant

communities because I believe that's the context in which the misconception evolved but wayward youth from observant homes are not the only ones whom such a myth affects. Right off the bat there are *baalei teshuvah* (those raised non-observant, who later become observant), converts and those who were forcibly tattooed against their wills, such as prisoners in the concentration camps. Regardless of one's level of religious observance or how a tattoo was acquired, it does not affect one's burial site.

Now, I may seem to be tattoo-friendly—indeed, I have many friends with tattoos—but don't mistake that for an endorsement. I must stress that, ability to be buried notwithstanding, getting a tattoo is still an overt Torah prohibition (Leviticus 19:28). Dispelling the myth about tattoos doesn't mean that it's permitted, just that it's not inherently any worse than anything else the Torah forbids.

Yarmulkes

Q. *When and why did Jewish boys and men start wearing yarmulkes? Must they always be worn?*

A. The practice of wearing a yarmulke is an ancient tradition that has its roots as a *middas chasidus* (an act of piety) before becoming accepted as normative practice for Jewish men and boys. There are a number of references to the practice in the Talmud. One of these is Rav Huna the son of Rav Yehoshua, who would not walk four cubits (about six feet) with his head uncovered as a reminder that God's Presence is always above us (*Kiddushin* 31a). The word "yarmulke" actually comes from the Aramaic *yarei Malka*,—"reverence for the King."

Another reference to covering one's head is found in tractate *Shabbos* (156b). There, Rav Nachman bar Yitzchak relates how his mother told him always to cover his head, the way that Torah scholars do, so that awe of God would always be upon him. On one occasion, he was studying under a date tree and his hat came off. Looking up, he was tempted by the dates and took a bunch, even though the tree did not belong to him. He learned from this that the yarmulke served to suppress his negative natural tendencies.

While originally a higher standard of behavior, the practice spread and eventually became codified in *halacha*. The Rambam (12th century) considered covering the head to be an act of modesty for scholars (*Deios* 5:6). The *Shulchan Aruch* (16th century) ruled that one may not walk four cubits bareheaded (*OC* 2:6). The Maharashal (also 16th century) wrote that he saw little to indicate that the practice should be considered obligatory except for the fact that it had been accepted by the masses. It's actually very powerful when the people accept a practice upon themselves.

While many early authorities considered wearing a yarmulke to be an act of piety, the *Taz* (*OC* 8:3) ruled it to be wholly obligatory because the non-Jewish practice was to remove headgear as a sign of respect and we are enjoined not to copy other nations' ways (Leviticus 18:3). Many modern authorities follow this approach.

Nowadays, the accepted practice in Ashkenazic communities is for men and boys to wear the yarmulke pretty much all the time. Exceptions include such activities as swimming, showering and sleeping. Many Chasidim, however, even wear a yarmulke when sleeping. There's a special yarmulke ("*shlof-kapl*"), better designed for the task.

On the other hand, Sephardic communities did not adopt the practice of wearing a yarmulke to the same extent as Ashkenazic communities. Many observant Jews of Sephardic descent are only strict about wearing a yarmulke when eating and davening.

Speaking of the Ashkenazic community, the question arises as to whether one must wear a yarmulke for a job interview if he is concerned that it will negatively affect his chances. Rav Moshe Feinstein addressed this question and concluded that one need not incur a major financial loss, such as not obtaining a job, for the sake of wearing a yarmulke (*Igros Moshe* 4:2). Of course, this creates the awkward situation of getting the job and showing up on the first day with a yarmulke, so one has to use their best discretion as to when and whether to employ this leniency.

Optimally, the yarmulke should be worn at all waking hours when one is not under water. This is the widely-accepted practice, which has a strength comparable to laws actually legislated by the rabbis. However, since it is technically an act of piety rather than a full-blown obligation, one may employ certain leniencies when called for. Just remember that the yarmulke is intended as an important reminder of God's Presence above us. Every year, hundreds of Jewish students bravely wear their yarmulkes to public schools. Over the decades, many have fought to earn us the right to wear our yarmulkes in court rooms, in the military, and in other places where personal headwear choices are normally not permitted. Therefore, we should not be quick to treat the practice lightly by overlooking it unnecessarily.

Hats

Q. Why do Jewish men wear hats?

A. This question has been asked before:

> A man asked his rabbi, "Why do we Jews wear hats?"
> The rabbi replied, "Because our forefather Abraham wore a hat."
> "How do we know that?" the man inquired.
> "The Torah says, 'And Abraham went out.' Would Abraham go out without a hat?"

I address why we wear hats in general above, so here I'll address why we wear black hats in particular.

Black hats (fedoras, homburgs, et al.) are worn by many Orthodox men for prayer and such formal occasions as weddings. Even before the practice of covering the head was universal to the point of becoming obligatory, we see a Talmudic opinion that one could not lead services bareheaded (Sofrim 14:15). This practice was likely popularized by the Christian practice to remove hats when entering a church, placing the Jewish practice in contradistinction. The Shulchan Aruch (Orach Chaim 91:3-5) discusses not praying, reciting blessings or entering a shul with one's head uncovered. The Mishnah Brurah (91:12) says that nowadays the yarmulke one wears under his hat is insufficient to wear for prayer. Rather, one must wear the hat that he wears when he walks in the street. After all, we wouldn't meet with important people without wearing a hat, so how could we even dream of talking to God with just our little skullcaps?

And here's where things fall apart a little. In previous generations, it truly was inconceivable to go out without a hat. This changed in the 1960s with the result that people now walk in the street bareheaded and do indeed meet with important people that way. Those who now daven wearing only their yarmulkes are of the opinion that since the accepted cultural practice is no longer to wear a hat, the "nowadays" of the *Mishnah Brurah* no longer applies. Those who are strict to wear a hat are of the opinion that such has become the accepted Jewish practice and it is to be maintained even if our surrounding society has become more casual.

Wearing a hat did not become the accepted practice in many communities for no reason; it is seen as more formal and more dignified. Once based on the general cultural norms of the times, this is now an independent Jewish practice embraced by adherents for its own sake.

Wearing Black

Q. Why do Orthodox Jews wear black?

A. The short answer is, "Tradition… Tradition!"

For the longer answer, it should be noted that not all Orthodox Jewish men dress in black and white but for those who do, I can think of three reasons.

The first is *tzniyus* (generally translated as "modesty," although "propriety" might be better). We tend to think of *tzniyus* as a "women's mitzvah" but such is not the case. While the details may differ, *tzniyus* is also for men. The Talmud in tractate *Shabbos* talks about modes of dress for men and it includes such details as not to be overly concerned with fashion (except when it comes to wearing one's best for Shabbos—113a) and that it is shameful for a scholar to wear stained or patched clothing (114a).

From a *tzniyus* perspective, men wearing black jackets and pants is both simple and formal. It's not flashy like stripes, plaid or bright colors, and it's not casual like jeans and a T-shirt. The message it sends is that the person wearing it is both dignified and humble.

There's another reason. We have discussed elsewhere the Biblical prohibition against copying other nations' ways (Leviticus 18:3). As I mention there, if I were to wear a black shirt with a white collar to signify clergy status, we would all agree that it would constitute copying other nations' ways. But there's a lot of gray area here. Is wearing a suit and tie copying other nations' practices? How about jeans and a T-shirt? There are going to be different opinions but it's a safe bet that the way our ancestors dressed in Eastern Europe represents an acceptable "Jewish style." (Of course, not everyone's ancestors came from Eastern Europe but that's to whom the "wearing black" thing generally pertains.) Some communities go further—long coats, knickers, fur hats, buttons on the opposite side—but black-and-white is a common baseline of an established Jewish look.

Finally, there are those who dress that way simply because it has become a recognizable look for certain Orthodox communities. When we affiliate with a community, we dress in a way that shows it. For example, if you see someone wearing a large colorful yarmulke, a small knit yarmulke, an oversized white crocheted yarmulke, or a black velvet yarmulke, you could probably make some educated guesses about with which community they affiliate. In such a case, it's not from a sense of obligation so much as from a desire to show that one is part of the team.

Ultimately, the way one dresses is a matter of personal choice. One's reasons can range from "this is the way my grandfather dressed" to "I like the way it looks." Like the clothes themselves, there's not necessarily one size of answer that fits all.

Payes

Q. Why do Orthodox men have sidelocks?

A. Those sidelocks are called *peiyot* in Hebrew, meaning corners. This is commonly Yiddishized as *peiyes* and is usually rendered in English in a variety of less-phonetically-accurate spellings, including *payes* and *peyot*. I'll stick with *payes* here.

Jewish men wearing *payes* is a pretty straightforward Biblical obligation. Actually, it's a prohibition as Leviticus 19:27 tells us, "Do not round the corners of your head...," which prohibits removing the hair that grows in this spot. While most prohibitions apply equally both to men and to women, this particular prohibition applies to men only. This is because the verse continues with the prohibition against destroying the corners of the beard. The two are so interrelated that the prohibition against rounding the corners of the head only applies to those who are prohibited to destroy the corners of the beard, i.e., men.

Now, people sometime mistakenly think that only Chasidic Jews wear *payes*. This they do visibly, in a variety of styles, including straight, curled and behind the ear. But Hasidim aren't the only ones who wear *payes*:— all Orthodox Jewish men do, just not as visibly. While some interpret the rule in a way that encourages them to grow their *payes* long, others see it merely as prohibiting altogether removing the hair that grows there. So, while a Jewish man would not be able to shave his head or to get a mohawk without violating this prohibition, most secular haircuts would not pose any sort of problem. In other words, modern Orthodox men also have *payes*, they're just generally indistinguishable from their neighbors' haircuts.

Now, this last point might seem counterproductive given that, according to the *Sefer HaChinuch*, the purpose of *payes* is to distinguish us from our neighbors. The reality is that sometimes our styles align with what's popular in the society around us, while other times they conflict. For example, hemlines go up and down; sometimes they align with our halachic practices and other times they don't.

Similarly, if one wanted his hairstyle to emulate Elvis or the Beatles in their heydays, that would have coincided pretty nicely with our halachic requirements. That wouldn't be the case if one wanted to emulate Yul Brynner, Telly Savalas, Patrick Stewart, Vin Diesel, etc. The reality is that sometimes crew cuts and shaved heads are in style, so this mitzvah absolutely does inform our style choices, if not all the time.

Beards

Q. Why do so many Jewish men have beards?

A. As mentioned above, Leviticus 19:27 contains two prohibitions: not to round the corners of the head—which is why Jewish men wear *payes*—and not to destroy the corners of the beard. There's a surprising amount to talk about here, and the sources I'm going to cite are really just the tip of a much bigger iceberg.

For starters, according to the Talmud in *Makkos* (21a) the halachic definition of "destroying" is with a razor. Ostensibly, it is therefore permitted for a man to remove his facial hair with scissors or a depilatory. This is the conventional wisdom on the matter but things are rarely that cut-and-dried.

The Rambam (Maimonides) codifies this law in *Hilchos Avodas Kochavim* 12:7. There he writes that one would be liable to the penalty of lashes for shaving with a razor but he would be exempt from punishment if he uses scissors. In 12:8, Rambam calls trimming the mustache permitted. Contrast his language of "permitted" in 12:8 with "exempt" in 12:7. Many authorities infer that the Rambam's position is that trimming beard with scissors is what we call *patur aval asur*—exempt from punishment but still prohibited. (It should be noted that this is not a stretch by any means; it's actually the simplest reading of the text.) But of course, not all authorities reach this conclusion, nor would Maimonides' interpretation of this law necessarily be the only one.

Let's leave aside the matter of Jewish law for a second and look at some philosophical thoughts on beards in Judaism:

- The Midrash in *Bemidbar Rabbah* (10:1) tells us that the Torah distinguishes every aspect of Jewish behavior from that of other nations. This extends even to the way we wear our facial hair, based on the aforementioned prohibition in Leviticus 19:27;
- The Talmud in *Shabbos* (152a) refers to the beard as "the splendor of one's face";
- The Radak, a 12th-13th-century authority, comments on events

in which some Jews were forcibly shaved by the enemy in order to humiliate them (II Samuel 10) that the Jewish practice since Biblical times was not to cut the beard, not even with scissors.

Since our traditional sources place so much emphasis on having a beard, and if lack of a beard was considered shameful, how did we get to the point of people even wanting to remove their facial hair? And how did it become so accepted in both practice and philosophy?

The *Chasam Sofer*, an 18th-19th-century authority, writes that the practice of Jews cutting their beards started in Germany in 1096, the time of the Crusades, as the result of harsh decrees against the Jews. For reasons of security, Jews needed to be less conspicuous, so they started cutting their beards and dressing in styles more in line with the surrounding culture. The authorities of the time permitted this, so there was a reason to employ the "permissible" (or "exempt") forms of hair removal. It's quite possible that others later relied upon this leniency, perhaps inappropriately in that they lacked the context of compelling extenuating circumstances.

One could argue that removing one's beard with something other than a razor is inherently permitted, or that it's inherently prohibited but acceptable in certain situations. According to the latter position, "extenuating circumstances" doesn't have to mean Nazi-like oppression. For example, the Talmud on *Sotah* 49b tells us that the household of Rabban Gamliel were permitted to wear their hair in non-Jewish fashions because they worked closely with the secular authorities. Arguably, such a situation would also apply to trimming the beard without use of a razor. (For similar reasons, many Jews in the public arena might shave during *sefirah* or the Three Weeks.)

Lest one think that the anti-shaving position is "fundamentalist" or "extremist," the Chofetz Chaim—author of the *Mishnah Brurah* (which is about as mainstream a contemporary *halacha* work one could find)— wrote an entire treatise against cutting the beard, called *Tiferes Adam* (*The Glory of Man*).

It should also be noted that, halachic issues aside, many grow their beards longer for kabbalistic reasons. According to the *Zohar* and other sources, one's beard is a conduit for Divine favor and mercy, with the result that trimming it at all is a pretty big deal! Kabbalistic reasons need not influence halachic practice but many feel that if Kabbalah and *halacha* don't conflict (as they don't in this case), then it is advisable to follow the kabbalistic rationale.

Finally, there's the matter of electric shavers. Assuming that one may shave with something other than a razor, electric shavers are kind of a gray area. Some would be acceptable but some are too razor-like to be permitted even according to the lenient positions. If one is in doubt about the permissibility of a particular model of shaver, it is advisable to contact one's own rabbi for guidance.

Bottom line, some maintain that it is permitted to remove facial hair other than with a razor, some maintain that it is prohibited except in extenuating circumstances, while others feel very strongly that, questions of permissibility aside, it's just an extremely bad idea and should be avoided. Whatever one's position, they do have halachic precedent to rely upon and we should always be respectful of one another's practice.

Pretty Woman

Q. I understand that Jewish law requires modest dress and behavior but does it require looking unattractive? Are there Torah sources to support this?

A. I have to admit, this is the first time I've ever been asked this! I can think of Torah sources that suggest the opposite. For example, Genesis 12:11 tells us that Sarah was beautiful; Rashi on Genesis 23:1 reiterates this point. Similarly, Esther 2:7 stresses the beauty of Esther. Neither of these sources seem to be criticizing the women in question.

Shir HaShirim is an allegory written in the form of a love story between a woman and a man. Chapter 4 is entirely the man's praises of the woman's beauty. Now, we can quibble over how literally or how metaphorically we should take this book but the fact remains that if being beautiful were a bad thing, it would make for a poor allegory of praise.

The sixth chapter of the Talmudic tractate of *Shabbos* is all about what jewelry and ornaments women can wear outside of an *eiruv* on Shabbos because, you know, women are allowed to wear such things to beautify themselves. There are also many rules about what cosmetics may and may not be used on Shabbos but the bottom line is that, certain Shabbos restrictions notwithstanding, women are allowed to use cosmetics!

The Talmud in *Kesubos* (17a) describes a difference of opinion as to how we should praise a bride. One opinion is to praise her as beautiful overall, even though this may not be quite true; the other opinion is to praise her for whatever beautiful characteristics she may actually possess. This is a debate about how truthful to be in praising her but both focus on her beauty. We are not told that a bride needs to "uglify" herself.

I could go on but you get the idea. Yes, you will find Talmudic and halachic references to things that women do to make themselves attractive to their husbands but that's because husbands and wives should want their spouses to be attracted to them. It doesn't suggest that a person should only be attractive behind closed doors and hideous in public. In fact, the Talmud in *Kesubos* on page 59b discusses things a man can do to beautify his wife—and things he can do to beautify his unmarried daughters! They may not be the same things because their situations are different but no one is meant to be repulsive.

Modest and attractive are not mutually exclusive. Look at pictures of Princess Diana, Nancy Reagan or other world leaders. Generally speaking, you will find them dressed both modestly and attractively. Then look at pop stars who often sport fashions that are both immodest and unattractive. Just because something's revealing, that doesn't automatically make it appealing.

There are limits to physical beauty, for both women and for men. The Talmud in *Nedarim* (9b) discusses a man with a particularly beautiful head of hair who became a *nazir* (a nazirite in English, if that helps). His hair led to vanity and temptation so he took a nazirite vow, which ends with having one's head shaved. He did this specifically to combat the evils he perceived to be a consequence of this physical feature of his. While it need not be taken to this extreme, everyone should try to be self-aware and to beautify themselves appropriately. (King David's son Avshalom also had a gorgeous head of hair about which he was very vain. It was literally the death of him in II Samuel 18.)

I don't believe that the laws of modesty were given for the sake of what other people think. The idea of modesty applies to both men and women, both in public and in private (albeit with obvious differences). Micah 6:8 tells us to walk modestly with God, which means to behave modestly even when it's just Him and me.

So, yes, one might want to dress up extra special for their spouse but that shouldn't be taken as an obligation to be extra-frumpy in every other context. One can be completely modest and still be attractive in appropriate attire.

Living in an Immodest Society

Q. I've heard people say that standards of modesty are based on the time and place you're living in. If that's true, why do we still have to follow them?

A. I would say that that "time and place" thing works as a stringency, not as a leniency, as I'll explain with an excerpt from one of my books, the aptly-named *The Tzniyus Book*. In it, there's a chapter entitled "Community Standards," which addresses this very issue. Here's a selection, very mildly edited:

When I was in high school, my friend Aviva, who was a few grades ahead of me, came back from a year of study in Israel. The summer was hot and humid (as it tends to be) and she complained of the relative discomfort of wearing stockings in the summer, a practice that was still new to her.

"So why wear them?" I asked.

"You have to wear stockings in a place where it is the *minhag* (custom)," she explained.

"And is it the *minhag* on Long Island?" I inquired.

"It's the *minhag* everywhere," she informed me.

The logic of that proposition eluded me then as it eludes me now, but it introduces an important principle, that of community standards. Not everything is black or white. There is some leeway in one's practice, but what is acceptable in one place may not be acceptable in another.

Rabbinic not
to BE
the period
Biblical
from Torah
Custom

When it comes to *tzniyus*, there are three levels of *ervah*, private areas. Parts of the body that are Biblically-required to be covered include a woman's entire torso, a married woman's hair and the genitals of both genders. Parts that are Rabbinically-required to be covered include areas such as a girl's upper arm. The necessity to cover some other body parts, such as the calf of the leg, and the acceptable methods of covering certain parts, may fall into categories of accepted practice in a given community.

Let's take Aviva's stockings as a perfect example. In some communities, the accepted practice is to wear opaque stockings with seams in the back. In other communities the practice is to wear regular tights (not with seams), but only opaque (so that one will not mistake flesh-colored pantyhose for bare skin). Still other communities accept flesh-colored tights, others accept knee socks, and still others permit ankle socks. And, of course, there are those whose practice is to wear no lower leg, ankle or foot covering whatsoever. This does not undermine the integrity of any community's practice. Communities differ in many accepted practices.

For example, matzah that has been soaked in water, such as is used to make matzah balls, is called *gebrukhts*. Some communities eat *gebrukhts* on Pesach, while others do not. Similarly, there are many differences in community practice when it comes to issues of *tzniyus*. In some communities, women only cover their hair with a *tichel* (head scarf). Others permit a *shaitel* (wig). Still others may only permit a *shaitel* to be worn if there is a hat on top. Skirt lengths, sleeve lengths, and other issues differ from community to community.

Here endeth our excerpt.

In our recent discussions on Orthodox Jewish men wearing black and wearing hats, we discussed the concept of "accepted Jewish style." This is a real thing in *halacha*. For example, the Talmud in tractate *Sanhedrin* (74a-b) tells us that if an oppressive government is forcibly converting Jews, one must die rather than violate even a minor practice. The example given of a "minor practice" is not even to change the style of how we wear our shoelaces. Rashi explains that in this example the Jews tie their shoelaces one way and the non-Jews tie them differently; Tosfos explain it that the Jews wear black laces and the non-Jews wear white laces. The principle is the same either way: if we have an accepted community style, it's a real thing and we're expected to abide by it.

Some things are black and white. Women wearing skirts, for example, is explicit *halacha* and nothing changes that. Other things—like stockings, socks, sandals, sleeve length, and other things that need not necessarily start with the letter S—may vary from community to community. If a community has an accepted standard, members of that community are obligated to abide by it regardless of what styles may be popular in other communities, and certainly regardless of what may be popular in the general society around us.

Addendum

Q. *Some of my classmates quote this Rambam (attached) as the source of why tzniyus is according to the times.*

A. For the benefit of those not privy to my email attachments, the paragraph I have been sent is *Hilchos Ishus* 13:11. The context there is the clothes that a husband is obligated to provide his wife at each holiday. One of these "baseline" garments, as listed in *halacha* 13:1, is a hat. *Halacha* 13:11 adds the following: in a place where women don't go out wearing just a hat, but they also wrap themselves in a cloak-like veil, he must also provide her with such a veil.

So this *halacha* doesn't discuss *tzniyus per se*, so much as it does a husband's obligation to provide his wife with clothing that conforms to local community standards. All this does is say that one can take the baseline halachic obligations (in this case, a hat) and add community stringencies to them (in this case, a veil), and that such stringencies are binding—in other words, exactly what we've been saying all along! There is no basis to suggest that a community can subtract from the baseline obligations. (If the Rambam had said that in a place where women go out without a hat, the husband need not provide her with one, it would be another story. To my knowledge, however, such an approach is unprecedented.)

Head-Shaving

Q. Why do Orthodox women shave their heads?

A. They do? To say that Orthodox Jewish women shave their heads is a huge generalization, and not a particularly accurate one. What the majority of Orthodox women do is *cover* their hair.

The parameters of the laws of *tzniyus* (modesty) are not explicit in the Torah. They are part of the *Torah she'b'al peh*—our oral tradition, which was communicated teacher-to-student until finally being committed to writing in the Talmud. There are, however, allusions to the laws of *tzniyus* in the Torah.

Perhaps the best-known allusion to the law of women's hair occurs in *parshas Naso*, in the section of the *sotah* (the suspected woman). Numbers 5:18 tells us that the *kohein* stands the suspected woman before Hashem and uncovers her hair; the Talmud in *Kesubos* (72a) observes that the Torah takes it for granted that a married woman's hair is normally covered.

The parts of the body that are considered *ervah* (private because they are potentially sexually-attractive) are alluded to in Shir HaShirim (Song of Songs). This includes the hair, as per verse 4:1, "You are beautiful, my love, you are beautiful. Your eyes are like doves, your hair inside your kerchief is like a flock of goats that stream down from Mount Gilad" (*Brachos* 24a). Of course, the details of different types of *ervah* differ. For example, a woman's singing voice is considered private in *halacha* but not her speaking voice. Similarly, uncovered hair is considered private for a married woman but not for a single woman. (It's also not retroactive; married women don't have to hide photos of themselves from before they were married.)

We see the concept of married women's hair covering taken as a given throughout Talmudic literature:

- Ohn ben Peles was saved from being part of Korach's rebellion by his wife. When Korach's men came to fetch Ohn, she sat at the entrance to their tent with her hair uncovered, causing the messengers to turn around and walk away (*Sanhedrin* 109b-110a);

- The Rabbis asked a woman named Kimchis what she had done to merit having seven sons serve as Kohein Gadol (High Priest). She responded that the beams of her house never saw her with her hair uncovered. While the Rabbis rejected her hypothesis (because many other women have acted likewise), the extent to which she observed this law is still presented as an example of meritorious behavior (*Yoma* 47a; see Yerushalmi *Megillah* 1:10 for the accepted opinion as to the merit of Kimchis);

- Rabbi Akiva once fined a man 400 zuz (an exorbitant sum) for uncovering a woman's hair in public. The man subsequently demonstrated that the woman did not hesitate to uncover her own hair in public but Rabbi Akiva refused to reduce the fine saying that the woman's willingness to uncover her own hair does not give the man license to do so (*Bava Kamma* 8:6).

There are other examples I could cite but the point is clear: our Sages universally agree that a married woman covering her hair is part of the laws of *tzniyus*. But shaving hair off? That's a practice observed in a few particular communities; it's not a sweeping societal norm among Orthodox Jews in general.

According to some Hasidic authorities, the only way to ensure that a woman's hair doesn't eventually stray from under her hat/turban/scarf/kerchief/wig/etc. is not to have any. There's also a concern that hair might create an interposition when using the *mikvah*. Ostensibly, this practice is based upon a statement in the *Zohar* (*parshas Naso*) to the effect that the *mikvah* should not see a woman's hair.

The fact that there may be such a source is hardly a "slam-dunk" in favor of head-shaving for a variety of reasons. The Talmud in several places either implies or states explicitly that the practice of women is not to shave their heads. For example, *Eiruvin* 100b says that one of the "curses of Eve" is that women grow their hair long, while *Nazir* 28b says that a man can cancel his wife's vow to shave her head if he finds it unattractive. Furthermore, the *Shulchan Aruch* expressly prohibits women from shaving their heads (*YD* 182:5). The *Zohar*, while important, is not a halachic work so ruling from when it contradicts the Talmud or works of *halacha* is not a simple thing, and Hasidic communities act differently in such situations than non-Hasidic communities. So this matter goes beyond acting leniently vs. acting stringently. (There are also authorities who say that that's not even what that *Zohar* means.)

This is not even the practice of all Hasidic communities. There are some Hasidic sects where the leadership may consider it obligatory for their adherents, others where it may be an optional practice, and still others where it may be virtually unheard of.

So is head-shaving a thing? Yes, but chiefly among women who belong to communities that follow that understanding of the *Zohar* in this matter. The majority of Orthodox women do not shave their heads. Rather, they cover their hair in a variety of ways and to a variety of degrees.

Is *Tzniyus* Overblown?

Q. I've heard people in the Orthodox community talk about tzniyus (modesty) as if it's a woman's most important mitzvah, like what she exists for. While I'm a fan of tzniyus, this perspective doesn't sit well with me, like our greatest goal as women should be to disappear. Which position do the sources support?

A. There is a point of view, sometimes espoused on the more right-wing end of the Orthodox spectrum, that what Torah does for men, *tzniyus* does for women. I know this because a certain (fairly controversial) book on modesty actually has a section titled "What Torah Does for Men, Tznius Does for Women." (That author transliterates *tzniyus* differently than I do.) The intention of this statement is as follows: the Talmud (*Kiddushin* 30b) teaches us that the mitzvah of Torah study protects men from the *yeitzer hara* (evil inclination). This position states that since women do not have an obligation to study Torah comparable to that of men, *tzniyus* fulfills the same function. But what is the source for such an assertion?

I am not aware of any Biblical verse or Talmudic dictum in support of this concept. The only real support the author brings is a statement of the Vilna Gaon. The Gaon, who was traveling, sent a letter home to his family with words of encouragement against all sorts of negative traits and behaviors—all except for his mother, whom he excluded because of her great modesty. The inference is that her adherence to the standards of *tzniyus* protects her from temptation. The author notes that "some versions" of the Gaon's letter spell this point out explicitly. Even so, and with greatest deference to the Vilna Gaon, an unsourced opinion expressed in 18th-century personal correspondence does not carry the same force of law as the Talmud, the Rambam's *Mishneh Torah* or the *Shulchan Aruch*.

It's actually impossible to answer "what is the most important mitzvah?" We intuitively "feel" that certain *mitzvos* like Shabbos and keeping kosher are more important than most. Similarly, we may not spend as much time thinking about things like *shaatnez* (not wearing garments of mixed wool and linen), burning a portion of our dough or not charging interest. But any such distinctions come from our own minds and not from the Torah. In fact, the Mishna in *Pirkei Avos* (2:1) tells us to be as careful in what we perceive to be "small" *mitzvos* as we are in what we consider to be "big" *mitzvos* specifically because we don't know the relative importance of *mitzvos*.

Along these lines, we see two *mitzvos* that promise a "long life" (in *Olam Haba*) for their fulfillment: honoring one's parents (Exodus 20:12) and sending a mother bird away before taking the young or eggs from her nest (Deuteronomy 22:7). Honoring one's parents is very difficult—it takes decades of constant vigilance! Shooing a bird away takes but a moment of one's time. It's very telling that the Torah promises the same reward for these two very different *mitzvos*!

Now, *tzniyus* is not just a "women's mitzvah" and it's not just about what we wear. *Tzniyus* is for everyone and it's ultimately about how we act. Micah 6:8 tells us, "It has been told to you, humanity, what is good and what God asks of you: only that you act justly, love mercy, and walk humbly with your God." (The word "humbly" in this verse is *hatzneia*, same as the word *tzniyus*.) So do people overemphasize the women's clothing aspect of this mitzvah? Some do, especially when they try to impose standards that exceed what *halacha* actually expects.

Since we can't say definitively what the most important mitzvah is, there are people who dedicate their lives to a wide array of *mitzvos*. Some people fight *lashon hara* (gossip and slander). Some encourage *hachnosas orchim* (hospitality). Some educate people about family purity while others work to arrange proper burials for the deceased. The list goes on and on. And yes, some people feel that the area of *tzniyus* is one where the community needs education and they work in that area, to various degrees of success. We need that, just like we need the others. There are those, however, who promote expectations beyond what's actually called for by *tzniyus*. That's where the problem lies.

So can I tell you that *tzniyus* is the most important mitzvah for women? Absolutely not. I also can't tell you that it isn't. This information is specifically withheld from us so that we should take all the *mitzvos* seriously! But just as we don't tell people to refrain from all speech in order to avoid *lashon hara*, or to spend all day in bed on Shabbos in order to avoid performing forbidden activities, we should ensure that the things we promote in the name of *tzniyus* are actually appropriate for achieving the goal and not counterproductive or unnecessarily burdensome on the community.

Love and Marriage

Q. *What are the halachic requirements of attraction in a prospective marriage?*

A. Let's discuss two types of "attraction"—emotional attraction (which we'll call "love") and physical attraction (which, for the sake of literary balance, we'll refer to as "lust").

Is love important in marriage? You might say "Of course!" but this is actually one of those questions that we're seeing through the goggles of our modern preconceptions. For most of recorded history, marrying for love was an anomaly, not an ideal. According to Stephanie Coontz, author of *Marriage, a History: From Obedience to Intimacy, or How Love Conquered Marriage*, the idea that a couple might marry for love bordered on subversive; parents might even disown their children for doing it.

Couples used to marry in order to forge political alliances, to pool their families' financial resources, to expand their workforces, and for a variety of similarly practical purposes. Women needed men to plow the fields; men needed women to spin the wool. A wise marriage choice was important to survival and love wasn't inherently part of the equation.

I like The Beatles but it would be foolish for me to take an accounting job just because a company's office music is a Beatles playlist. I'm not an accountant so that's a bad job for me and I would starve to death. If I get a job that's appropriate for me and that also happens to accommodate my musical tastes, that's great but, unless I'm a musician, it would hardly be a prerequisite. Similarly, if one found love in marriage, that was as a nice perk but not generally a deciding factor.

Look at how Chamor pitched the idea of intermarriage with the Israelites to the people of Shechem in Genesis 34:21: "Let them dwell in the land and do business in it because the land is large enough for them. We can take their daughters for wives and give them our daughters." This wasn't an insidious plot *per se*; it was the natural order of things.

Historically, objections to love as a basis for marriage weren't only practical, they were also philosophical. The Greeks considered lovesickness to be a form of insanity, a viewpoint that persisted in Medieval Europe. Some philosophers considered excessive love towards one's spouse to be akin to adultery; Catholic and Protestant theologians considered it to be a form of idolatry. According to Coontz, "Too much love was thought to be a real threat to the institution of marriage."

A number of factors contributed to changing attitudes towards marriage, including the American Revolution, the French Revolution and the industrial revolution. The political Revolutions and the enlightenment promoted the concept of a right to personal happiness; the shift to a wage-labor economy and urbanization helped to make economics less of a factor in marriage. Once our concept of marriage had shifted towards love, Coontz says, "We convinced ourselves that was the traditional ideal."

Even today, the idea of marrying for love is not universal; it's primarily a value in affluent, Western nations. In many peasant societies, too much marital love is considered disruptive because it causes the couple to withdraw from the wider web of dependence that enables the society to function. A 1975 survey of college students in the Indian state of Karnataka found that only 18% strongly approved of marriages made based on love, while 32% completely disapproved of such marriages.

The cultural norm of the students who replied to the 1975 survey was to marry first and (hopefully) subsequently to fall in love. This was also the standard in early-modern Europe. 16th and 17th philosophers assumed that if a husband and wife were each of good character, they would probably come to love each other. You can imagine that, historically, Jews were also part of this mindset. This comes as no surprise to anyone familiar with the score from *Fiddler on the Roof*:

> **Tevye:** But my father and my mother said we'd learn to love each other.
> So, now I'm asking, Golde…
> Do you love me?
> **Golde:** I'm your wife!
> **Tevye:** I know. But do you love me?
> **Golde:** Do I love him?
> For twenty-five years, I've lived with him,
> Fought with him, starved with him.
> For twenty-five years, my bed is his.
> If that's not love, what is?

For more traditional texts, consider that there are two Talmudic tractates dealing with marriage: *Kiddushin* and *Kesubos*. These tractates are about betrothal and marriage contracts, respectively, and they have a lot to say about the various parties' financial obligations. Between them, however, these two tractates mention love between the bride and groom as a precondition for marriage exactly zero times.

Also consider this passage from the 19th-century work *Aruch HaShulchan* (EH 2):

If he marries an upstanding woman for the sake of money—
meaning that if not for the money he would marry somebody
else—this is not a sin. Just the opposite: it is appropriate to do so
if he is a scholar (because it will help to support his studies).

So there's nothing wrong with marrying for pragmatics but you'll note
that it's limited to "an upstanding woman." Love may not have been the
sole driving motivation in marriage but neither was a mercenary attitude.
In Judaism, the traditional focus has always been on finding a likeminded
spouse with compatible spiritual goals.

The Biblical archetype of one who married for love is the Patriarch
Yaakov, who loved Rachel at first sight and agreed to work seven years
for her father in exchange for her hand in marriage. After seven years of
labor, when he was deceitfully given the wrong bride, Yaakov was willing
to invest another seven years to marry Rachel (Genesis 29). [Please note
that this suggests an important lesson: love doesn't mean having to get
married right now, it means being willing to wait.] But if Yaakov married
Rachel because he loved her, what are we to make of his father, Yitzchak?
Genesis 24:67 says, "Yitzchak brought her into his mother Sarah's tent.
He married Rivka, she became his wife and he loved her." For Yaakov, love
led to marriage but for Yitzchak, marriage led to love. In both cases, what
they have in common is that the husband and wife shared the same values
and goals.

This is something that our "love conquers all" society tends to
overlook. Anecdotally, I am aware of far too many couples who felt that
way but, once the honeymoon phase was over and real life began, quickly
discovered that their life goals were incompatible. Differences in religious,
political or social outlooks may seem insignificant when you're 22 or 23
and madly in love. Things look very different five years later, after the
initial infatuation has cooled.

As far as purely physical attraction—i.e., "lust"—you may be surprised
to hear me speaking up for it, especially after I threw cold water on the
idea of marrying strictly for love. The Mishna in *Kesubos* (chapter 7)
lists various physical defects for which a man may divorce his wife—or

a woman may demand a divorce from her husband and still be paid the value of her marriage contract! No one expects a couple to live together if there's no physical attraction. That's a necessary component of a marriage. But, as with love, it's by no means a sole basis for a relationship.

The archetype for a lust-based relationship is Amnon's lust for Tamar in II Samuel 13. As the Mishna in *Avos* (5:19) points out, once Amnon got what he was after, he had no more use for Tamar. Boaz, on the other hand, was attracted to Ruth but what attracted him was her behavior (see Ruth 2:5 and Rashi there), which is a more lasting basis for a relationship.

The penultimate verse in Proverbs (31:30), familiar from the song *Eishes Chayil*, is "Grace is deceptive and beauty is meaningless; it is a woman with reverence for God who is to be praised." There's nothing wrong with beauty *per se*; Sarah and Esther are both described as beautiful and they're two of our greatest heroines. It's just that beauty is superficial. It's what inside that counts most.

Regarding the creation of man, Genesis 5:2 says, "male and female He created them." Midrashically, man and woman were created a single being that was divided and we are each in search of our "missing piece," which will complete us spiritually. So, yes, love is important—and even a little lust is important—but each of these pales in priority to finding a mate whose priorities and goals align with our own.

Shaking Hands

Q. *Why don't Orthodox Jews shake hands with members of the opposite sex?*

A. This is a loaded question in that it makes a number of assumptions and you're going to meet people who don't meet those expectations. I agree with the basic premise, though: as a general rule, observant Jews do not shake hands with members of the opposite sex.

The root of this practice is Leviticus 18:6, which tells us that no person may draw near to a forbidden relationship in order to initiate sexual congress. The forbidden relationships are already clearly delineated. What's added by this verse is the "do not draw near" part, which is understood as a prohibition against any form of affectionate contact (*derech chibah*) with a forbidden relationship (*Sifra Acharei Mos 9, et al.*).

Rambam (Maimonides) considers the prohibition against affectionate contact to be Biblical in origin, while Ramban (Nachmanides) considers it to be a rabbinic enactment. All authorities agree that it is prohibited, but there may be some differences in extenuating circumstances depending on whether the prohibition is Biblical or rabbinic in nature.

"Affectionate contact" clearly includes hugging and kissing but does it include shaking hands? Handshaking is definitely a sign of camaraderie; just look at the way the public reacts when a public figure does or doesn't shake hands with a political rival or unpopular world leader. In our society, handshaking is a sign of brotherhood, and that's *chibah* (affection) even if it's not romantic.

A common—but far from universal—practice is to accept a hand if offered by a person of the opposite gender who is unfamiliar with the Jewish practice. This is done so as not to embarrass the other person, which may seem curious. After all, if someone offers us non-kosher food, we're not allowed to eat it to avoid embarrassing them! The difference is that there are a lot of gray areas in this matter. Not only is there the question of whether the law is Biblical or rabbinic in nature, there are different opinions on just how affectionate handshaking is, some authorities considering it "just business" and not affectionate at all. So while leaping straight for the handshake is not the normative Orthodox practice, there is room to be lenient in extenuating circumstances. (If it's going to be an ongoing relationship, it's advisable to advise someone about one's religious practice.) It should be noted that some authorities, such as Rabbeinu Yonah, consider any form of inter-gender physical contact to be prohibited, so defining handshakes as affectionate or not would be moot in their opinions.

Here are some examples of what's excluded by limiting the prohibition to affectionate contact: helping a fallen person to get up, helping someone who needs assistance to walk, a dental hygienist putting their hands in your mouth, a doctor or a physical therapist of the opposite gender, a lifeguard rescuing someone. Generally speaking a professional person in the course of their duties is considered non-affectionate. We see this from the Talmud Yerushalmi (*Sotah* chapter 3), which discusses the matter of how a *kohein* would wave a woman's *mincha* (flour) offering by placing his hands under hers and guiding her. He touched her hands but the contact was non-affectionate and permitted. (There may be limits to what is considered "professional services." Getting a haircut from a member of the opposite sex is a gray area in that the need is less compelling than when seeing a medical professional; ask your rabbi. A non-medical massage would certainly be considered a step too far.)

Rav Moshe Feinstein has a well-known responsum (*Igros Moshe EH* II:14) in which he addresses men sitting next to women on crowded transportation like subways and buses. He rules that such unintentional contact is not affectionate in nature and therefore permitted. He does point out one important exception: if one is doing it intentionally because he enjoys it, then it is prohibited. This is an important principle: the things that are permitted are only permitted because one does not get a sexual sensation from them. If a particular person does get a sexual thrill from sitting next to a person of the opposite sex, a handshake or a haircut, then for that person it would be considered *derech chibah* (an affectionate manner) even if such is not the intention of the other party.

Finally, it should be noted that if a man declines to shake hands with a woman, it's not because they're being sexist. This law works both ways: men don't shake hands with women and women don't shake hands with men.

So that's the short form on why Orthodox Jews don't generally shake hands with members of the opposite sex and why you may see some exceptions. There are those who consider it a Biblical prohibition and those who consider it rabbinic. Some consider handshaking to be affectionate, some consider it business as usual, and for some that distinction is irrelevant. Some will accept a hand if offered in ignorance while others will decline in all circumstances. Adherents of each practice have valid reasons to act as they do.

"Negiah" Exemptions

Q. I work at a school and a nurse there refused to perform a medical procedure because it meant touching a woman. Does halacha require someone to avoid touching the opposite sex even for work or medical procedures?

A. I'm confused by this question. The nurse refused to perform a medical procedure because it meant touching a woman? So the nurse was a man? That's certainly possible—one of my closest friends is a male nurse—but it's such a woman-dominated field, I don't see how anyone with such strong objections could enter the profession and go through nursing school while accommodating his self-imposed limitations. (And student nurses have to deal with patients, too, and they don't get to pick them.) In any event, a nurse has to be prepared to deal with patients of both genders—and by "prepared," I mean both professionally and halachically.

The laws of *kiruv basar* ("nearness of flesh"—colloquially referred to as "*negiah*," though the term grates on my ear) prohibit affectionate touch. The Rambam (*Hilchos Issurei Biah* 21:1) writes that one who engages in acts of physical intimacy with a prohibited person deserves lashes for violating a Biblical prohibition. He gives the examples of hugging and kissing and extrapolates from Leviticus 18:6 ("Do not draw near...") that the prohibition applies to any kind of affectionate physical contact. (*Even Ha'Ezer* 20:1 says pretty much the same thing as the Rambam; I'm not going to quote both but interested parties can look it up.)

What this prohibition doesn't include is professional contact, though what that means can vary.

Going to a doctor or a dentist is certainly professional because it's a health necessity. There's nothing affectionate about a dental hygienist sticking his or her fingers in your mouth or a nurse cutting off your circulation with a sphygmomanometer (that inflatable cuff thing).

What about getting a haircut from a member of the opposite sex? To me, that's a gray area—I think that it might seem like nothing to some people but it might feel a little too affectionate for others.

I think all authorities would agree that a massage from a masseuse or a masseur (as opposed to from, say, a physical therapist) is certainly too intimate despite the professional nature of the relationship. [Note: When this article first appeared online, a massage therapist objected because he perceived that I was implying that massage therapy is unacceptable. Actually, I intentionally avoided mentioning massage therapy because many people are not familiar with the field.]

My basis to make such a distinction in the latter two cases is from Rav Moshe Feinstein, *ztz"l*. In *Igros Moshe* (*Even Ha'Ezer* II:14), Rav Moshe addressed the question of taking public transportation during rush hour, when all the commuters are squeezed together like human sardines. Rav Moshe said that being pressed up against other commuters, even of the opposite gender, does not qualify as affectionate contact. (As a New York City commuter, I can verify that there's nothing remotely provocative about it.) However, Rav Moshe cautioned, if one is sexually stimulated by such contact, then one must avoid it.

Along these lines, I think it's safe to say that if the opposite-sex barber cutting your hair gives you sexual thoughts, then such a haircut is just not for you.

But the medical profession? That's the very definition of permitted cross-gender contact. Obviously, if a woman isn't comfortable with a massage from a male physical therapist, she can go to a female physical therapist. (And there's a reason that women OB-GYNs now outnumber the men.) But practitioners may not have that luxury. According to the AMA Code of Medical Ethics Opinions on Patient-Physician Relationships (1.1.2 Prospective Patients), "Physicians must also uphold ethical responsibilities not to discriminate against a prospective patient on the basis of race, gender, sexual orientation or gender identity, or other personal or social characteristics that are not clinically relevant to the individual's care."

So, bottom line, I don't believe there's a "religious exemption" for medical practitioners not to treat patients of the opposite gender, nor does *halacha* require such a thing.

Around the Calendar

Rosh Hashana

Is Rosh Hashana Meant to Be Scary?

Q. *I was raised to see Rosh Hashana as a terrifying time of year, when I would be judged by God but I've met people who approach the holiday in a more positive way. What's the correct mindset?*

A. Emotions are funny things. Weddings are unambiguously joyous occasions but, stereotypically, plenty of people cry at weddings. While the jury is still out on exactly why that is, the theory is that we emotionally contrast the joy of the wedding with experiences of loss, such as one's own failed romance, the divorce of one's parents, the absence of a deceased loved one, an anticipated change in relationship with the bride or groom, etc.

Conversely, a funeral is an unambiguously sad occasion (unless one *really* disliked the deceased) but plenty of people laugh—often uncontrollably—at such things. That's because death and mourning make them anxious and laughter is a psychological coping mechanism. Life events can be different, often conflicting, things. Laughter and tears often intermingle.

We see this in *halacha* as well. When someone enjoys a significant benefit, like buying a house, he recites either the bracha of *shehechiyanu* (that God brought us to this occasion) or *haTov vehaMeitiv* (that God is good and He does good things for us). [The difference in which bracha is recited hinges on whether one is the sole recipient of the good fortune or one of multiple beneficiaries.] When a close relative dies, we recite the bracha of *Dayan ha'emes* (that God is the truthful Judge). The Talmud in *Brachos* (59b) discusses a case in which one's parent dies and leaves him a significant inheritance. First one recites *Dayan ha'emes* on the death, followed by *shehechiyanu* or *haTov vehaMeitiv* on the inheritance. This is not to say that a death is in any way a good thing, just that life consists of both black and white, swirled together.

Which brings us to Rosh Hashana. Is it a happy day or a sad day? The answer is a little of both—and a little of neither.

Consider that we normally recite Hallel (Psalms of praise) on Rosh Chodesh (the first day of the new month) and on *yom tov*. Well, Rosh Hashana is both *yom tom* and the first day of Tishrei, and yet we don't recite Hallel! According to the Talmud (*Rosh Hashana* 32), that's because it would be inappropriate for us to sing joyfully when the books of life and death lie open before God.

But that doesn't make it a sad day! Tisha b'Av is a sad day. On Tisha b'Av, we fast, we sit on the floor, we don't wear shoes and we refrain from greeting one another. On Rosh Hashana, we wear our finest clothes. We indulge in all sorts of delicacies. Fasting is actually prohibited on Rosh Hashana! We wish one another a good *yom tov* and a good year. It's clearly a happy time.

But it's not Purim. It's not Simchas Torah. It's not Pesach. Rosh Hashana is not a time for celebration and it's certainly not a time for frivolity. Our judgment before God is serious business.

Consider the eighth chapter of the Book of Nechemiah, which takes place on Rosh Hashana:

Ezra the priest brought the Torah before the congregation—both men and women—all who could hear and understand, on the first day of the seventh month (i.e., 1 Tishrei—Rosh Hashana). He read from it from the square before the Water Gate from the time it got light until midday in front of the men and the women and those who understood, and the ears of all the people listened to the Torah. Ezra the scribe stood on a wooden platform that they had made for the occasion.... Ezra opened the scroll in front of all the people, because he was above them, and when he opened it, all the people stood. Ezra blessed Hashem and all the people answered, "Amen, Amen," raising their hands, bowing their heads and prostrating themselves to Hashem on their faces to the ground.... The Leviim explained the Torah to the people, and the people stood in their place. They read in the scroll of God's Torah clearly, and they explained and made the reading understandable to the people. Then Nechemiah, Ezra and the Leviim who explained it to the people said to them, "This day is holy to Hashem your God, so do not mourn or cry" because all the people were crying when they heard the words of the Torah. He said to them, "Go eat delicacies, drink sweet beverages and send portions to those who have nothing prepared because today is holy to Hashem. Don't be sad because Hashem's joy is your strength." The Leviim calmed the people, saying, "Hush, today is holy, don't be sad." So all the people went to eat, drink, send portions and rejoice because they understood the words that were explained to them (excerpted from verses 2-12).

Is Rosh Hashana a sad day? No. The Bible passage excerpted above tells us explicitly that it isn't. Is it a happy day? Yes, but not a frivolous one. What it is, is a solemn day. It's serious, because we're being judged, so we should take it seriously. But we are also optimistic of a favorable outcome. We should be in awe but not in mourning. We should have some healthy anxiety but not incapacitating fear.

Weddings, childbirth, dissertations, certain medical procedures— these are all things one might undertake voluntarily but not without some degree of anxiety. We work through the nervousness because we believe that good things await us on the other side. Rosh Hashana is the same way. It is a big deal and the outcome is serious business but we are optimistic that great benefits will be waiting for us once we've gotten through it.

Rosh Hashana's Symbolic Foods

Q. *Where do the* simanim *("meaningful omens") foods come from?*

A. While I've seen the translation used, I personally wouldn't call the *simanim* "omens," which suggests something of prophetic significance. In my opinion, to call them "omens" is to imbue the *simanim* with superstitious powers:—"if we do X, Y and Z, we'll have a good year; if we don't, we won't." While some people may feel that way, the *simanim* don't really have that ability. Rather, they are merely symbolic gestures we make that are representative of our hopes for the coming year. Performing the *simanim* will not guarantee one a good year, nor will failure to do so condemn one to a bad year. What they are meant to do is to remind us to shape up and to do a good job on Rosh Hashana and in the Ten Days of Repentance in order to earn good things in the year ahead.

When we speak of the *simanim*—literally "signs"—we refer to the foods that we eat for symbolic reasons on Rosh Hashana, accompanied by prayers for the coming year. These foods are of two types: foods that are symbolic because of their inherent properties and foods that are symbolic because of wordplay.

The source of the custom is the Talmud in tractate *Krisos* (6a) in which Abaye says, "Having established that symbolic gestures are significant, on Rosh Hashana one should eat things like gourds, fenugreek, leeks, beets and dates."

The meaning of these symbols is as follows:

- The Talmudic word for "gourds" is *kra*, which sounds like the word meaning "to read" and also the word meaning "to tear." We pray that our merits should be read before God and that any evil decrees against us should be torn up;
- The word for "fenugreek" is *rubia*, similar to the word meaning "to increase" (*yirbu*). We pray that our merits should increase;
- "Leeks" is *karsi*, similar to the word meaning "to cut off" (*kareis*). We ask that our enemies should be cut off, i.e., destroyed;
- "Beets" (*silka*) is similar to the word for "removal" (*siluk*). We ask that

our opponents should be removed;

• Finally, "dates" is *tamrei*, similar to the word "to be consumed" (*yitamu*). Again, this is something we ask be done to our enemies. (Historically, we have had a lot of enemies!)

The Talmudic list is just a list of suggestions. Over the generations, many other customs have arisen. Here are a few of the more popular ones:

By far the most well-known Rosh Hashana food is an apple dipped in honey, which is symbolic of our desire for a sweet year. (The honey is an ancient tradition; apples, despite their current ubiquity, are a relatively recent addition to the custom, having been adopted by Jews in Eastern Europe where they were widely available as summer turned to autumn.)

Pomegranate is another common Rosh Hashana food, because of its many seeds. We pray that our merits should increase until they are as numerous as the seeds in a pomegranate.

Fish is yet another *siman*, followed by a prayer that we should be as prolific as fish.

Formerly, one might have seen the head of a sheep on someone's Rosh Hashana table. Nowadays, it's much more likely that you'll see a fish head. This is accompanied by a prayer that we should be like the head rather than the tail.

Finally, there are carrots. In Yiddish, carrots are *mehren*, which also means "to increase." Accordingly, we pray for our merits to increase. Those who shun our Yiddish heritage for whatever reason might still employ carrots on Rosh Hashana, relying on their Hebrew name, *gezer*. This sounds like the word for a decree (*gezeira*), and they pray that God discard any negative decrees against us. In any event, aside from carrots' use in the *simanim*, a sweet carrot *tzimmes* is a traditional Rosh Hashana side dish.

I say "finally" even though this list is not exhaustive. There are still other practices, both historical and contemporary. Once upon a time, it was customary to eat liver on Rosh Hashana because the word for livers in Yiddish (*leberlach*) sounds like the phrase "live honorably" (*leb ehrlich*). In considerably more modern times, my children had a teacher who used to joke about eating lettuce, half a raisin, and celery ("let us have a raise in salary"). That may sound like making fun (and I don't know anyone who actually does this) but it's exactly the kind of clever wordplay that led to the many of the customs we actually have today.

Not that you asked, but there are also foods that we are accustomed not to eat on Rosh Hashana. Most well-known is no doubt nuts. People will tell you that the reason we avoid nuts is because the numerical value of *egoz* (nut) is the same as *cheit* (sin). (It is if you spell "cheit" wrong.) While this explanation is certainly recorded in halachic literature, I suspect that it is likely an explanation after the fact. I believe the other explanation is more likely the origin of the practice: nuts generate phlegm, which could impede one's ability to pray during the much-longer-than-usual service.

There is also a practice to avoid vinegar and other sour or bitter foods, like horseradish. This is not an ironclad prohibition, as some believe that "fish without horseradish is like a wedding without music" (i.e., if it's going to spoil your enjoyment of the fish, don't refrain from the horseradish). Consult your rabbi for guidance in this matter.

Eating the *simanim* is an ancient custom but it's not an obligation like eating matzah and *maror* at the Seder. If you don't like carrots, fish heads or fenugreek (whatever that is), you don't have to eat them and failure to do so will not condemn you to a lousy year. Just try to internalize the message that the *simanim* are meant to impart and bring it to life in your prayers and in your actions.

Yom Kippur

Kaparos and Animal Cruelty

Q. *Every year I read about Jews who use chickens in some sort of atonement ceremony. It seems incredibly cruel to have chickens handled like this. Is there no law against animal cruelty in Judaism?*

A. The ceremony in question, called *kaporos*, when done properly is no more cruel than picking up your dog or cat when your dog or cat may not care to be picked up. The problem is that not everybody performs the ceremony properly.

First, a little background: The practice of *kaporos* ("atonements") is more than 1,300 years old. Despite opposition from some early authorities (not based on animal cruelty issues), the practice has become near-universally accepted by Ashkenazic and Sephardic Jews alike. In the original practice, a person would circle a live chicken around his head. The chicken is then slaughtered and given to a needy family for a meal. In more modern times, many people use money, which is then donated to charity. I use cash but I don't begrudge people who use chickens. I do, however, urge them to do so properly.

The issue is not the "waving" of the chickens *per se* (which is not cruel if done properly), nor is it the slaughtering of the chickens (which is always done for consumption); it's the incidental mistreatment that's a problem. For example, chickens might be left crated in the hot sun without water. They might be left within the reach of children, who might abuse them. One might hold them improperly while performing the ceremony. (It has also come to my attention that sometimes the chickens are discarded rather than being distributed to needy families. That's not an issue of animal cruelty *per se*, but it's still a problem.)

There is a Jewish concept called *tzaar baalei chaim*, which means that we are to avoid causing needless suffering to living things. The operative word is "needless." God told Adam to conquer the Earth and to rule over the various creatures (Genesis 1:28). From this we see that the world's resources are here for our benefit and they should be enjoyed. But God also told Adam to work the Garden and to guard it (Genesis 2:15). From this we see that we also have an obligation to protect the world. In short, we are permitted to *use* the world's resources but we may not *abuse* them. Putting this idea into practice, we may slaughter a chicken for food ("use") but we may not mishandle the chickens, leave them in the sun without water, or allow children to mistreat them ("abuse").

The Talmud (*Bava Metzia* 85a) tells us a famous story about *tzaar baalei chaim*. Rabbi Yehuda HaNasi (AKA "Rebbi," the compiler of the Mishna) once observed a calf being led to the slaughter. The calf ran to him and sought shelter by sticking its head under Rebbi's garment. "What do you want from me?" the Sage responded. "This is why you were created!"

Rebbi's answer wasn't necessarily inaccurate but it was unsympathetic to the calf's plight. In order to teach him a lesson in compassion, God afflicted him with an ailment that would last for 13 years. The punishment ended when Rebbi saw his maid about to sweep away a nest of baby rodents. He stopped her, citing Psalms 145:9, "God's compassion is over all His creatures." At that point, God determined that the message had been received and He healed Rebbi's symptoms.

So, while one is permitted to "wave" a chicken overhead and even to slaughter it for food, that is not license to mistreat the chicken, neither actively nor passively. The reason one performs *kaparos* in the first case is to help atone for his sins and to get closer to God. It should go without saying that if one cannot perform the ritual without causing unnecessary suffering to the chickens, then it may be advisable to forgo chickens altogether in favor of waving and donating cash.

Planning to Sin Again

Q. *The Yom Kippur prayers perplex me. What if we didn't do the sin we apologize for, and what if know that we're going to do it again?*

A. The first part of your question doesn't really bother me for two reasons. The first is because it's always possible that you did something you don't even know about. Maybe you took something from a store thinking it was a free sample but you accidentally stole it. Maybe you said something rude in public and made a *chillul Hashem*. Maybe we excused ourselves from fulfilling our responsibilities thinking that we were unable to perform them when God knows that we were actually able. There are plenty of ways we could have erred and not even been aware of it.

For the other reason, think about the text we recite. In one place it's "*ashamnu, bagadnu…*" ("We have sinned, we have acted treacherously…") and in the other it's "*al cheit shechatanu…*" ("For the sin that we have sinned…"). You'll note that, like Shemoneh Esrei (in which we say things like "heal us," "bless us," etc.) the confession is in the plural. It's a collective, communal prayer. Maybe you didn't perform a particular misdeed but *someone* did. We don't exist in a vacuum; we're all just organs in one greater body and something that brings one of us down brings us all down.

I'd like to focus on the second half of your question: what if one knows that he's going to continue performing the sin after Yom Kippur? This is a particularly good question in light of the fact that one of the things we confess is "For the sin we have committed before You through insincere confession," which could render the act of confession itself sinful if performed insincerely! The trick, therefore, is to do so sincerely!

On Rosh Hashana, we focus a lot on our forefather Avraham's relationship with his son Yitzchak but let's take a look at his other son, Yishmael. After Sarah had Hagar and Yishmael expelled, Yishmael wasn't doing so well. He was in danger of dying from thirst but God miraculously saved him with a well. Genesis 21:17 says:

> God heard the boy's voice, and an angel of God called to Hagar from Heaven, saying to her, "What troubles you, Hagar? Do not fear because God has heard the boy's voice in the place where he is."

The words "in the place where he is" cry out for explanation. In his commentary on this verse, Rashi cites the Talmud and the Midrash as follows:

> "A person is judged according to his current deeds and not according to what he will do in the future (*Rosh Hashana* 16b). God's ministering angels accused Yishmael, saying, 'Master of the Universe! You're going to create a well to save one who will eventually kill Your children with thirst?' God replied, 'What is he now, righteous or wicked?' The angels replied that he was currently righteous, to which God replied, 'I will judge him according to his present deeds' (*Genesis Rabbah*)." (Rashi goes on to cite the historic incident referred to in which Yishmael's descendants killed Jews through thirst, which occurred following the exile by Nebuchadnezzar and is foretold in Isaiah 21:13-15.)

We see from here—and from the Gemara cited—that a person is judged according to how he is at the moment, not according to what he will do in the future. If, at the time of reciting *vidui* (confession) on Yom Kippur, one intends to continue in the improper path, that would be a problem of insincere confession. But if one honestly intends to try changing his ways, he is judged as righteous. This does not preclude the possibility of backsliding—people are human after all—but it's one's intention at the time that makes the difference.

Contrast this with the *ben sorer u'moreh*, the stubborn and rebellious son. On Deuteronomy 21:18, Rashi cites the Talmud in *Sanhedrin* (72a-b) that he actually is judged according to what he's destined to do. (This is also the case with one who breaks into a house to rob it.) In these cases, it's fair to judge them according to their future deeds because they are already on those paths and making progress towards those goals. Yishmael, in his time of distress, was not yet on such a path and therefore judged according to how he was at the moment.

And that's the secret. Yom Kippur does not demand perfection in the coming year, and failure to achieve perfection does not invalidate what we say on Yom Kippur. The question is what's in our hearts. If we are sincerely interested in improving ourselves and changing our ways, then we will be judged as righteous. If we're only interested in just getting through Yom Kippur so we can get back to our sinning—well, that's another story.

Succos

Reading Koheles

Q. *Why do we read the book of Koheles on Succos?*

A. Tanach, the Jewish Bible, includes five *megillos* (scrolls), which are read on various occasions. The most famous of these is the book of Esther, which tells the story of Purim and is read, appropriately enough, on Purim.

A close second is Eicha (Lamentations), in which the prophet Jeremiah foretold the aftermath of the Temple's destruction and the exile from Jerusalem. This is read on Tisha b'Av, which commemorates that destruction and exile.

Rus (Ruth) is read on Shavuos; the holiday celebrates the giving of the

Torah and Rus, as a convert, accepted the Torah upon herself. Additionally, Rus was an ancestor of King David and we have a tradition that Shavuos is King David's *yahrtzeit*.

Shir HaShirim (alternately known as Song of Songs, Song of Solomon and Canticles) describes the relationship between God and the Jewish people in the form of a love story between a man and a woman. Shir HaShirim is read on Pesach (Passover), which marks the formation of Yaakov's descendants into a nation and the beginning of our unique relationship with God.

Which brings us to Koheles, known in English as Ecclesiastes. Koheles is a most unusual—and, frankly, depressing—book, in which Shlomo HaMelech (King Solomon) examines various aspects of life and determines that they are "*hevel.*" (Often translated as "vanity," *hevel* means that things are temporal, fleeting, or insignificant.) Shlomo concludes that "The end of the matter, after everything has been heard, is revere God and keep His commandments because this is the entirety of a person" (12:13).

The reading of Koheles on Succos appears to be a later addition. Tractate *Sofrim* (14:3) mentions the practice of publicly reading the other four *megillos* but omits Koheles. Nevertheless, the practice can be found in Medieval sources. A cynic might argue that Koheles is read on Succos simply because we are left with a megillah that has no holiday and a holiday that has no megillah but that's no basis for a match; there must be a thematic connection. And there is. (Several, actually):

- Koheles reminds us that all things are fleeting except for God and His Will. On Succos, we leave our homes—which give us a feeling of permanence and security—and dwell in booths that are of an inherently temporary nature. All of this underscores the same message: we're just "passing through" this world and heading for a more permanent place. (This is the explanation I favor);

- Succos is a harvest festival, which serves as the basis for another hypothesis. According to this explanation, the message of Koheles on Succos is to be happy with one's harvest and not lust after greater riches, which are actually meaningless;

- According to another explanation, the idea of Koheles on Succos is to temper the joy of the holiday, lest we get carried away by it. Koheles reminds us that the joy of this world is insignificant so that we don't let it interfere with our Divine service;
- Still other explanations tie the reading of Koheles on Succos to events in the lifetime of its author, King Solomon. For example, it has been suggested that Shlomo read Koheles at *hakhel* (a ceremony held on Succos on which the king read to the people from the Torah);
- Some see an allusion to Succos in Koheles itself. Koheles 11:2 says, "Divide your portion among seven, even among eight." Succos is a unique holiday in that it is seven days long, capped at the end by an eighth day, Shemini Atzeres.

The Sages who enacted the public reading of Koheles may have had one or several of these ideas in mind, or perhaps they had a different thought or thoughts altogether. Ultimately, the exact reason they instituted reading Koheles on Succos is unimportant. What's important is that we hear the profound message of Koheles and try to incorporate it into our lives.

Hoshana Rabbah and Beating Aravos

Q. *What is Hoshana Rabbah? Why are we beating willow branches?*

A. The bottom line is the Oral Law.

The Oral Law is an integral part of the Torah. It's absolutely impossible to observe the Torah without it. For example, the Torah tells us that performing labor on Shabbos is a capital crime but it doesn't define what labor is, which would be pretty useful information to have. The Torah also tells us to put on *tefillin*, which it calls "*totafos*," but it doesn't define them—and yet somehow we all agree on the black leather boxes containing certain Scriptural passages! My favorite proof of the Oral Law is from Deuteronomy 12:21, "...you shall slaughter from your herd and your flock, which God has given you, in the manner I have commanded you...." The Torah explicitly says that God has taught us the laws of *shechitah* (ritual slaughter) but they appear nowhere in the text, ergo there must be an Oral Law!

The Oral Law features prominently in the holiday of Succos. For example, Leviticus 23:40 says to take *pri eitz hadar*, literally "the fruit of a nice tree." So how do we know that this is an esrog and not a pear or an apricot? The Talmud (*Succah* 35a) cites several different authorities. One says that *hadar* is like *ha-dir* ("the stable"); just as a stable contains both large and small animals, the esrog can grow in a wide range of sizes. Another says that *hadar* is like *ha-dar* (the one who dwells); the esrog "dwells" on its tree in that it can remain there from year to year. A third sage says that the word *hadar* is etymologically related to the Greek word for water (*hydro*), and the esrog is a tree that requires a lot of irrigation.

Now here's what most people get wrong. The Sages did not use wordplay to conclude that "the fruit of a nice tree" is an esrog. They *knew* that it was an esrog! What the Sages are doing (and what they are typically doing in cases where they employ such wordplay) is taking a fact known from the Oral Law—in this case the identity of the *pri eitz hadar*—and attaching it to the text with a mnemonic device.

There are other facts that are known from the Oral Law that have no such hooks to connect them to the text. These are called *halachos l'Moshe miSinai*—laws communicated to Moses at Sinai. They are just as much a part of the Torah as the 39 categories of Shabbos labor, the meaning of tefillin, ritual slaughter and the identity of an esrog. The *aravos* ceremony was communicated to us as a *halacha l'Moshe miSinai*.

In Temple times, there was a daily processional on Succos. The Mishna (*Succah* 4:5) describes how the *kohanim* (priests) would lead the people in a circle around the altar reciting *hoshia na* ("please save"). On the seventh day of Succos—which we call Hoshana Rabbah—they would do so seven times. When the Temple was destroyed, the Anshei Knesses HaGedolah (Men of the Great Assembly) instituted that we should continue the practice with the *bimah* of our synagogues substituting for the altar.

The Midrash says that this ceremony, called Hoshanos, is a sign that we have emerged victorious from our judgment on Yom Kippur, mere days before. In the Temple, this ceremony was performed after offering the *korban musaf*—the special offering of the holiday. For this reason, most congregations perform Hoshanos as part of the Musaf service, which corresponds to that sacrifice. (Others perform it after Hallel, consolidating all parts of the service involving the four species into one big event.)

The seventh day of Succos is known as Hoshana Rabbah ("the great Hoshana"). While the name is of medieval origin, the day was unique even in Biblical times. The Mishna (*Succah* 4:6) calls it *"yom chibut chariyos"*—"the day of beating the palm branches." (The author of that statement was of the opinion that it was the lulav that should be beaten rather than the *aravos* but we do not follow his opinion.) Like the prayers recited throughout Succos, the bundle of *aravos* we beat is also referred to as "hoshanos."

After we make the seven processionals with the lulav and return the Torah to the ark, the bundle of *aravos* is beaten on the ground. (Five *aravos* are optimum, though three is sufficient and, in a pinch, even one will do.) Anything that would invalidate *aravos* for use on the lulav would also invalidate them for this purpose but even if a majority of the leaves fall off, it is still valid. In fact, as long as one leaf remains on the stem, it is valid, though the mitzvah is best performed when the *arava* has many leaves. When we come to "Answer Your faithful ones" in Hoshanos, we put down the lulav and esrog and pick up the *aravos*. After Hoshanos, we wave the bundle, then beat it on the ground five times. (Technically, we are not beating the *aravos*, we are beating the floor with the *aravos*.) It is optimum for at least some of the leaves to fall off, though it's okay if they don't. (It's also pretty unlikely that they won't.) The beaten *aravos* are not thrown on the ground because this is considered disrespectful to the mitzvah. It is better to put them aside and later use them as fuel for baking the Passover matzah. In this way, the *arovos*, which have been used for one mitzvah, can be used again for another.

There are other rituals associated with Succos that are not explicit in the text. For example, there were water libations on the altar and a water-drawing ceremony that was so festive that the Mishna tells us that one who did not witness it never saw real rejoicing in his entire life. We call our Succos parties *simchas beis hashoeva* (the joy of the place of water-drawing) in memory of these Temple celebrations.

Hoshana Rabbah is an especially holy day, on which the judgments of Rosh Hashana and Yom Kippur are ratified. Even though Hoshana Rabbah is not a *yom tov* (Festival), we recite the extra Psalms of praise that are otherwise only recited on Shabbos and holidays. Beating the *aravos* is only a small portion of a day of great significance that tends to get overlooked among the many days of *yom tov* that fall in the month of Tishrei. If it weren't surrounded (and overshadowed) by Rosh Hashana, Yom Kippur, Succos, Shemini Atzeres and Simchas Torah (all of which are *yomim tovim*), we would probably have a greater understanding of and appreciation for the gift of this very special occasion.

Chanukah

Yehudis: Warrior Princess

Q. I heard there was a female warrior in the Chanukah story. What's that about?

A. Chanukah, as you may be aware, is not overt in Tanach (the Jewish Bible). There are some hints to it in the Torah, and some prophecies in the book of Zechariah that appear to refer to the Maccabees and the miracle of Chanukah, but the actual event occurred after prophecy ceased, too late to include a historical, narrative account of the war and the miracle. But this doesn't mean that we have no account of it. In fact, we have several; they're just not part of the Bible canon.

We usually just point out that the Chanukah story is retold in the Talmud (tractate Shabbos) and leave it at that but let's take a look at some other sources.

For our purposes, the most authoritative is probably what we call Megillas Antiochus (the scroll that tells the story of Antiochus, who was the leader of the Syrian-Greek forces opposed by the Maccabees). This is generally dated to the second century, but it is popularly attributed to the scholars of the academies of Hillel and Shammai. If that attribution is accurate, it would actually date the scroll to more like the first century.

Following that, there are the various Books of the Maccabees. The first two are part of the Apocrypha. The Apocrypha are books of dubious canonicity, often falling between the Jewish and Christian Bibles. The Catholic Church generally accepts Apocryphal books in their canon but Jews and most Christian denominations do not. While we do not consider them to be holy, not having been authored with Divine inspiration, they can be an important source of historical information. (The third and fourth Books of the Maccabees are part of the Pseudepigrapha—the "false writings" that spuriously claim prestigious authorship. These books can also provide insights into the times in which they were written but are less useful than the first two. There are at least four more works that lay claim to the name but they provide continuingly-diminishing returns.)

Of interest to us here is another Apocryphal book, the book of Judith (Yehudis). I cannot stress enough that we do *not* accept this book as holy in any way but it does relate a story that is part of our tradition.

The first part of the work describes the rise of Nebuchadnezzar, though there is much reason to believe that it's actually talking about Antiochus; our tradition is that Judith occurs during the time of Chanukah so we'll just simplify things and say Antiochus. Antiochus had an enthusiastic general named Holofernes, who led a campaign through the town where Yehudis lived.

Yehudis, frustrated with her peers' lack of faith in God's ability to save them, took matters into her own hands. She went over to the enemy camp, pretending to be sympathetic to the invaders' cause. She ingratiated herself with Holofernes as a potential spy. Once she gained his trust, she allowed herself to be taken back to his tent. Getting Holofernes drunk on wine, Yehudis beheaded the general with his own sword. She took the head back to the Jewish camp and they used it as part of a PR campaign to demoralize the enemy over the loss of their powerful leader.

While the book of Judith is a non-Jewish source (or, perhaps, a non-Jewish translation of a lost Jewish source), the story of Yehudis is firmly part of the Jewish tradition:

- Rashi alludes to the story of Yehudis as a reason why women are obligated in the mitzvah of Chanukah: because the victory was brought about through a woman (Talmud, *Shabbos* 23a);

* The book of Judith doesn't mention it but we have a tradition that Yehudis fed Holofernes cheese in order to make him thirsty. For this reason, some have the tradition to eat cheese on Chanukah (Ran, *Shabbos* 10a);

* The prevalent practice is for women to refrain from performing acts of labor while the Chanukah lights are burning, at least for the first half hour (which is the minimum amount of time that the lights must burn). This is in the merit of Yehudis' actions (*Magen Avraham* 670:1).

So, even though we lack an existent Jewish narrative of the story of Yehudis, there is a strong oral tradition and, anachronistic misrepresentation of the enemy leader notwithstanding, a non-Jewish book that retells the story pretty much as we have it. Despite the lack of Biblical text, Yehudis is held as the model of a Jewish heroine, alongside the likes of Esther, Ruth, Devorah and Yael.

Tu b'Shevat

A Birthday for Trees?
Q. What is the meaning of having a birthday for trees?

A. Aside from the fact that "birthday" is something of a mistranslation, the idea of Tu b'Shevat is actually kind of a technical legal thing and not a day celebrating nature or agriculture *per se*. The very first Mishna in tractate *Rosh Hashana* (1:1) tells us:

> There are four new years: 1 Nisan is the new year for the kings and for holidays; 1 Elul is the new year for tithing animals, though Rabbi Eliezer and Rabbi Shimon say it is on 1 Tishrei; 1 Tishrei is the new year for counting years, Sabbatical years and Jubilee years, for planting and for vegetables; 1 Shevat is the new year for the trees according to Beis Shammai, though Beis Hillel say that it is 15 Shevat.

The idea of four "new years" isn't so unusual as you might think. We do the same thing. For example, our secular calendar year starts in January but your company's fiscal year might start in July, your child's school year might start in September and, if you invest in commodities, your crop marketing year might start in April.

So what are these four "new years" mentioned in the Mishna?

"1 Nisan is the new year for kings and for holidays" — The Torah tells us that Nisan is the first month for Jews because that's the month in which God took us out of Egypt. ("This month will be the head of the months to you; it will be the first month of the year for you" — Exodus 12:2.) Accordingly, the reigns of Jewish kings and the dates of Jewish holidays are counted from this date. Examples include Isaiah 36:1—"In the fourteenth year of King Hezekiah's reign"—and Leviticus 16:29—"On the tenth day of the seventh month you shall afflict yourselves and not perform any labor"—among many, many others.

"1 Elul is the new year for tithing animals, though Rabbi Eliezer and Rabbi Shimon say it is on 1 Tishrei" — Leviticus 27:32 commands us to give a tithe (10%) of our herds and flocks to God. Animals cannot be tithed from one year for another; they must come from that same year's stock. Accordingly, there has to be a cut-off point to determine what counts as last year and what counts as this year. The Sages chose 1 Elul as the cut-off because most animal births occur in the previous month, Av. (Rabbis Eliezer and Shimon thought it should be 1 Tishrei, to coincide with the cut-off point for the tithes of grain.)

"1 Tishrei is the new year for counting years, Sabbatical years and Jubilee years, for planting and for vegetables" — "Counting years" includes both the reigns of secular kings and the Jewish calendar years. While our "first month" is Nisan, Rosh Hashana—when the calendar changes from 5779 to 5780—occurs in Tishrei. (This is why the "Jewish new year" occurs in the seventh month of the year!) This is also the turning point for agricultural milestones: the Sabbatical year (every seven years) and the Jubilee year (every 50 years)

start on 1 Tishrei. One can't use fruit from a tree for its first three years, using this date as the dividing line, and it's also the deadline for which vegetables are tithed in which year.

"1 Shevat is the new year for the trees according to Beis Shammai, though Beis Hillel say that it is 15 Shevat" — Shevat, when the rainy season is mostly over, is the cut-off for in which year fruits are to be tithed. Beis Shammai selected 1 Shevat as the cut-off but Beis Hillel favored the midpoint of the month, 15 Shevat; we follow the opinion of Beis Hillel. In Hebrew, 15 Shevat is known as Tu b'Shevat, "tu" being the Hebrew letters tes and vav, whose numerical value equals 15.

It has always struck me as strange that we celebrate fruits on Tu b'Shevat but not vegetables on Rosh Hashana, or flocks and herds on 1 Elul, but there it is. If you don't live in Israel and are not eating Israeli produce, agricultural tithes are pretty inapplicable with the result that the only real halachic ramification of Tu b'Shevat is the omission of the *Tachanun* prayer from the daily services. There is, however, a nice custom.

The practice on Tu b'Shevat is to celebrate God's creation by partaking of various fruits, with special emphasis on the species for which Eretz Yisroel (the land of Israel) is praised in Deuteronomy 8:8: grapes, olives, dates, figs and pomegranates. Some people have the custom to eat carob in accordance with a statement by Rabbi Nechemiah in the Talmud (*Rosh Hashana* 15b). When eating these fruits, we praise God by reciting the *bracha* of *Borei pri ho'eitz*, that God created the fruit of the trees. If one eats enough of the fruits of Israel, he recites the concluding *bracha* of *al ho'eitz*. (This is just like the *bracha* of *al hamichya*, which is recited after baked goods but for the fruits of Israel.) Finally, reasonable effort should be exerted to eat at least one fruit that one hasn't eaten that entire season in order to be able to recite the *bracha* of *shehechiyanu*, that God has kept us alive to reach this occasion.

So, while Tu b'Shevat largely marks a legal deadline for which most of us have no practical application, it has been adopted as an opportunity to thank God in a most delicious way for one of the many gifts He has given us.

Purim

Celebrating a Massacre?
Q. How can we celebrate a victory in which women and children were killed?

A. Were they? Let's examine.

When Haman first organized his pogrom, King Ahasuerus granted him authority "to destroy, kill and cause to perish all the Jews, both young and old, little children and women, on one day, on the thirteenth day of the twelfth month, which is the month of Adar, and their spoils to be taken as plunder" (Esther 3:13). When Haman was revealed to not actually have the king's best interests at heart, Ahasuerus granted the Jews the right "to assemble and to protect themselves, to destroy, to slay, and to cause to perish the entire host of every people and province that oppress them, small children and women, and to take their spoils for plunder" (Esther 8:11).

You will note that the Jews were fighting a strictly *defensive* war. While the other citizens of the Persian empire had license to kill Jews at their whim in order to take the Jews' property, the Jews were only permitted "to assemble and to protect themselves" by doing what others sought to do to them.

So what did they do? We are told that on the first day, "in Shushan the capital, the Jews slew and destroyed five hundred men" (Esther 9:6). On the second day—"Shushan Purim"—"they slew in Shushan three hundred men" (9:15). Both of these verses stress that the Jews killed men—i.e., combatants—and not collateral victims.

Esther 9:16 gives the casualties for the entire 127 provinces of the empire as 75,000 and doesn't specify men but nowhere in the megillah does it indicate that they killed women or children. The megillah does stress several times (chapter 9, verses 10, 15 and 16) that they Jews didn't lay hands on the spoils, which they were entitled to do. Since they didn't touch the spoils, it is apparent that they were sincerely fighting a defensive battle—all they were interested in was survival. It would certainly suggest that they were careful about not involving non-combatants. At least, that's the logical conclusion to draw without any evidence to the contrary.

If you are talking about the general commandment to eradicate Amalek, that's another story altogether.

Allow me to quote myself, from my book *The Taryag Companion*:

We are commanded to eradicate the nation of Amalek, wiping any vestige of them from the face of the Earth. The reason, as discussed in the previous mitzvah, is because of the cowardly attack that the Amalekites made against God when He took the Jews out of Egypt. Apparently, God knows that certain traits are ingrained within the descendants of Amalek. Nevertheless, many people find this to be a very troubling mitzvah. As historic victims of inquisitions and pogroms, they ask, don't we find it inconsistent to justify genocide?

We can understand this mitzvah better if we realize that the Amalekites had the opportunity to turn their backs on the ways of their nation and be spared their fate. (This is very different from the way in which Jews were treated in, say, the Holocaust.) As with other nations, Amalek had the opportunity to accept the seven universal (Noachide) laws and submit to Israel's rule. Not only that, they could convert. The Talmud in Gittin (57b) famously tells us that Haman had descendants who taught Torah in B'nei Brak. (Many authorities believe this to include the renowned sage Rabbi Akiva, who was known to be from B'nei Brak and who was descended from converts.)

This brief explanation may not satisfy contemporary sensibilities but that's okay; most of human history did not share modern sensibilities. For us, the mitzvah to eradicate Amalek is strictly an academic exercise with no practical application to worry about. It may take some doing to grasp this mitzvah but the first step is to recognize that it's not what we initially imagined it to be. With further study, we can hopefully better understand what it actually entailed and why God required it of our ancestors.

Pesach

Kitniyos

Q. What's the deal with kitniyos since we now know it's not chametz?

A. *Kitniyos* is typically translated as "legumes" and the Ashkenazi practice is not to eat them on Passover. This isn't because we used to think that they were *chometz* ("leaven") but now we know better. The situation is comparable to the universal practice not to eat poultry with dairy.

The Torah prohibits eating meat with dairy. The language it uses refers to eating meat cooked "in its mother's milk," so it's pretty clear that it's only referring to mammals, since only mammals produce milk. However, the Sages created a rabbinic prohibition against having chicken and other fowl with milk as well. This wasn't because they mistakenly thought that chickens give milk. We always knew that wasn't the case. They made the rule because human beings are fallible and they wanted to help people keep far away from sin. There are plenty of people who can't tell a veal cutlet from a chicken cutlet, so why take chances?

Similarly, the practice not to eat *kitniyos* on Passover is a rabbinic enactment designed to keep people from the possibility of transgression. Things can be classified as *kitniyos* because:

1. They are harvested and processed in a manner identical to *chometz*; and/or
2. They can be ground into flour and baked like *chometz*; and/or
3. They may have grains of *chometz* mixed into them.

So, like chicken with milk, reasons #1 and #2 are because people can get confused. People are not so expert in what they're eating as you might expect. Watch the confusion over what *bracha* to make over different kinds of cereal, or whether to wash before eating a wrap. Reason #3 is because people might actually come to eat *chometz*.

This is a post-Talmudic practice, dating back to the Middle Ages. Yes, there was originally opposition to adopting the practice but it has long since become universally accepted by all Ashkenazi communities. Types of produce classified as *kitniyos* include (but are not limited to) rice, lentils, beans, peas, mustard, corn, green beans, and sesame seeds. Non-*kitniyos* foods include coffee, tea, garlic and nuts. (Peanuts, despite the name, are not actually nuts. There is some disagreement as to their status but the general practice is to treat them as *kitniyos*.)

Because of the way the practice was instituted, it is generally limited to the foods originally designated as *kitniyos*. (There are exceptions, such as corn, which is considered the "local grain.") Potatoes, had they been known in Europe at the time, would no doubt have been declared *kitniyos*. Because they were only discovered later, potatoes are not included in the prohibition. (This is also the basis to permit quinoa, although that is a much tougher call to make based on its similarity to other grains.)

Actual *chometz* is prohibited to be eaten on Passover, of course, but one may likewise not derive benefit from it, nor even own it. The Rabbis only prohibited *kitniyos* to be eaten; one need not sell it or destroy it before Passover. One may not feed an animal or an infant *chometz* on Passover but he may feed them *kitniyos*. (Please note that there are many *halachos* regarding *kitniyos*; we're not even scratching the surface here.)

But why do some Jews eat *kitniyos* on Pesach and others not? That's because of history. The Talmud was the last time that all the halachic authorities were able to be together to debate and decide on matters of law. Accordingly, whatever the Sages of the Talmud ruled is universally binding on all of Jewry. After that, the communities were dispersed and not able to communicate so easily. Two of these communities are what we call "Sefardi" (Spanish Jewry) and "Ashkenazi" (Eastern European Jewry). Each community was able to legislate for itself, regardless of what was going on elsewhere. This is what's called *minhag*.

Minhag is commonly translated as "custom," which does a disservice because people infer that customs are optional, while *minhag* is actually binding on the members of its community. This is not contradictory. You can open carry in Texas but not in New York; even though they're both in the US, each state can make its own laws. Similarly, the Sefardi and

Ashkenazi communities can develop different *minhagim*, each binding on members of their respective communities.

And that's the deal with *kitniyos*.

Does the Haggadah Call for Violence?

Q: *In the Haggadah, it says "Pour out Your wrath upon the nations that do not call out Your Name." Since when do we call out for violence?*

A. The first thing one has to realize is that the line in question isn't just some sentiment expressed by the authors of the Passover Haggadah. Rather, it comprises two Biblical verses from the book of Psalms. Psalms 79:6-7 reads:

> Pour out Your wrath upon the nations that do not know You and upon the kingdoms that do not call in Your Name, for they have devoured Jacob and laid waste his habitation.

This sentiment is echoed by the prophet Jeremiah. (I say "echoed" because, while the book of Jeremiah appears earlier than Psalms in the Bible canon, the prophet Jeremiah lived about 400 years after King David, the author of Psalms.) Jeremiah 10:25 reads:

> Pour out Your wrath upon the nations that do not know You and upon the families that do not call in Your Name, for they have devoured Jacob; yes, they have devoured and consumed him, and have laid waste his habitation.

So, once the idea actually appears in your Bible—not once but twice—you have to give it a certain amount of credence. Nevertheless, this concept doesn't sit well with many of us because we've been raised with the idea that we're all God's children and He loves us all. So why would we wish ill on others? What we have to understand is that context matters a lot. I'll illustrate.

Let's look at Psalms 97-98. Psalms 97:5 reads, "The mountains melted like wax at God's presence." However, Psalms 98:8 says, "Let the mountains sing for joy." Mountains are a symbol for the mighty kings of various nations. So which is it? Will they melt like wax or sing for joy? The answer depends on context: those kings who insist on considering their own might to be supreme will ultimately be shamed and melt like wax; those who learn to subordinate themselves to God will ultimately join together in joyful song to Him.

The same is true regarding "pour out Your wrath." We don't pray that God arbitrarily wipe out other nations. So what's the context here?

On Psalms 79:6, the commentary called *Metzudas Dovid* explains "Pour out Your wrath upon the nations that do not know You" to mean "Remove Your wrath from us and pour it out on the nations that don't want to know You." So the first thing we see is that the nations to whom this verse refers are not just ignorant of God, they're *willfully* ignorant, which is a different matter entirely: they *choose* not to recognize God so that they may persist in their not-so-good ways.

The Radak also sheds some light on this verse. Regarding "the kingdoms that do not call in Your Name," he says that we ask God to remove His wrath from us and to place it on those aforementioned nations because, even though we may sin (and therefore be deserving of *some* wrath), we still call in His Name. We may not be perfect—no human is— but at least we're trying.

Furthermore, the Radak specifies that the reason these other nations deserve God's wrath is because they dismantled Jewish sovereignty when they destroyed Jerusalem and exiled the Tribe of Judah. This sounds to me like only certain very specific nations are intended.

Which brings us to Psalms 79:7, "for they have devoured Jacob and laid waste his habitation." The ibn Ezra explains that it wasn't enough for these nations simply to ignore God; they felt the need to attack Israel, who *did* recognize God. So they're not just people who choose not to know God, they're overtly antagonistic to God and they try to destroy those who do have a relationship with Him.

So, yes, in general we do prefer the paths of peace but context is important. After WWII, should we not have tried and executed Nazi war criminals? Who would say that "forgive and forget" is the appropriate course of action in the face of such atrocities? Similarly, the call of "Pour out Your wrath" is directed specifically at those nations that chose to self-identify as enemies of God and to commit unprovoked acts of brutality against us because of it.

Sefiras Ha'Omer

The Omer Without a Temple

Q. *If there's no Temple anymore, why are we still counting an omer that's not even being brought?*

A. Leviticus chapter 23 tells us the following: Passover starts at night following the 14th day of the month of Nisan. The first day of Passover (i.e., 15 Nisan) and the seventh day of Passover are holidays with Sabbath-like restrictions on performing labor. On the day after the first holiday (i.e., 16 Nisan), the *kohein* would wave a particular sheaf offering. This sheaf is called an *omer*. From the day that the *omer* was brought, there is a mitzvah to count seven weeks (49 days); the 50th day is the holiday of Shavuos, which celebrates the giving of the Torah at Sinai. So "counting the *omer*" is really counting from 16 Nisan until Shavuos.

It is true that there are aspects of ritual that we cannot perform in the absence of the Temple but we still do what we can. For example, we cannot currently offer the Passover sacrifice but we still eat matzah and *maror*. We cannot perform the special Yom Kippur service but we still fast and repent. Similarly, bringing the *omer* and counting seven weeks are independent *mitzvos*. Even if we can't do everything, we do what we can.

As noted, "counting the *omer*" is really counting from the *omer* to Shavuos. The reason for this mitzvah is to underscore the importance of the Torah. The Jews were not redeemed from Egypt simply to relieve them of the burden of slavery. Rather, the redemption was just the first step in a process that was to culminate in the Jews receiving the Torah at Sinai seven weeks later. We count the days from Passover until Shavuos to demonstrate how precious the Torah is to us and how anxiously we await its transmission to us.

Here's something interesting. "Everyone knows" that the date of Shavuos is 6 Sivan—or is it? Counting the *omer* extends from the last two weeks of the month of Nisan, through the entire month of Iyar, and into the first few days of Sivan. Under our current fixed calendar, Nisan always has 30 days and Iyar always has 29 days, with the result that Shavuos always falls on 6 Sivan. But such was not always the case! When there's a Sanhedrin, the months are set based on witnesses testifying as to the sighting of the moon. Under that system, Nisan and Iyar could be 29 days each, placing Shavuos on 5 Sivan. Or Nisan and Iyar could be 30 days each, placing Shavuos on 7 Sivan. There were about 300 years from the destruction of the Second Temple until the fixed calendar was adopted. This means that even after sacrifices ceased, counting the *omer* wasn't just a symbolic gesture, it was a very practical means of figuring out when Shavuos was.

Leviticus 23:15 says *usfartem lachem*—"count for yourselves." Whether we're counting for the practical purpose of determining the date of Shavuos or for the moral lesson about the importance of Torah, ultimately counting the *omer* is something we do for ourselves—no sacrifices required!

Rabbi Akiva's Students

Q. What did Rabbi Akiva's students do wrong? Isn't killing 24,000 of them a bit much?

A. The *sefirah* period, which lasts from Pesach through Shavuos, is a period of quasi-mourning during which we don't get haircuts, listen to music, or engage in other behaviors associated with joy. (The exact dates during which the mourning is observed is a matter of various customs.) The reason for this mourning period is explained in the Talmud (*Yevamos* 62b) as follows:

Rabbi Akiva had 12,000 pairs of students from Gevat to Antipatris (in the North), all of whom died in the same period of time because they did not show one another the proper respect. The future of Torah was in jeopardy until Rabbi Akiva went to the South and taught Torah there. His later students included Rabbi Meir, Rabbi Yehuda, Rabbi Yosi, Rabbi Shimon and Rabbi Elazar ben Shamua, who preserved the study of Torah and transmitted it to future generations. Rabbi Akiva's earlier students died in the period between Pesach and Shavuos. Rav Chama bar Abba— some say Rabbi Chiya bar Avin—said they all died an ugly death; Rav Nachman clarified that this refers to diphtheria.

It should be noted that the Talmud was compiled during the era of Roman occupation and many stories are written in code to avoid censorship or political repercussions. It has been suggested that Rabbi Akiva's students died in battle as part of the Bar Kochba revolt, or were executed as a consequence of it. Rav Sherira Gaon (d. 1006) suggests that they were martyred; Rav Yosef Eliyahu Henkin (d. 1973) said explicitly that "died of a plague" is code for "died fighting the Romans." There are others who say this, and it's widely accepted in academic circles, so it's surprising to me that this interpretation is not better known. But whether Rabbi Akiva's students died of a literal plague or of a plague-as-code-for-the-Romans is immaterial as, either way, our original question remains.

From the fact that we observe a period of mourning for these students, we can easily infer that they were righteous despite this particular shortcoming. That being the case, it honestly doesn't surprise me if they were held to a higher-than-average standard, because that's consistent with God's "standard operating procedure."

Imagine a brand-new shirt, sparkling white. The tiniest spot on it is a glaring stain. When you've had the shirt for a while and it's getting kind of dingy, the spot doesn't show as noticeably and it won't bother you as much. By the time the shirt is all gray and covered with oil and grease from working on your car with it on, you don't even care if you drip soup on it because who's going to notice? Spiritually speaking, people are also like that. Most of us are gray and stained, or at least a little dingy—a tiny spot like not extending sufficient honor to our colleagues is barely going to show. But the righteous are like new white garments—a little stain is really going to stand out. It totally ruins it. So a defect that's minor to you and me is glaring in truly great people.

Consider how Moshe was punished for hitting the rock in Numbers chapter 20. There is some discussion as to what Moshe "really" did wrong. I favor the explanation that his "sin" was that he lost his temper with the Jews when he yelled, "Listen up, you rebels!" at them in verse 20:10. But regardless of the interpretation, all the potential "sins" of Moshe have one thing in common—they all seem pretty minor. Certainly not deserving of Moshe being unable to enter Israel after all he had done! The answer is because Moshe was Moshe. Everyone looked to him as their role model. Accordingly, he was obligated to adhere to a much higher standard of behavior.

The same is true of Nadav and Avihu, the sons of Aharon who died during the inauguration of the Mishkan (Tabernacle). Their crime was apparently bringing an incense offering that was not commanded (Leviticus 10:1). As with Moshe, there is some discussion as to what their sin *really* was (ruling in front of their teachers, asking when they would assume leadership, drinking before performing the service, etc.) but the same fact remains: none of their potential "sins" really seem to be deserving of death. Again, this is not because they were lesser, it's because they were greater. The Torah tells us as much when God says, "I will be sanctified through those who are close to Me" (10:3). Nadav and Avihu were held to a higher standard specifically because of their greatness.

We see elsewhere in Chumash (and throughout Tanach) that the righteous are held to higher standards, so it's not a great leap that Rabbi Akiva's students might have been punished harshly for a minor flaw because of their greatness.

I have seen other explanations, such as that Rabbi Akiva's students were being groomed to be the Torah leaders of the next generation but they demonstrated that they lacked one of the character traits necessary for proper acquisition of Torah (see R. Chaim Vital). Another idea is that what seems like proper respect to you and me is insufficient when one is a student of Rabbi Akiva, who is famous for the opinion that "love your neighbor as yourself" is the central theme of the Torah.

I would like, however, to share an idea that occurred to me for which I have seen no support.

Imagine I said to you, "Bob died in his sleep because he didn't have a carbon monoxide detector." You might derive a lesson from that—that it's important to have a carbon monoxide detector in your home—but you would not infer that Bob was Divinely punished with death over his lack of such a detector. We recognize that Bob's death was a natural occurrence (as much as any death is) and that Bob merely lacked the means to protect himself against it.

That being the case, let's re-read the Gemara's first sentence: "Rabbi Akiva had 12,000 pairs of students from Gevat to Antipatris, all of whom died in the same period of time because they did not show one another the proper respect."

Maybe that doesn't mean that God actively smote them because of this flaw. Maybe death from the diphtheria epidemic (or the Roman occupation) was the "natural" course of events. Rabbi Akiva's students were so great that they might have been deserving of miraculous salvation except for one thing: they didn't honor one another sufficiently. According to this reading, they weren't killed because of their shortcoming but this shortcoming kept them from meriting Divine intervention.

I think that such an approach is not unprecedented. Consider, for example, the *mei'il* (robe) worn by the Kohein Gadol, the hem of which was ringed with small bells. Exodus 28:35 says, "It shall be upon Aharon to perform the service; its sound shall be heard when he goes into the holy place before Hashem, and when he comes out, so that he not die." From the language, it would seem that dying was the natural consequence of entering the Holy of Holies and the *mei'il* served as Divine protection against this reality.

Like I said, applying this logic to Rabbi Akiva's students is my own idea; if any well-versed readers know of a source who theorizes such an approach, I'd love to hear it. But even if you don't accept my hypothesis because I can't cite precedent for it, my earlier point still stands: greater people are held to higher standards. If the students of Rabbi Akiva did indeed perish for such an offense, then they were on a truly high spiritual level and mourning the loss of what they could have contributed is an appropriate response on our part.

Shavuos

The All-Nighter

Q. As I get older, it gets hard to stay up all night to learn on Shavuos. Am I obligated to?

A. Shavuos is in many ways an atypical holiday. There are three Festivals in the Torah: Pesach, Succos and Shavuos. Pesach and Succos each last a week or so, with intermediate quasi-holidays that we call chol hamoed; Shavuos is just one day (two outside of Israel). The Torah is explicit about why we celebrate Pesach and Succos—to commemorate that God took us out of Egypt and caused us to dwell in huts, respectively—but it does not tell us outright that Shavuos commemorates the giving of the Torah at Mount Sinai. Even the date of Shavuos is obscured. Rather than just telling us the date as it does for other holidays, the Torah instructs us to count seven weeks from Passover.

Seeing how different Shavuos is from the other Festivals, it should not surprise us that it differs in another way. Pesach and Succos each have unique *mitzvos*. On Passover, we recount the Exodus from Egypt, and we eat matzah and *maror*. On Succos, we eat in a succah and wave the four species. But the practice to stay up all night learning Torah on Shavuos? That's not of Biblical origin, nor is it an obligation.

The practice to stay up all night learning Torah is attributed to Rav Yosef Karo, the 16th-century codifier of the *Shulchan Aruch*, though its roots are much older. The *Zohar* speaks of Rabbi Shimon bar Yochai, who lived in the second century, staying up all night. His reason for doing so is compared to an attendant helping to prepare a bride prior to her wedding. (A wedding between God and the Jewish people is the common metaphor for the giving of the Torah at Sinai.) The ultimate basis for the tradition is a Midrash in *Shir HaShirim Rabbah* that describes how the Jews overslept on the morning when God was to give them the Torah, which showed a lack of enthusiasm. Throughout the generations, we rectify this national flaw through the many enthusiastic volunteers who spend the entire night engaged in study to show their appreciation to God for the gift of His Torah.

No particular course of study is prescribed. The Medieval kabbalist known as the Arizal organized a selection of Biblical and Talmudic passages into a text called the *Tikkun Leil Shavuos* ("Order for the Night of Shavuos"). Some have colloquially come to refer to the all-night study session itself as *tikkun leil Shavuos*. While not technically accurate, it is not inappropriate. The word *tikkun* in Hebrew can also mean a repair or a correction. While such was not the intention of the Arizal, it is perhaps a fitting way to refer to the night's activities, seeing as they are intended to make up for the oversight of our ancestors.

The custom was originally to stay up learning the *Tikkun Leil Shavuos*, which contains excerpts from the various books of Tanach, as a means of preparing to receive the Torah in the morning. Nowadays, the practice in most modern American synagogues is to hear speakers and/or to study in small groups. This is a completely voluntary practice. It is much to be praised but it's definitely not for everyone. In fact, it's preferable that some people *do* sleep. The recitation of the morning blessings is complicated by not sleeping, so one who has slept typically serves as leader for that portion of the morning service.

On Shavuos morning, when we read about the revelation at Sinai, we re-enact in microcosm the transmission of the Torah to the Jewish people. By studying Torah all night the night before, we prepare ourselves, emotionally and intellectually, to appreciate this gift. But if one doesn't want to stay up for whatever reason—whether because one lacks the physical stamina, has children to watch in the morning, or will just feel lousy without a good night's sleep—then there's no reason to feel bad, because this practice is completely optional.

American Holidays

Is Independence Day Unlucky?

Q. *Two people have told me that July 4, 1776 was on the 17th of Tammuz. Wikipedia confirms this. Does that indicate something negative about America?*

A. Rav Salman Mutzafi (a student of the Ben Ish Chai and the author of *Siddur HaRashash*), Rav Shmuel Yaakov Weinberg (a student of Rav Hutner, the son-in-law of Rav Ruderman, and later the rosh yeshiva of Ner Yisroel) and Rav Yaakov Yitzchak Spiegel (a student of Rav Ahron Kotler) were all born on 17 Tammuz; does that imply something negative about them? For that matter, we have a tradition that Moshiach will be born on Tisha b'Av (Yerushalmi, *Brachos* 2:4, *Eicha Rabbah* 1:51); does that suggest something bad about Moshiach? Clearly not!

While bad things did happen on 17 Tammuz and 9 Av, not everything that happens on those days is necessarily bad. Things that happen on those days can also be good. Remember such verses as Psalms 30:12 ("You turned my mourning into dancing for me, You removed my sackcloth and dressed me with gladness") and Jeremiah 31:12 ("...I will turn their mourning into joy, comfort them, and make them rejoice from their sorrow"), among others. These are sad days but not everything that happens on them need necessarily be a portent for disaster.

Celebrating Thanksgiving

Q. *Is it kosher to celebrate Thanksgiving since it's a non-Jewish holiday?*

A. You'd think this would be a straightforward yes-or-no question. You'd be wrong. One of my all-time favorite theological quotes is from that profound modern-day philosopher of *The Simpsons* fame, Reverend Timothy Lovejoy: "Short answer, 'yes' with an 'if;' long answer, 'no' with a 'but.'"

Many of the things we discuss depend on whom you ask. For example, whether *chalav Yisroel* milk (meaning that the cow was milked under Jewish supervision to ensure that it's not, say, camel's milk) is obligatory in our society or a stringency. According to the latter position, M&M's, Hershey bars, Ben and Jerry's ice cream and Entenmann's cakes are all perfectly kosher. Those who follow the former position, however, would consider these things (and many more) to be non-kosher. That's not to say that anyone is wrong *per se*; each group is following the rulings of their halachic decisors. By way of analogy, can a person turn right on red, open-carry a weapon or marry their first cousin? It all depends on where you live, as the legality of these things depends on the rulings of the local authorities.

The issue driving the Thanksgiving question is a *halacha* called *b'chukoseihem* (Leviticus 18:3), in which the Torah adjures us not to copy other nation's ways. As with a number of other laws (such as "you shall be holy"—Leviticus 19:2), the parameters are not clearly defined, so the authorities are going to differ on some of the details.

We agree on this: we cannot copy other religions' theological practices. It might occur to me to wear a black shirt with a white collar so that passersby could easily identify me as clergy but that is a decidedly non-Jewish practice. Decorating your home with an evergreen tree in December likewise carries theological implications. Everyone agrees that these things would be violations of *b'chukoseihem*.

Accordingly, we may not celebrate holidays with origins in other faiths. These include (but are not limited to) Christmas, Halloween, and St. Patrick's Day. No matter how secular these days may have become, they continue to be religious in their roots. This would also be the case with the Hindu holiday Diwali and the Islamic Eid. If you're inclined to fast for Ramadan in solidarity with your Muslim friends, your heart might be in the right place but it would be a violation of *b'chukoseihem*.

So, Thanksgiving may not be Jewish in origin but is that the same as being "non-Jewish?" Therein lies the crux of the matter, and in this the authorities differ. Rav Yitzchak Hutner ruled that any annual holiday established according to the Gregorian calendar is *de facto* a non-Jewish holiday and would be prohibited. He calls this conclusion "simple and obvious." There are certainly those who follow this position but there are other, equally great authorities who ruled otherwise.

Rav Moshe Feinstein addressed this question several times, always concluding that Thanksgiving is a secular rather than a religious holiday. While Thanksgiving may have (allegedly) been instituted by the Pilgrims (who were English Dissenters—a breakaway from the Church of England—and not Puritans *per se*), it was not instituted as a religious obligation. In other words, there were plenty of English Dissenters—and Puritans—back in Europe who did not observe this holiday. It fulfills no religion's obligations to eat turkey, stuffing and cranberry sauce on the Thursday preceding the last Saturday of November.

Rabbi Joseph B. Soloveitchik ("the Rav") also ruled that Thanksgiving is a secular rather than a religious holiday and that it is permissible to eat turkey on that day. In fact, his students reported that he always held class on Thanksgiving but that he started and ended earlier than on other days so that he could fly home from New York to Boston, presumably to participate in a family meal.

There are other nuances of opinion, such as Rav Yehuda Herzl Henkin, who advises skipping the Thanksgiving meal every few years in order to demonstrate that one does not consider it a religious duty. Rav Dovid Cohen rules against celebrating Thanksgiving not because it has non-Jewish religious connotations but because *b'chukoseihem* also prohibits doing things that have no rational basis, and feeling obligated to eat turkey on a random Thursday certainly qualifies. (However, Rav Cohen says, if a family wants to get together because they are off work and they happen to enjoy eating turkey, it's certainly permissible to do so.) Even Rabbi Feinstein, who ruled that observing Thanksgiving is permitted, said that particularly pious individuals should refrain.

In short, there are a wide variety of positions but, since Thanksgiving is celebrated by Americans of all faiths and is of religious import to no particular denomination, it may be "not Jewish," but that doesn't make it "un-Jewish." If one wants to eat turkey with all the trimmings, he certainly has who to rely upon (though one should always follow the advice of his own religious exemplars). The Thanksgiving feast need be no more religiously problematic than having a barbecue on the fourth of July. In this author's opinion, observing Thanksgiving is far less problematic than celebrating New Year's Day (also known as "Feast of the Circumcision of Christ," "Feast of the Holy Name of Jesus" and "Octave of the Nativity," among other names), a day with far more religious implication than Thanksgiving ever had.

Spiritual Matters

Predetermination vs. Free Will

Q. *We are told that everything that happens, even if it appears to be detrimental, is ultimately for the good and meant to be. How is that reconciled with humans having free choice? Does that apply to when Jews don't follow the Torah? Are those who persecute Jews doing so because it was predetermined (like God hardening Pharaoh's heart) or are they using their free will? Was Hitler predetermined to engineer the Holocaust or was it his free will? When someone speaks to you, is it them speaking from their free will or are the words they're saying predetermined by Hashem (and therefore a Divine message)?*

A. You are working under some misconceptions. The Talmud tells us "everything is in the hands of Heaven except for the fear of Heaven." In other words, God will decide your health, your financial success, etc., but you will decide whether or not you observe the Torah. The second thing is, the Talmud tells us "all that He (God) does, He does for the good." Everything *He* does is for the good, but not necessarily everything that *we* do! So, with these two clarifications in mind, (1) not everything is predetermined and (2) not everything that happens is necessarily good.

Before I go any further, allow me to add that God is not bound in space or in time. Just as He is simultaneously in New York, St. Louis, Cape Town and Madagascar, He is also simultaneously in the years 2014, 1936, 2525 and 3500 BCE. He knows what you're going to do because He's already seen you do it, but He didn't force your hand.

So, with all this in mind:

1. Does that apply to when Jews don't follow the Torah?

As we said, "everything is in the hands of Heaven except for the fear of Heaven." They have free will and they are choosing to exercise it in a manner contrary to what the Torah says. We may disagree with their course of action but they have the power to make their own choices.

2. Are those who persecute Jews doing so because it was predetermined (like God hardening Pharaoh's heart) or are they using their free will?

The heart-hardening thing is misunderstood. It doesn't mean that God took away Pharaoh's free will, it means that He restored it. If every time you tried to eat a cheeseburger, you received an electric shock, you'd stop trying to eat cheeseburgers. This would not be using your free will—you're being compelled not to eat the cheeseburgers! Similarly, the frogs, blood, locusts, etc. bullied Pharaoh into agreeing to release the Jews against His will. "God hardened his heart" means "God strengthened his resolve." He restored Pharaoh's ability to do what he wanted, despite the plagues.

3. Was Hitler predetermined to engineer the Holocaust or was it his free will?

The famous question about Pharaoh is "Why was he punished?" After all, God told Avraham that the Jews would be enslaved, so wasn't Pharaoh just fulfilling God's will? Yes and no. Just because the Jews were destined to be enslaved, that doesn't mean that Pharaoh had to be the one to do it. (If I kill someone, doesn't that prove that that person's time is up and God wanted to take them? Maybe, but it's not my job to act as God's agent. It's my job to do what God said and not kill people.) Even if you want to say that God specifically desired Pharaoh to do it, Pharaoh didn't have to go overboard with all the oppression and baby-killing. Same thing with Hitler. If God wants us punished, that doesn't make it Hitler's job. Even if you say God specifically wanted Hitler to do it, Hitler didn't have to be so over the top. Hitler's job—like all of ours—was to do what God says, in this case, not to kill.

4. *When someone speaks to you, is it them speaking from their free will or are the words they're saying predetermined by Hashem (and therefore a Divine message)?*

Free will. We don't have prophecy nowadays and, even when we did, it was limited to—you know—prophets. (In general, it's a good idea not to assume that other people's words are Divine messages—that's a great way to drive yourself crazy!)

Bris Milah

Q. *Why would God create man needing a bris? What is Judaism trying to tell us about why we need circumcision? Why can't we be proud of who we are without needing to change?*

A. Let me start by recommending my book *The Taryag Companion*, which addresses the reasons underlying the 613 *mitzvos*, at least insofar as we understand them. Let's examine the rationale underlying the mitzvah of *milah* (circumcision).

In Genesis 17:10, God says, "This is My covenant that you must honor, between Me and you and among your descendants: every male among you must be circumcised." God promised Abraham great things for him and his descendants. In exchange, He commanded that all males be circumcised—optimally at the age of eight days old—as a sign of this covenant. By performing this act, we partner with God in completing the act of creation.

The reason for this mitzvah according to the *Sefer HaChinuch* is that it forms a permanent, physical sign of our covenant with God. The Talmud in *Menachos* (43b) stresses this point when it relates a story involving King David. On one occasion, David entered the bath house and was saddened when he considered that he was bereft of his *tallis, tefillin,* the Torah scroll that a Jewish king is commanded to carry with him, and all the other symbols of the Jewish people's commitment to fulfilling God's will. When he looked down and saw the place of his circumcision, however, he was comforted.

Now consider the alternative: if we were not commanded to circumcise (or if we were born pre-circumcised), God would have promised great things to Abraham and his descendants, in exchange for which He would have asked for... nothing. Seems pretty one-sided! The permanent sign of our covenant would be... nothing! David would have been comforted by... nothing! We would partner with God in completing the act of creation by doing... nothing!

This doesn't sound like there's any shame in how we're born. Rather, it's doing something to take us to the next level as a sign of our membership in an exclusive club. We don't tattoo (doing so is actually prohibited by the Torah) but consider this analogous to a Marine getting a "Semper Fidelis" eagle tattoo. There's nothing wrong with his bicep without it, he just chooses to use it to display his pride of membership.

Now, there are certainly others who circumcise for a variety of other reasons—religious, health, aesthetic or otherwise. The fact that we are not exclusive in this practice doesn't take away from it at all. Elsewhere, I discuss how cultural hairstyles sometimes favor *payes* (sidelocks worn by Jewish men) and sometimes these styles go against them; we grow our hair a certain way regardless of what's popular. Well, the same is true of circumcision. We had the better part of a century in which circumcision was popular in the US thanks to Dr. John Harvey Kellogg, who, in addition to being inventor of the corn flake, was an anti-masturbation crusader and a circumcision proponent. (This is not a joke.) The popularity pendulum started swinging the other way—in the US and in Europe—in the 1990s and 2000s. In recent years, a number of European countries have instituted or considered circumcision bans. So, popularity or lack thereof notwithstanding, we consider circumcising to be our right, privilege and duty.

One last thought: We have a tradition that Abraham observed the entire Torah, based on Genesis 26:5 ("because Abraham heeded My voice, and kept My charge, My commandments, My statutes, and My laws"). If Abraham was able to intuit all the laws of the Torah and observe them voluntarily, why didn't he circumcise himself before God commanded it? The reason is because he intuited the prohibition against self-injury (Deuteronomy 14:1). If not for God's command, we would not be permitted to circumcise, except as might be required in cases of medical necessity.

That being the case, it should be evident that, while Judaism considers circumcision to be the fulfillment of God's will, it simultaneously considers female "circumcision" to be a form of mutilation. The women's morning blessing that God "formed me according to His will" is not intended as the "consolation prize" that some like to frame it. Rather, it is a statement that God made women—the pinnacle of creation—physically perfect, as He desires them.

Such is not the case with men, whom God formed not according to the way He ultimately wants us. Rather, He designed us requiring a small alteration, enabling us to partner with Him as a sign of the covenant. And there's no shame in that.

The Benefits of Keeping Kosher

Q. What are the benefits of a kosher diet, strictly from a health perspective?

A. Not to be glib but, who says there are any?

I'm not saying that a kosher diet doesn't have health benefits, just that such is not necessarily the reason for keeping kosher.

I'll give you an example. There are those who lobby to declare meat unkosher if the animals were mistreated before slaughter (such as by being kept crated) or if the workers are not paid a living wage. Treating animals properly is an important Jewish value. Equitable pay for labor is an important Jewish value. It's just that neither of these values affects whether or not food is kosher. If bad things are happening in a factory, it's a problem and they should be fixed but not everything is tied up in whether or not food is kosher.

The same is true when it comes to health. Safeguarding our health is an important Jewish value but it's not part of the kosher-diet package. If a person gets up in the morning and starts his day with a kosher hot fudge sundae, followed by a loaf of kosher garlic bread, a pan of kosher lasagna, a kosher cheesecake, etc., etc., etc., that may be a violation of the directive to protect one's health but his diet is perfectly kosher. (This is not to justify such a lifestyle. A glutton is considered a *naval birshus haTorah*—one who acts inappropriately within the Torah's parameters. The act of eating kosher food—even if it's unhealthy food—is permitted. Doing it to excess, however, is just wrong.)

That having been said, historically there have been health benefits to a kosher diet, although these are merely "fringe benefits." For example, trichinosis is a disease caused by a parasite found in pork. Those who keep kosher have been unaffected by trichinosis outbreaks because they don't eat pork. The 14th-century Black Plague occurred long before germs were discovered, so hand-washing was not regularly practiced. Observant Jews wash their hands for religious reasons before eating, so they were largely unaffected by the plague. (The downside of this was that, because the Jews weren't dying, they were blamed for causing the plague and persecuted. All in all, it was probably still the better scenario.) The various kinds of shellfish carry a large number of pathogens and parasites that kosher consumers avoid. Some say that kosher meat was safer during the mad cow disease outbreak, though others disagree. Generally speaking, the inspections associated with kosher food supervision help to ensure the purity of our food's ingredients.

But, as noted, any health benefits that may have arisen from a kosher diet are purely ancillary; they are not the reason for the mitzvah. The danger in conflating kosher food with health is that as medical science progresses, people under such misconceptions tend discard the *mitzvos*. If someone thinks that the reason God prohibited pork was to save us from trichinosis, then he could potentially replace that mitzvah with a regimen of antiparasitic medications.

The ultimate reason for any mitzvah is "because God said so" but we look at the *mitzvos* and try to discern lessons. There are many such lessons that can be derived from our kosher food laws. For example, we're allowed to slaughter animals for food but we may not slaughter an animal and its young on the same day. The lesson of this mitzvah is that, while we may be permitted to kill an animal as needed, we must be aware of God's providence over all species and not be wantonly destructive. Other *mitzvos* likewise carry meaningful lessons.

Does kosher food have health benefits? Sure. But any physical health benefits are incidental. The real health benefits of keeping kosher are spiritual, as is the case with all *mitzvos*. God gave us the *mitzvos* as a means to purify our souls and get closer to Him. If you're looking to trim down and tone up, try fresh fruits and vegetables, lean proteins, proper hydration and maybe some light cardio. Cheese snacks and chocolate pie won't do the trick, no matter how kosher they might be.

Infallibility of the Righteous

Q. Can a tzaddik make a mistake?

A. Of course! We see that our greatest, most righteous leaders were capable of errors of various kinds! This can include both factual errors and errors in judgment. Just a few examples include:

- Avraham and Sarah disagreed about how to handle the situation involving Sarah's servant Hagar and her son with Avraham, Yishmael; God told Avraham that Sarah was right (Genesis 21:12);
- Yitzchak favored his older son, Eisav, as his successor but his wife Rivka knew that their younger son, Yaakov, was the true heir, a fact to which Yitzchak eventually conceded. (In Genesis 27:33, he ratified the blessing that he had originally given to Yaakov in error);
- Yaakov appears to lose an argument with his sons in Genesis 34; at the very least he lets them have the last word. Also, some questionable parenting decisions (as described in Genesis 37) appear to be responsible for the strife between Yoseif and the rest of the brothers;
- Moshe erred when he said that the Jews wouldn't believe him (Exodus 4:1), for which he was punished with a mild case of *tzaraas*. He lost his temper at the Jews, yelled at them and struck the rock, for which he was denied entry to Israel (Numbers 20). He wasn't even infallible in matters of *halacha*. For example, Aharon corrected Moshe in a matter of *halacha*, to which Moshe immediately conceded (Leviticus 10:20). Moshe was known to have forgotten halachos on other occasions, as well, such as during the incident with Tzelofchad's daughters (see

Numbers 27:5 and Rashi there);

- King David clearly erred in the matter of Batsheva (II Samuel 11) but he also didn't know who was telling him the truth in II Samuel 19—Ziva or Mephiboshes—so his solution to divide the property between them was unfair to whoever was the innocent party. He was also played by his son Avshalom, who staged a coup (II Samuel 14-15); after the coup was put down, David's mourning for his rebellious son's demise was so bad for his own troops' morale that his officers had to tell him to knock it off (II Samuel 19).

I could provide countless examples of righteous Biblical personages making errors of various kinds but I think you get the idea. Errors on the part of the righteous can also be found in Talmudic literature. For example:

- Rabbi Meir was corrected by his wife Bruriah when he prayed for local hooligans to die rather than repent (*Brachos* 10a);
- Bruriah also reprimanded Rav Yosi HaGlili for being chattier than necessary with women (*Eiruvin* 53b);
- Rabbi Yehoshua ben Chananiah was chastised by a little girl for taking a shortcut across a field (also in *Eiruvin* 53b).

You can also find much more contemporary examples, such as one famous incident involving the Steipler Gaon (d. 1985). The Gaon once reprimanded a young child for learning Gemara in *shul* instead of davening. The child showed the Gaon that his "Gemara" was actually a very large siddur and he was in fact davening. The Gaon immediately apologized for jumping to the wrong conclusion. But the story doesn't end there! Six years later, the Gaon showed up at the boy's bar mitzvah just to apologize again. The forgiveness of a child not being halachically effective, the Steipler made sure to apologize a second time as soon as the boy reached the age of majority.

We believe that our Torah leaders are great people, gifted with insight and wisdom often many orders of magnitude beyond our own. But they're not perfect. No human being is. (Koheles 7:20—"For there is no righteous person on Earth who only does good and never sins." In other words, "nobody's perfect!") To suggest that a human being is infallible borders on idolatry because perfection is exclusively God's domain.

The test of a *tzaddik* is not perfection; that's an unachievable standard. The difference between the righteous and the rest of us is in how we handle our shortcomings. When you and I are wrong, we tend to double down on our mistakes. We get sucked into flame wars online defending and justifying our mistakes even after they've been brought to our attention. But that's not how *tzadikkim* react. Moshe acknowledged when Aharon was right. David conceded when Nathan the prophet chastised him about Batsheva. Rather than burying stories in which he was corrected by women and children, Rabbi Yehoshua ben Chananiah shared them so we could learn from them. The Steipler Gaon went out of his way to apologize to a child who didn't even remember his "offense."

The righteous aren't great because they never make mistakes. They're great because they own their mistakes. They admit them, they try to make things right, and they grow from the experience.

We can potentially do that, too. We just have to get over ourselves first, and that's the hard part. But that overcoming of ego is a huge part of what makes someone a *tzaddik* in the first place. Being righteous isn't about being right all the time; it's very much about being able to see beyond the "I."

Miracles, or Lack Thereof

Q. *I've been thinking about the ten plagues and how these awesome miracles happened for the Jewish people in the Passover story, as well as throughout the Torah. Why don't we have miracles anymore?*

A. To answer that, we have to go back to idolatry. And before idolatry, we have to talk about sex.

Look at our society and see how preoccupied it is with sex. Look at TV, magazines, the Internet, fashion, etc., etc., etc., and you'll know what I'm talking about. Even if you, personally, are not preoccupied with sex, you are no doubt aware that such a preoccupation is common, even prevalent.

Well, believe it or not, people used to have an equally strong desire for idolatry. If you read your way through the books of the Prophets, you'll see that this is the case. For some reason, people were just crazy about idols—they couldn't control their urges!

This was already history by the time of the Talmud. In one famous incident, the Talmudic sage Rav Ashi made a disparaging remark about the Biblical King Menashe. That night, Menashe appeared to Rav Ashi in a dream and demonstrated his Torah knowledge. Surprised, Rav Ashi asked the king, "If you're such a Torah scholar, how could you worship idols?" "You don't know the temptation we had for idolatry," Menashe replied. "If you had lived in my day, you'd have picked up the hems of your garment to run after idols!" (*Sanhedrin* 102b)

So what happened to reduce this desire to serve idols? Early in the Second Temple period, the Men of the Great Assembly (whose ranks included the final prophets) prayed that the desire for idolatry be given over to them. This request was granted and the idolatrous impulse appeared to them like a fiery lion. They were able to destroy it except for a "lock of its hair" that fell out. These descriptions, of course, are symbolic images intended to illustrate how they disabled the overwhelming majority of idolatry's power—something like 99.99999999999999% of its previous lure. If what we have worldwide today represents a "lock of idolatry's hair," you can imagine how strong the "fiery lion" must have been! (This story is recounted in the Talmud, *Yoma* 69b).

Okay, so what does all this idolatry stuff have to do with miracles? I'll explain.

Human beings are placed in this world with a mission: we are meant to perfect ourselves by choosing between good and evil. In order for us to go through life, good and evil have to have a fairly level playing field. There used to be two very strong but opposite attractions. One of these was the lure of idolatry, as we have discussed. The other was prophecy. The prophets spent most of their time railing against idol-worship to varying degrees of success. However, once the urge to serve idols was all but eradicated, that gave the positive pull of prophecy too strong an edge. Accordingly, prophecy ceased shortly after the urge for idolatry was conquered. (The prophets actually predicted the end of prophecy. One famous verse on this subject is Amos 8:11, "Behold, days are coming, says God Hashem, that I will send a famine in the land—not a famine for bread or a thirst for water but rather to hear to the words of Hashem.")

Now, prophecy and miracles typically go hand in hand. God split the sea—but He did so through Moses. God made the sun stand still—but He did so through Joshua. God revived the dead—but He did so through Elijah, etc. Even without using a prophet as His agent, the principle would be the same: the forces that pull us towards good and towards evil have to be commensurate.

The ironic thing is that we do have miracles today, they're just of a different kind than the ones you're thinking about. If you went back 3,500 ago to the time of the Exodus and you saw the clouds of glory and the manna, you would no doubt be duly impressed. But bring someone from that era back with you. Show them your smart phone. Take their picture with it. Play them a few songs, record a video, show them Google—how many miracles is that? Now show them a video of the moon landing—wasn't that a miracle? You can hop on a plane and be on the other side of the globe in 12 hours—is that not a miracle?

Before you dismiss our miracles as the simple application of naturally-occurring scientific principles, remember that mankind has always excelled at dismissing miracles.

"Remember that flood that wiped the world out a few generations ago? That was some freaky storm, huh?"

"You see the Red Sea split? Yeah, that happens sometimes."

"That sure was some palpable darkness we had last week—almost as bad as the flaming hail!"

"Manna? Sure, that's a natural phenomenon!"

We're surrounded by miracles. We're just as able to justify miracles like the ten plagues and the revelation at Sinai as we are to dismiss miracles like strawberries and your endocrine system.

God still works miracles. They're all around us. They just have to be appropriate for the times in which we live. Our miracles may be less overt in some ways than those of our ancestors but in both cases people have the ability to embrace them or dismiss them and to live their lives based on the implications of those decisions.

Noah's Ark

Q. Are we really supposed to believe that all of those animals were in that ark? As rational thinkers, how are we to come to terms with a story that doesn't make sense?

A. Thanks for your question. My answer is potentially going to anger everybody. There are those who will read the first 90% of what I'm going to say and decide that I'm a fundamentalist. Others will read the last 10% and decide that I'm a heretic. What that boils down to is that I'm a moderate and a moderate approach takes both sides of such questions into account, albeit not necessarily in equal measures.

First, allow me to speak in favor of the flood story. Virtually every culture has a flood myth that includes a number of elements found in the story of Noah, including the wrath of God (or of "the gods"), righteous people being saved, animals being collected, longevity, sacrifices, rainbows and more. Here's a small sampling of examples (and it was really hard to pare this list down to a manageable size!):

In India, there's the story of Manu. The god Matsya (an incarnation of Vishnu) appeared to Manu and warned him about an impending flood. Manu was instructed to collect samples of all types of grains and animals in a boat. The flood destroys the world and Matsya guides the boat to safety.

In Hopi mythology, the god Tawa destroyed the world in a flood. Spider Grandmother saved the few righteous people by sealing them into hollow reeds.

In the Aztec flood myth, a human couple survives by hiding in a hollow vessel.

In the Hawaiian version of the story, Nu'u builds an ark to escape the flood, eventually coming to rest on Mauna Kea. Nu'u mistakenly credited the moon for his salvation and offered sacrifices to it. The creator god came down to earth on a rainbow and corrected his misconception.

In Greek mythology, Deucalion is told to build a chest to escape the flood. Deucalion and his wife, Pyrrha, are saved and eventually come to rest on Parnassus (or Phouka, or Mount Othrys—versions differ). After the flood, Deucalion offered sacrifices to Zeus. Zeus then had Deucalion and Pyrrha throw stones that turned into men and women, respectively.

In the Andaman Islands version, the god Puluga sent the flood to punish people for forgetting his law. Two men and two women survived.

Only one man and one woman survived in the Incan version, in which the god Viracocha sent the flood.

Aside from the story of Noah, the best-known flood story is probably that of Utnapishtim in the epic of Gilgamesh. While Noah lived an extremely long life, Utnapishtim is said to have been granted immortality by his gods.

From the Chinese story of Yao to the Norse myth of Bergelmir, from various African tribes to the arctic Inuits, nearly every culture has a similar story, most incorporating many of the same details found in the Biblical account of the flood. So, is there something inherent in mankind that makes people compelled to compose and disseminate this particular story? Or is it possible that this reflects an oral history transmitted to all of mankind by a common ancestor who was actually there?

As far as the number of animals on the ark, the first thing to consider is that there were far fewer animals in Noah's day than there are now. For example, there are 339 breeds of dog in the world today—and most of these were created within the past 200 years by man imposing selective breeding on them! Noah didn't have a pair of Afghans, a pair of Airedales, a pair of Malamutes, a pair of Terriers, a pair of Corgis, etc. He had a pair of archetypical dogs, from which all such breeds were later descended. Similarly, Noah didn't have Jersey cows and Guernsey cows and Brahma bulls, etc.; he had a pair of archetypical cattle, from which these breeds later descended. The same is true of elephants, horses, chickens, pigs, snakes—you get the idea. Bottom line, Noah needed *wayyyy* less space than most people typically think. (Science accepts the concept of micro-evolution but would no doubt attribute it to a much longer time frame for many species. So let Torah and science quibble over the details!)

Now, let's assume that you're still skeptical that all those rats and cats and bats and gnats could fit on the ark. Bottom line, it all boils down to one thing: it was a miracle. Making things fit into spaces where they shouldn't is actually one of God's specialties, as we see in many places.

The Mishna in *Avos* (5:5) gives two such examples: (1) even though the people in the Temple stood pressed closely together, when they bowed down and prostrated themselves, each person had four cubits of space (about six feet) around him; (2) even though the whole nation came to Jerusalem for the various Festivals, no one was ever unable to find a place to stay. There are additional examples. The Gemara in *Gittin* (57a) tells us that Israel is like a deer. The explanation of this is that when one skins a deer, it's incomprehensible how the carcass could ever fit inside that skin and yet somehow it did. Similarly, the tiny country of Israel shouldn't be able to accommodate the throngs of Jews who live there, yet somehow it does. Finally, the Gemara in *Yoma* (21a) and *Megillah* (10b) tells us that the *aron* (the ark, as in "Raiders of the Lost...") took up no room in the Holy of Holies. If you measured from the *aron* to the wall, you would find that it was 10 cubits on either side—and yet the entire width of the Holy of Holies was only 20 cubits! Somehow the *aron* occupied no space whatsoever! (It's beyond our scope but these dicta mirror the physics concept of a singularity. From Israel to Jerusalem to the Temple to the Holy of Holies, the phenomenon of spatial dilation intensifies with each increasing degree of holiness until one reaches the holiest point, in which matter occupies no space at all.)

If God can take people who are standing shoulder to shoulder and give each one a six-foot diameter when they bow down, and if He can make a box of acacia wood coated in gold occupy no space, I think it's a no brainer that He can figure out how to fit some giraffes, aardvarks, rhinoceroses and mongooses on a boat!

All of the above is the stuff that probably makes me sound like a fundamentalist. Now for the stuff that probably makes me sound like a heretic: if it bothers you, don't worry about it. I'll explain.

Many things in the Torah are allegorical. For example, the Torah speaks of things like "the hand of God" even though He has no physical body. It also says things like "the sun rose," which are not technically accurate, because from our perspective, that's what happens. ("The Earth rotated until the sun could be seen" is rather cumbersome.) So the concept of allegory exists. Hold that thought.

Nowadays, we all accept that the universe was created, we just quibble over how long ago it may have been. In the Rambam's day, however, the debate was about whether the universe was created or whether it always existed, the science of his day arguing for an always-existent universe. Despite his belief in the Torah account, the Rambam says that if the eternity of the universe were proved beyond the shadow of a doubt, he would have no problem relegating the creation account to the realm of allegory. He accepts the Torah account as presented but he's also open to the possibility that we may be misunderstanding it. If the Rambam says that about the Creation account, I don't see why the flood should be any different.

Don't get me wrong: many parts of the Bible are allegorical but the overwhelming majority are meant to be taken literally. I believe that the flood story—like the Creation account, the stories of the Patriarchs and the Exodus—are among those that are meant to be taken literally. But the Torah is not primarily a history book or a science book. If, for some reason, you can't reconcile such a Biblical account with your other knowledge and understandings, try to compartmentalize things. Focus on the moral lessons that the Torah tells the story in order to impart rather than on the cognitive dissonance created by trying to reconcile all the details. (For the record, it wasn't until the 20th century that science caught up to the Torah and decided that the universe actually was created after all, so never be too sure about what really "makes sense!")

Prayers vs. Wishes

Q. *What's the difference between prayers and wishes? I know that Hashem is no genie to do our bidding, but what are we supposed to pray for?*

A. I think the first part of the question that we need to address is the assumption that we're necessarily "supposed" to pray "for" anything at all. Yes, we do pray for things, and appropriate requests are built into the daily prayers that were composed for us by the Sages, but the purpose of prayer isn't to present a wish list. It's an opportunity for us to get close to God.

The Talmud in *Yevamos* (64a) discusses the infertility initially experienced by a number of notable Biblical personages. There, it tells us that the reason God had them endure this trial is because the prayers of the righteous are desirable to Him. This isn't because God "needs" our prayers (He doesn't). Rather, He loves us and wants what's best for us. The best thing in the world is for us to get close to Him and prayer is one of the ways we can accomplish that.

Along similar lines, Genesis 2:5 tells us that the plants and grass had not yet sprouted because God had not yet caused it to rain; this was because there weren't any people yet. Rashi explains the connection as follows: God withheld rain until there were people because there was no one to recognize the goodness of rain. Once God had created Adam, the man realized how useful rain would be and requested it of God. This wasn't for God's benefit, nor was it for the benefit of the grass and trees. Rather, God put Adam in a position to pray because doing so was good for Adam.

Let us now turn the ninth *bracha* of *Shemoneh Esrei*, in which we ask God to bless the year for us with abundant produce. The first thing you'll notice is that we specify "for us." It would do us little good if the trees were full of fruit and the fields were full of grain but we were unable to enjoy it. Beyond asking that we be able to partake in an abundant crop, we ask that it be "for good." That's to keep things from turning out like the story of "The Monkey's Paw," in which one's wishes are granted, albeit in an ironic fashion.

Anything we ask for can be given to us for good or for bad. A person can pray for rain but he doesn't want it to turn into a destructive flood (refer to the story of Choni in *Taanis* 19a). A lost camper freezing in the woods might pray for a fire to warm himself but he doesn't want a devastating forest fire. Everyone wants to win the lottery but those who actually do end up declaring bankruptcy at rates significantly higher than those of us who don't. The bottom line is that we ask God to give us the things we ask for in a way that's good for us, assuming that they're actually good for us at all.

For this reason, the practice is to ask God, for example, to send one an appropriate match, rather than to marry a specific person; this is because He knows whether or not that other person will actually be good for us.

We ask God to help us earn a living rather than to ensure we secure a specific job because, again, He knows whether or not that job would be a good fit. So while we do ask God for forgiveness, health, peace, and other things, we don't dictate terms. We leave it up to Him to do so in the way that He determines to be best. And if He decides that the things we ask for are not in our best interest? That's okay because He knows what we need.

As you noted, God is not a genie. He's not Santa Claus. He's not a leprechaun, so He owes us neither a pot of gold nor a box of marshmallow cereal. What He gives us is a golden opportunity: the chance to get close to Him, which is inherently good. These meetings give us an opening to share how we're feeling and what's troubling us, in addition to thanking Him for all He has already provided. The mere act of unburdening to God can be cathartic, but it might also be transformative. By getting closer to Him, we may become more deserving of the things we desire, or perhaps we may come to reassess our priorities and realize that we don't really need the things we thought we did.

The bottom line of prayer is that it's not a wish at all. It's an audience with the Omniscient One, Who knows what's good for each person and can be relied upon to provide it. Prayer provides us with quality time in which we can provide input on our situations. But our input should never be any kind of a demand that God do or give us a particular thing. It should always be qualified by the sentiment, "if You deem it a good idea." If He does, you might get the thing you sought. If He knows otherwise, you're invariably better off without that thing, even if you don't know why that is.

Witchcraft and Magic

Q. I was wondering what the Jewish view on witchcraft and magic is. Is it mentioned anywhere in Jewish texts? Do you need to believe in it to be an observant Jew? The ancients might have believed in it but we now know that magic is a hoax.

A. The Torah certainly talks about magic and sorcery, but the jury is out as to whether or not these things are real. But the very fact that they're discussed is not proof in and of itself that they exist.

The Torah prohibits such things as fortune-telling and necromancy. There are two schools of thought on this matter: one is that the practitioners of such arts actually tap into dark forces. The other is that they're frauds, deceiving people into believing nonsense. Either one would be sufficient reason to prohibit sorcery.

The "magic is a fraud" position is not a modern, rationalist invention. This was actually the opinion of the Rambam (Maimonides). He discusses the relevant laws in the *Mishneh Torah* in *Hilchos Avodas Kochavim* (Laws Pertaining to Idolatry), chapter 11. Examples of his comments there include:

> One is not permitted to tell fortunes; this is so even though he performs no action, but merely tells lies that foolish people think contain wisdom. ... This prohibition (Leviticus 19:26—"Do not tell fortunes") also includes one who performs magic tricks and deceives others into thinking that he performs wonders; such a person is liable for the penalty of lashes (*Avodas Kochavim* 11:9).

> Incantations and spells do nothing—they can neither harm nor help (*Avodas Kochavim* 11:10).

Descriptions of magic and sorcery in Tanach are likewise subject to dispute. The Torah describes Pharaoh's astrologers duplicating the earliest of Moshe's feats; the Book of Samuel describes how the "witch of Endor" summoned the spirit of the prophet Samuel for King Saul. Some authorities take these narratives at face value, while others—including the Rambam—say that these magicians were engaged in acts of trickery and only made it appear as if they accomplished these things. This is not unreasonable. I might say that I saw a magician saw a lady in half, although we are all well aware that he actually did no such thing.

Mediums, astrologers and Tarot readers exist even today, but that doesn't mean that they have supernatural power. In 1983, I saw David Copperfield make the Statue of Liberty disappear. Thousands of people were watching and it was pretty darn impressive. But nobody thinks he actually did it. We all know it was a trick. This kind of "magic" is permitted because, unlike an unscrupulous huckster who tries to control people with horoscopes or Tarot cards, stage magicians aren't really trying to convince anyone that they have supernatural powers. It's just a form of entertainment. The problem is the intention to deceive.

"Soothsaying" is a more difficult area. It is clearly prohibited to base one's actions on signs and omens, such as "turning back because a black cat crossed one's path." Yet we see some "kosher" people engaged in the practice. The best-known example would be Avraham's servant Eliezer. When dispatched to find a bride for Yitzchak, he said, "I'll ask the girl for some water. If she offers to water my camel as well, I'll know she's the one." As we know, things did work out as Eliezer planned with Rivka, but was he guilty of relying on signs?

There are two ways to reconcile this dilemma. One approach is that Eliezer was wrong, but that God made it work out okay for Avraham's sake. The other approach is that Eliezer wasn't relying on signs at all. He knew what Avraham was looking for in a daughter-in-law. Rather than trying to prompt a Divine signal, he was actually testing Rivka's character to see if she shared Avraham's trait of generosity. Her response to Eliezer's request was intended strictly as a test of her hospitality.

Similarly, Yonatan appears to rely on a sign in order to determine whether or not he should attack the Philistine camp in I Samuel chapter 14. At first glance, he appears to be relying on a sign but upon the barest inspection, it becomes apparent that he was actually testing the enemy's defenses.

So, are you required to believe in magic? Absolutely not. And if you don't, you'd be in some very fine company indeed. Let us conclude with the Rambam's final thoughts on this topic: "All the forms of sorcery discussed in this chapter are lies that idolaters used to deceive the nations in order to get them to follow their idols. It is not appropriate for Jews to follow such nonsense, nor to attribute any value to them. Numbers 23:23 says, 'There is no divination found among Jacob, nor soothsaying within Israel.' Deuteronomy 18:14 likewise states that 'The nations you are driving out follow astrologers and diviners but God has not given you things like these.'

"If a person believes in sorcery like these, thinking that they are true and wise, albeit prohibited by the Torah, then he is foolish. Wise people know that all these magics that the Torah has forbidden are simply forms of emptiness that attract feeble-minded people and cause them to abandon the path of truth. This is why, when the Torah prohibits all these things, it adds (Deuteronomy 18:13) 'Be of perfect faith with Hashem, your God'" (*Avodas Kochavim* 11:16).

Dreams

Q. *What is the Jewish perspective on dreams? Are we meant to take them as any form of prophecy or is it just an exercise of the subconscious?*

A. Oh, boy. Here we go again.

The reason I say that is because, as we have discussed before, there are *shivim panim laTorah*, seventy approaches to Torah (not necessarily literally 70 but, you know, many). When I discuss things like this, I take a rationalist approach. This doesn't sit well with those who adhere to more mystical approaches. They invariably respond with "what about this" and "what about that?" I know about "this" and "that," I just don't happen to agree with them. When there are multiple approaches, following one typically precludes following them all. So, the opinions I express primarily reflect those to which I adhere. If you disagree, that doesn't make either of us wrong *per se*, it just means that we disagree.

That having been said, there are basically two schools of thought about dreams: either they're a little taste of prophecy or they're utterly meaningless. I, personally, subscribe to the position that dreams are, with rare exception, essentially meaningless.

That's not to say that such has necessarily always been the case. With the exception of Moshe, who was able to converse with God while wide awake, prophets received their messages in dreams and visions (Numbers 12:6). For example, Yaakov had his famous vision of a ladder to Heaven in a dream (Genesis 28) and Shlomo's dialogue in which he requested wisdom occurred in a dream (I Kings 3). Most famous, however, are the series of dreams that occurred in the story of Yoseif.

Yoseif himself dreamed two dreams—one in which his brothers' sheaves of grain bowed to him and one in which the heavenly bodies bowed to him. While in prison, Yoseif interpreted the essentially similar dreams of Pharaoh's baker and wine steward. Later, Yoseif interpreted Pharaoh's own dreams—one of thin cows consuming fat cows and one of parched stalks devouring healthy stalks. One question remains unanswered, though. The story begins with Yoseif having dreams; later he's interpreting dreams. We all have dreams but that doesn't qualify us as interpreters. So where did Yoseif get this ability?

In his book *Between the Lines of the Bible*, Rabbi Yitzchak Etshalom points out that all the dreams in the story of Yoseif are repeated. He hypothesizes that Yoseif might have received a tradition from his father regarding the significance of recurring dreams. (You will note that Yoseif's father, Yaakov, discounts the significance of his son's dream in Genesis 37 but that Yaakov had only been told of one dream. Had he been told of both, he might have felt differently!)

Aside from speaking to prophets, God used dreams to send coded messages to monarchs regarding the fates of their nations. Not only did He communicate with Pharaoh through dreams interpreted by Yoseif, He communicated with Nebuchadnezzar through dreams interpreted by Daniel. There are many other dreams throughout Tanach.

But here's the thing: we don't live in Bible times. We're not *tzaddikim* like Yoseif, we're not supreme rulers like Nebuchadnezzar and, even if we were, prophecy has departed. Dreams may indeed be a little taste of prophecy (Talmud, *Brachos* 57b) but the state of prophecy ain't what it used to be.

The Talmud in *Brachos* spends a lot of time discussing dreams (pages 55-57). On page 55b, we are told that a dream follows its interpretation— it can be interpreted in either a positive or a negative way. On 55a, we are told that an uninterpreted dream is like an unread letter, i.e., it has no meaning whatsoever. On the same page we are also told that a dream always includes nonsensical elements and that a dream is never completely fulfilled.

My favorite insight on dreams, however, is on page 56a. There, Rav Shmuel bar Nachmani tells us that one only dreams about things that he thought about during the day. This is what Daniel told Nebuchadnezzar (Daniel 2:29), "your thoughts came to you upon your bed." Such an approach is not unlike our current outlook, in which dreams are considered an outlet for our unconscious thoughts and our anxieties.

The bottom line in the time of the Talmud was that most dreams were utterly meaningless. Nowadays, I think we can upgrade that to "virtually all dreams are utterly meaningless." (I don't feel qualified to rule out "all dreams" but I can't name any specific exceptions.)

Let's take a look at a halachic question impacted by dreams. In *Sanhedrin* (30a), the Talmud discusses a case in which a man's father told him in a dream that he had hidden a certain sum of money in a certain location and that it was earmarked for *maaser sheini* (second tithe). Even though the man found that sum of money in the place described, the Sages said he could use it for any purpose (i.e., not limited to second tithe). This is because dreams are considered to be of no consequence. The Rambam in *Hilchos Zechiah u'Matana* (10:7) adds that one may also ignore such a dream if it says that the money belongs to another person.

On the other hand, the *Shulchan Aruch* says that if a person dreams that he takes a vow about a certain matter, he should have the vow annulled (*Yoreh Deah* 210:2). The *Chasam Sofer* explains that this is based on the aforementioned dictum about a person dreaming about the thoughts he had during the day. We are therefore concerned about the possibility that a person may have made such a vow but consciously forgotten about it (*YD* 222).

Even if dreams are essentially meaningless, the Talmud tells us that bad dreams can be physically debilitating (*Brachos* 55b). Worrying over a nightmare can wreck a person; we are therefore given steps to help ourselves feel better in the aftermath of a disturbing dream.

One course of action after a bad dream is to fast (called a *taanis chalom*). This fast, undertaken on the day after a troubling dream, is optional; one need not fast if he is unconcerned about a dream regardless of how upsetting it may have been. However, if one is distressed enough about a bad dream, he might be permitted to fast even on Shabbos or *yom tov*—days on which fasting is normally prohibited. (See *Shulchan Aruch, OC* 288:5 for what kind of dreams might qualify.) As with all fasts, a person undertaking a *taanis chalom* should also perform *teshuvah* (repentance) and give charity.

The other course of action is called *hatavas chalom*, the rectification of a bad dream. Based on a procedure recommended in *Brachos* (55b), the dreamer assembles a panel of three friends and reports having had a disturbing dream. (The details of the dream are unimportant and need not be shared with the panel.) The participants recite various verses and prayers expressing the hope that the dream should have a favorable interpretation.

On the other hand, when the amora Shmuel would have a bad dream, he would merely recite Zechariah 10:2, "...dreams speak falsely..." (*Brachos* 55b).

In closing, let me share a completely true story about dreams that some may feel undermines my rationalist approach. Years ago, a neighbor came over on a Saturday night. She had had a disturbing dream so we convened a panel and performed *hatavas chalom*. She died a week later, on Shabbos Shuvah. Some might want to establish a correlation between her bad dream, whatever it might have been, and the fact that she died shortly after. From my perspective, many people die without having had bad dreams first, and many people have bad dreams without dying soon after. It follows logically that some small percentage of people will both have bad dreams and pass away; that doesn't prove the dream was prophetic.

So why should I mention this incident at all, knowing that there are those who will see it as proof against my own position? I mention it because I always try to be intellectually honest. I have a position to which I subscribe and I don't see this incident as disproving it. As always, however, every reader is free to draw their own conclusions.

Prove to Me...

Q. *I grew up religious but haven't kept Shabbos in ten years. How do I know that there's a World to Come? Keeping Shabbos doesn't make me feel more holy, so why is it important for me to keep it?*

A. Thanks for your question. You don't need to satisfy yourself that there's an *Olam Haba* (World to Come) so much as you should satisfy yourself that there's a God. Once you've done that, the ramifications—such as the existence of an afterlife—will fall into place.

Actually, satisfying ourselves that there's a God is one of the *aseres hadibros*. (These are commonly known as the "Ten Commandments," though there are really more than ten commandments in those ten statements.) The very first of these is "I am Hashem your God, Who brought you out of the land of Egypt, out of the house of bondage" (Exodus 20:2). What kind of commandment is "I am…?" It's understood as an obligation for us to know that there's a God.

The Rambam's *magnum opus* is called the *Mishneh Torah*, a 14-volume work comprising 15,018 *halachos*. And the very first of these, in *Hilchos Yesodei HaTorah* 1:1, is:

> The most basic premise and the foundation of all wisdom is knowing that there is a Creator Who brought the universe into being. Every creature in the heavens, on the earth, and everywhere in between only exists because of this Creator.

You'll note that our obligation is not just to believe in God, but to *know* that there's a God. This is a thing that we must research for ourselves until we are intellectually satisfied.

As far as how we come to know this, everyone is different. Some people look at nature. They see, for example, that the human eye is more complicated than any camera ever invented. If you would never believe that an iPhone could evolve naturally, how could you assume that about our eyes, which are many orders of magnitude more advanced? The same is true when we look at the wisdom of the strawberry, whose seeds are on the outside, and the watermelon, whose seeds are on the inside, each perfectly suited to perpetuate that particular species.

Some people are moved by things like the "Torah codes." Known as Equidistant Letter Search and nowadays performed by computers, the "Torah Codes" actually represent an ancient method of Torah interpretation called *dilug osiyos* (letter skipping) in which words can be found encoded within the text, many defying statistical probability. One of my favorite examples involves the search for Yoseif's goblet in *parshas Mikeitz*. The Hebrew word for goblet is *geviyah* (*gimmel-veis-yud-ayin*). The word *geviyah* is only encoded one place in the entire book of Genesis. It can be found in eight-letter intervals in Genesis 44:12—"He searched, beginning with the eldest, and ending at the youngest. The cup was found in Benjamin's sack"—the very verse describing the search for the missing cup!

Others are most impressed by the continued existence of the Jewish people, despite any historical precedent for a nation to be constantly exiled and still endure, let alone thrive. Counterintuitively, the Torah foretells that the Jews would be exiled, persecuted, and perpetually a small nation, but that we would always endure. This goes counter to the experience of any other nation in history and yet that's exactly what has come to pass!

There are many other approaches that one might take based on their own personal interests and individual temperament. Any number of things in this world could satisfy a person that there's a God. But there's never going to be concrete proof. God always gives those who want to "opt out" the justification to do so. As it says in *Bereishis Rabbah* 5:8, God puts the evidence in front of us; if people want to willfully ignore the logical conclusions, He gives them the ability to do so. To force belief on someone would be to deny them their free will.

Non-Jewish authorities have also grappled with the issue of determining that there's a God. They have come up with different approaches that largely boil down to "hedging one's bets." Let us consider, for example, Pascal's wager, named for 17th-century mathematician Blaise Pascal. In it, he determines mathematically that it's in one's own best interest to assume there's a God and to act accordingly because the consequences of being wrong outweigh any possible benefit. (Basically, he posits that if there's no God but you live as if there is one, you miss out on a finite number of things in life. However, if there is a God and you act as if there isn't, you're forfeiting an infinite reward. Any effort is worth the investment for the possibility of an infinite payout.)[4]

Along similar lines, 20th-century philosopher Albert Camus (an atheist) wrote, "I would rather live my life as if there is a God and die to find out there isn't, than live as if there isn't and to die to find out that there is."

There are many fine books that can help you with this. I'd like to recommend *Permission to Believe* by Rabbi Dr. Lawrence Kelemen, followed by his other book, *Permission to Receive*. The former is subtitled "Four Rational Approaches to God's Existence," and that's exactly what it is. That latter is subtitled "Four Rational Approaches to the Torah's Divine Origin" and it illustrates how believing in the revelation at Sinai actually makes more sense than trying to explain it away.

Once you have satisfied yourself that there's a God, keeping Shabbos should be an obvious next step. We can speculate on God's reasons for giving us Shabbos—to disconnect from the world and recharge our batteries, to have an opportunity to get closer to Him, etc.—but ultimately it doesn't matter. If we recognize that there's a Creator (God) and that He gave us a user's manual (the Torah), then we accept that Shabbos comes under the category of "required maintenance" whether we understand how it works or not.

There's a familiar Talmudic dictum, *"mitoch shelo lishma, ba lishma"*— "if one performs a mitzvah for an ulterior motive, he will ultimately come to perform it sincerely" (*Pesachim* 50b). Similarly, I think that if a person observes Shabbos because he accepts that there's a God Who told us to do this because it's somehow for our benefit, he will ultimately come to appreciate what Shabbos has to offer.

Ghosts

Q. *Someone close to me recently died and I never got to say goodbye. Does Judaism believe that the dead know what's going on in this world?*

---

4. Pascal's own faith was predicated not on his famous wager but on personal experience; the wager was a useful tool for him to present to others. Its staying power speaks to its presumed efficacy.

A. I am not the final arbiter of what Judaism believes; I can only tell you things as I understand them. In this case, I'm afraid it won't be what you're hoping to hear.

Whenever we talk about spiritual and metaphysical matters, I am quick to point out that there are generally two schools of thought about such things. Let's call them "literalists" and "rationalists." I am what one would consider a rationalist. Accordingly, my approach will typically shy away from parapsychological phenomena. Sometimes that may require taking a less literal approach to the text but here I think I ultimately have the simple understanding of things on my side.

There is a prohibition in the Torah against necromancy, i.e., trying to communicate with the dead (Deuteronomy 18:11). Some authorities (e.g., Nachmanides) believe that this activity is possible but prohibited. Others—notably Maimonides—believe that contacting the dead isn't even possible but we are prohibited to mislead the gullible through such frauds as seances. In fact, the Rambam decries all forms of fortune-telling as foolishness and superstition. It should come as no surprise that I subscribe to the latter opinion, that seances are literally smoke-and-mirrors.

The only overt appearance of a "ghost" in Tanach is ostensibly the spirit of the prophet Shmuel in I Samuel chapter 28.[5] King Saul went to the "witch of Endor" to raise Shmuel from the dead because he needed guidance that he felt only the recently-deceased prophet could provide. But did the "witch" truly summon Shmuel's spirit from beyond? There's a three-way difference of opinion on the matter. Some, like the Radak, say that the "witch" did as the Navi describes. Others, like the Rambam, say that, as always, such deeds were mere parlor tricks. Then there's Rav Saadia Gaon, who opines that, under normal circumstances, necromancy is pure fraud but in this particular case, God miraculously facilitated it.

Until now, literalists may think that my skepticism about ghosts might require me to ignore the simplest understanding of the texts but I think that things are about to turn in favor of my approach.

The Talmud in *Brachos* (18a-19a) has a lengthy discussion about

---

5. The spirit in I Kings 22 is identified by commentators as the ghost of Naboth but, being an extra-textual interpretation, it doesn't really need addressing here.

whether or not the dead know what's going on here on Earth. It starts when Rabbi Chiya chided Rabbi Yonason to be careful of a behavior that might be offensive to the dead. Rabbi Yonason responded by citing Koheles 9:5, "the dead don't know anything." Rabbi Chiya responded that Rabbi Yonason didn't really understand that verse, the "living" and "dead" in it actually referring to the righteous and the evil, respectively. (You'll note that in this case, the "rationalist" is also the "literalist!" It's Rabbi Chiya, with the more spiritual approach, who understands this verse allegorically.)

In a subsequent incident, Rabbi Chiya's sons got a little preoccupied with their business endeavors and they forgot some of their Torah studies. One asked the other whether their now-deceased father was aware of this turn of events. The other replied by citing Job 14:21, "His sons come to honor and he (i.e., the deceased) doesn't know it; they are brought low but he is unaware."

Towards the end of the Talmud's lengthy discussion on this subject, the question is raised whether the dead talk to one another. The Gemara cites Deuteronomy 34:4, in which God says to Moshe, "'This is the land that I swore to Avraham, Yitzchak and Yaakov, saying, 'I will give it to your descendants....'" The word *leimor*, typically translated as "saying," is understood as God's command to Moshe to go repeat what he has been told. Usually, he was to repeat things to the Jewish people but here the Talmud understands that Moshe—who was about to die—was being instructed to go tell Avraham, Yitzchak and Yaakov that God had fulfilled His promise to them. As Tosfos in *Sotah* 34b (s.v. *avosai bakshu alai rachamim*) citing this Talmudic discussion makes clear, even our late Patriarchs don't know what's happening on Earth.

At the end of this discussion, the Gemara makes the following observation: the dead either don't know what's going on in the world of the living or they just don't care. (If they don't care, it's presumably because they've moved on.)

We do believe in an afterlife. We believe that the soul lives on and we can help to elevate it in the Next World by performing *mitzvos* on its behalf. But is a soul aware of what's going on in this world? While there are no doubt those who believe that it is, I'm afraid that such is not my understanding based on the traditional texts. This doesn't surprise me. After all, our souls were somewhere before they came here (God's "storehouse," called the *guf*). How in touch are we now with wherever our souls were previously? Similarly, if the deceased reside in a completely different world—the Next World—why should we expect that they have any interest in keeping tabs on this world, let alone the capacity to do so?

However, as with all things pertaining to the afterlife, our understandings are speculative, based on what has been revealed to us. We'll find out for sure when we get there!

The Devil

Q. What's the Jewish view of the Devil?

A: The Jewish view of the Devil? That's easy: there's no such thing.

Now, if you had asked me about Satan, it would be another story. You see, Judaism does have a concept of Satan but he's no Devil. He's an angel—and not a "fallen" one, either!

Satan makes his big appearance in the Biblical book of Job. Let's look at his debut in chapter 1, verse 6:

> There came a day when the sons of God came to present themselves before Hashem, and Satan was among them.

The first thing you'll notice is that the angels are called "sons of God" and Satan was one of them. Let's now continue with verses 7-12:

> Hashem said to Satan, "Where are you coming from?" Satan answered God, saying, "From going back and forth on the Earth, and from walking up and down in it."
>
> Hashem said to Satan, "Have you noticed My servant Job? There is no one like him on Earth—such a wholehearted and upright individual, who reveres God and avoids evil!"
>
> Satan replied to God, saying, "Does Job revere God for

nothing? Haven't You made a boundary all around him, his house and all his possessions? You have blessed everything he does and his wealth increases in the land. If You would only reach out and touch what he has, I bet he would curse You to Your face."

God said to Satan, "Okay, everything that he has is in your power, just do not put your hand on him personally." So Satan departed from before God.

The story escalates, with Satan being given increasingly freer rein until he is able even to bodily afflict Job, short of killing him.

I guess at this point it makes as much sense as any to point out that, while many of you have probably been reading that as "Satan" (pronounced "say-tin"), that's not the Jewish way of saying it. We actually call this concept "the Satan" (pronounced "sah-tahn," with a "the" in front of it). The Satan is "the accuser." He is not a demon, a fallen angel, or the ruler of Hell. He doesn't want your soul, nor would he have any use for it. Rather, the Satan is an angel like any other, a servant of God with an assigned job to do. His job is something like District Attorney—he prosecutes our sins in the Heavenly courtroom. That doesn't make him evil, at least no more so than the prosecutors on *Law and Order* and, generally speaking, we root for them to get a conviction.

The Talmud (*Bava Basra* 16) actually equates the Satan with both the *yeitzer hara* (the evil inclination) and the Angel of Death. The idea is that the Satan comes down to Earth to try and entrap humans into sin (as he did with Job), then he ascends to Heaven to testify against them. If the person is convicted, he serves as executioner. (This is inferred from the fact that God cautioned the Satan not to take Job's life, from which we see that such was otherwise within the Satan's purview).

Of course, one can use one's own judgment as far as how much (or how little) one chooses to personify the Satan, the *yeitzer hara*, and/or the Angel of Death. To clarify, let's talk about the *yeitzer hara*. Is that a spiritual being with its own consciousness and personality, or is it a part of each of us? Each of us has a *yeitzer hara* and a counterbalancing force in the form of the *yeitzer hatov* (good inclination). These could be understood as the little angel and devil that sit on a person's shoulders in cartoons, as a person's Id and Superego, or in other ways. There's no obligation to personify these metaphysical concepts as humanoid, that's merely a device to facilitate our understanding. Not everyone's religious disposition is quite so literal and that's okay.

So, does Judaism believe in a Devil? No. A Satan? Yes, but not the way you might think. His role as Heavenly prosecutor calls for fewer pointy tails and pitchforks than normally depicted. But if you've ever been in a courtroom, you know that expensive suits and attaché cases can also be pretty frightening.

Hell

Q. Do Jews Believe in Hell?

A. I don't know where the idea that Jews don't believe in Hell got started but we most certainly do believe in one. I've heard umpteen times on television that Jews don't believe in Hell—including on the venerable *Simpsons*. And people figure that if *The Simpsons* says it, it must be true—but it isn't!

America is predominantly Christian (as are Europe, Australia, *et al.*) so the Christian concept of Hell is culturally dominant. In Christian theology, Hell is forever; such is not the case in Jewish theology. So when people say that Jews don't believe in Hell, what they really mean (even if they don't know it) is that Jews don't agree with the Christian idea of Hell. We do believe in Hell. What we don't believe in is eternal damnation. (At least not for regular people. People like Hitler, Stalin, Pol Pot and Vlad the Impaler are another story.)

The Jewish idea is that God has placed us in this world for a limited time. While we're here, we're faced with a constant series of choices between right and wrong. At the end of our time here, we are rewarded according to the degree of perfection we manage to achieve. A person then enjoys the level of reward that he has earned forever (R. Moshe Chaim Luzzatto, *Derech Hashem* I, 3.3). However, since every person—even good people—invariably made some bad calls in life, we must first be cleansed of our misdeeds in "Hell," which we call Gehinnom (*ibid.*, II, 2.4).

Some people think that Hell isn't in the Jewish Bible but that's incorrect. It's not prominent because our focus is on the here and now rather than on the afterlife but it's definitely there if you know where to look. The Talmud in *Eiruvin* (19a) tells us that Gehinnom has seven names: *Sheol* (the pit), *Abaddon* (doom), *Be'er Shachas* (pit of corruption), *Tit haYaven* (clinging mud), *Shaarei Maves* (gates of death), *Tzalmaves* (shadow of death) and *Eretz haTachtis* (the underworld). These are largely derived from a variety of Biblical verses (see there). The name we typically use, Gehinnom, is not actually its name; it's more of a description. Gehinnom means "the valley of Hinnom" and is derived from an actual place name as seen in Joshua 15:8 and 18:16, *et al.* We see in II Kings 23:10, and possibly elsewhere, that atrocities were committed in this valley.

So what happens in Gehinnom? The Talmud in *Brachos* describes fire as one-sixtieth of Gehinnom, from which we can easily calculate that Gehinnom is sixty times as intense as fire. Of course, fire burns our bodies, which we won't have in the afterlife. We'll only be souls in the Next World so the "burning" of Gehinnom is of a spiritual nature.

I have often heard that the Gehinnom is like a movie theater in which we are shown two movies: one of our lives as we actually lived them and one of our lives as they would have been had we made all the right choices. According to this model, the "burning" of Gehinnom is the shame that we feel when we realize how far we've gone astray. Rabbi Dr. Asher Meir expresses such a concept in his series *Meaning in Mitzvot*:

> Our world is a world of significant moral ambiguity. Even a person who wants to do the right thing can often be confused into wrongdoing; furthermore, our base impulses are always tempting us into transgression. Very often the fog of uncertainty serves to assuage feelings of guilt. But when a person perceives his acts from the clear perspective of the World of Truth, he feels an intense burning remorse for all his misdeeds. This sense of shame tortures the person for a period of time until his atonement is complete.

I went looking for the original source of this widespread understanding of Gehinnom but I didn't find it—at least not overtly. I did find the following pieces, which can be assembled:

First of all, a number of Biblical verses equate afterlife punishment with feeling shame. For example, Isaiah 66:24 says, "They will go out and see the corpses of the people who rebelled against Me, because their decay will not cease, their fire will not be quenched, and they will be disgraced before all mankind."

Similarly, Daniel 12:2, speaking of the future revival of the dead, says, "Many who sleep in the dust of the earth will awaken—some for eternal life and some for shame, for eternal abhorrence." The Malbim on this verse explains shame to mean that the wicked will receive their punishments while observing the salvation of those who actually heeded God's word.

The Midrashic work *Tanna d'Bei Eliyahu Zuta* (12) says that children who study Torah will save their parents from the "shame, humiliation and disgrace" of judgment in Gehinnom. Nothing about pain and suffering, just "shame, humiliation and disgrace!"

Finally, the Medieval work of *musar* (self-improvement) *Shaarei Teshuvah* by Rabbeinu Yonah of Gerondi says that embarrassing someone is worse than death (3:139). I have seen later writers extrapolate from this that shame is worse than pain. If that's the case in the temporal world, in which we have bodies, it's all the more likely to be true in the Next World, where we are only souls.

If the punishment of Gehinnom is shame, then based on our earlier Gemara from *Eiruvin*, it must be sixty times more intense than the worst embarrassment a person could feel on Earth! That's an incredible degree of humiliation!

Of course, this interpretation is just that: one interpretation. Maimonides, in his introduction to the Mishnaic chapter called *Cheilek*, makes it clear that the nature of suffering in Gehinnom is not elaborated upon by the Sages of the Talmud. He cites one Talmudic opinion that the wicked will be burned by proximity to the sun (based on Malachi 3:19, "the day comes, burning like an oven") and another that the consuming heat will come from inside the wicked themselves (based on Isaiah 33:11,

"Your breath is a fire that will devour you"). The bottom line is that we just don't know. (The Talmud in *Gittin* 56b-57a describes some fanciful punishments in Hell but those appear to be reserved for the kinds of people who can exceed the normal time limits for sentences in Gehinnom. I would not presume that average people would merit the same degree of penalty.)

Speaking of limits to sentences, the consensus is that a normal person (as opposed to a Pol Pot or a Vlad the Impaler) is limited to a year in Gehinnom (Mishna, *Eduyos* 2:10; Talmud, *Shabbos* 33b and *Rosh Hashana* 17a). This is the reason that mourners recite Kaddish only for 11 months even though they're in mourning for a full year: to recite Kaddish for 12 months would suggest that the deceased was so bad as to warrant the full, harshest sentence.

We also have a midrashic tradition that those being punished in Gehinnom enjoy a reprieve for the duration of Shabbos. The *Zohar* (II, 89b) explains that the verse prohibiting lighting a fire (Exodus 35:3) applies both to us here and to the "fires" (however metaphorical they may be) that they light in Gehinnom. (Whether the time of the Shabbos reprieve corresponds to Jerusalem time, the deceased's local time or something else is a question beyond our scope.)

Finally, the Ramchal describes *kareis* (excision—the most extreme form of punishment) as the soul of the offender being discarded altogether (*Derech Hashem* II, 2.3). As unpleasant as the punishments of Gehinnom may be, they still seem to be preferable to non-existence.

Lest all this sound too good to be true, keep in mind that Nachmanides writes that an hour in Gehinnom is worse than 70 years of suffering as Job did (*Shaar HaGemul*—I couldn't find this in the original but I saw it cited by a number of reputable secondary sources). So, while the Jewish version of Hell is definitely way better than an eternity of being stabbed by devils with pitchforks while you stand in a lake of fire, it's still something that one should try to avoid.

NEW! Life is Unfair

Q. Why isn't life fair?

A. Are you sure you don't want to ask me a difficult question?

This is something that bothered even Moshe Rabbeinu, who understood God better than any other human before or since. In the fourth *aliyah* of *parshas Ki Sisa* (Exodus 33:17-23), God told Moshe that He was very pleased with the job he had been doing and was favorably inclined to grant his requests.

"In that case," Moshe said, "I'd like to understand Your ways."

"I'm afraid I can't do that," God replied. "Humans are simply incapable. From your point of view, My ways are going to appear pretty arbitrary."

"Even so...," said Moshe.

"Fine," God compromised. "I'll allow you to understand Me with the benefit of hindsight."

(The dialogue in the Torah has Moshe asking to "see God's face" and God allowing Moshe to see His "back" as He "passes by." These anthropomorphisms are metaphors for the concepts as I have phrased them.)

The Talmud (*Brachos* 7a) continues this discussion with the question of *tzaddik v'ra lo* and *rasha v'tov lo*—a righteous person who has it bad and an evil person who has it good. It concludes that:

- A righteous person who has it good is completely righteous—he therefore deserves reward in both this world and the Next World;
- A righteous person who has it bad is not completely righteous. He is therefore punished for his sins in this world in order to enjoy pure reward in the Next World;
- An evil person who has it good is not completely evil. He is therefore rewarded for his *mitzvos* in this world in order to receive pure punishment in the Next World;
- An evil person who has it bad is completely evil—he therefore deserves punishment in both this world and the Next World;

(For clarity, the above incorporates the explanation of the Maharsha.)

Even this may be more simplified than things actually are. Consider the explanation of Rabbeinu Bachya ibn Pekuda in *Chovos HaLevavos* (*Shaar HaBitachon* 3,II). There, he writes that a righteous person might be subjected to suffering because:

- It is punishment for a sin he previously committed, as per Proverbs 11:31, "Even the righteous are repaid on Earth";
- In order to increase his share in the Next World, as per Deuteronomy 8:16, "To do good for you at your end";
- To demonstrate his patience and faith in God as a lesson to others, as was the case with Job;
- To contrast this person with evil contemporaries in order to highlight his piety and devotion to God, as in Isaiah 53:4, "It was our illness that he carried, our pains that he endured";
- Because this righteous person failed to rebuke his evil contemporaries, as was the case with Eli, the High Priest, in I Samuel chapter 2.

Similarly, God might show favor to an evil person for many different reasons, such as:

- To reward him in this world for an earlier good deed, as per Deuteronomy 7:10, "He repays His enemies to their face in order to destroy them";
- The evil person is only given riches as a conduit to get them to a righteous person, as per Job 27:17, "He prepares it but the righteous will wear it," and Koheles 2:26, "to the sinner He gives the job to gather and to accumulate so that he may give it to one who is good before God";
- The evil person might be given wealth to be the cause of his undoing, as per Koheles 5:12, "There is a great evil I have observed under the sun—riches kept by their owner for his own injury";
- Wealth might be given to an evil person as a sign of God's patience, in the hope that he will repent and become worthy of what he has, as was

the case with Menashe, an evil king whose repentance is recorded in II Chronicles chapter 33;

- Wealth might be given to an evil person as repayment for the good deeds of his righteous father, as was the case with Yehu, who was granted four generations on the throne regardless of the worthiness of his successors (II Kings chapter 10);

- Finally, wealth might be granted as a test to a person who acts righteously but is inclined toward evil. When he sees how the wicked prosper, will he turn from the service of God and follow the path of evil? The *Chovos HaLevavos* cites examples involving the prophet Elijah and the wicked Queen Jezebel, and the prophet Jeremiah and the evil kings of his day.

The question of *tzaddik v'ra lo* and *rasha v'tov lo* doesn't only bother you and me, and it didn't only bother Moshe. It bothered Jeremiah ("Why does the way of the wicked succeed?"—Jeremiah 12:1). It bothered Habakkuk ("Why do You remain silent when the wicked devours one more righteous than he?"—Habakkuk 1:13). It bothered King David ("Behold, such are the wicked; they are always at ease and they increase their riches. Surely in vain have I cleansed my heart and washed my hands in innocence because all day long I have been plagued and I am chastised every morning"—Psalms 73:12-14). It's truly *the* age-old question.

We can never expect a nice, clean, one-size-fits-all answer to this question. The universe simply has too many variables. No person's life is like anyone else's so we can't objectively rank what anyone "deserves," let alone conclude that what he has is "unfair." This is why Moshe told us, "The concealed things are for Hashem our God, and the revealed things are for us and our children..." (Deuteronomy 29:28). Similarly, King Solomon advises, "When you see the oppression of the poor, and the perversion of justice and righteousness in the state, do not wonder about (God's) will..." (Koheles 5:7). Only God can keep track of all the moving parts.

Science Fiction and Fantasy

Harry Potter

Q. *Since witchcraft is prohibited by the Torah, how is it okay to read Harry Potter?*

A. Why should it not be okay to read? Witchcraft is prohibited in the Torah, reading about witchcraft isn't.

Along similar lines, murder is prohibited by the Torah; is it therefore prohibited to read Agatha Christie novels? Theft is prohibited by the Torah; is it prohibited to read the Hardy Boys? Eating shellfish is prohibited by the Torah; is it prohibited to read *Alice in Wonderland* because the Walrus and the Carpenter eat oysters? Could we even read the Bible, which describes people engaging in every form of illicit behavior from incest to cannibalism? Where would one draw the line?

Let's take a quick look at the Torah's prohibition against sorcery. There are actually a number of prohibitions addressing a variety of behaviors like divination, soothsaying and necromancy. The question is whether magic is real. There is an opinion that dark forces of sorcery do exist, practitioners accessing them through names of impurity and via other methods. I, however, favor the opinion of the Rambam that magic isn't real and that what the Torah prohibits is tricking people into thinking that one has supernatural abilities. He writes (*Avodas Kochavim* 11:16) that all the prohibited forms of sorcery are tricks intended to deceive people; if a person believes that the magic prohibited by the Torah is real, then he's a fool.

According to this understanding, even the magic attributed to Pharaoh's sorcerers in Egypt or to the witch of Endor might just be trickery, the Torah just describing the appearance of things. This is not difficult to understand. If you went to a magic show and someone asked you what tricks the magician performed, you might reply, "Oh, the usual. He sawed a woman in half." Of course you know that he did no such thing, you're just describing the appearance. Similarly, when the Torah says, "Then Pharaoh summoned his wise men and sorcerers, and the magicians of Egypt duplicated the feat with their secret arts" (Exodus 7:11), it might just be describing the way things looked. (I say "might" because there are a variety of opinions on the matter, including "magic is real," "all magic is false except for the magic described in the Torah" and "all magic is false including that described in the Torah." Take your pick.)

You might ask, if magic is prohibited because it's trickery, then how are birthday party magicians permitted? Rav Moshe Feinstein addresses this question in *Igros Moshe* (*Yoreh Deah* 4:13). There he explains that birthday party magicians aren't trying to trick anyone. They don't claim to have supernatural powers in order to mislead their audiences, they're just performing sleight of hand for entertainment purposes. It's inconceivable, Rav Moshe wrote, that the Torah would prohibit a person demonstrating his natural abilities even if they far exceed those of the average person. As examples, he mentions Naftali and Shimson (Samson), who had speed and strength (respectively) far superior to other people, bordering on supernatural. Using these abilities was not seen as problematic.

This brings us back to *Harry Potter*. Is the magic in *Harry Potter* the same kind of sorcery prohibited by the Torah? After all, in the world of *Harry Potter*, there are wizards, muggles and squibs. In other words, you're either born with the gift or you aren't. Harry intuitively performed acts of magic even before he knew he was a wizard. Filch, as a squib, is incapable of performing magic. A muggle, no matter how hard he tries, will never be able to cast a spell. So is this the witchcraft prohibited by the Torah or is it the kind of God-given innate ability that we can't expect one to refrain from using? I'll let readers form their own opinions.

Many years ago, when there were only five *Harry Potter* books, I wrote an article entitled "Harry Potter is Jewish!" (The original is long gone but it's referenced and reprinted multiple places on the web for those who care to look for it.) In it, I use the world of *Harry Potter* as a useful metaphor for Jewish concepts. Around the same time, someone else wrote an article decrying *Harry Potter* as antithetical to Jewish ideals. What amused me is that this person asked, "Why can't kids read wholesome books, like Mary Poppins?" The logic of this eludes me as I fail to see how the world of *Mary Poppins* is any less steeped in magic than that of *Harry Potter*!

Lest you think that my opinions are colored by a love for *Harry Potter*, allow me to clarify that I have little to no interest in the franchise. I read all 14 original *Oz* books by L. Frank Baum (plus numerous sequels by other hands), all seven of C. S. Lewis' *Narnia* books and all eight *Mary Poppins* books by P.L. Travers. I only read the second through the fifth *Harry Potter* books. When people ask me why I didn't read the first and how I could stop before the series was completed, I reply that "My wife read the kids the first one; by the time the sixth came out, they were all old enough it to read it for themselves."

Bottom line, I'm not sure that the characters in *Harry Potter* practice the same kind of magic that would be prohibited by the Torah if it were real and, even if they do, I don't think that reading about prohibited things is itself prohibited. (If it were, how could we read the Torah?) But a person has the right not to read things that offend their sensibilities, as well as the responsibility to monitor what their children read. Even if it's permitted to read *Harry Potter*, one is not obligated to do so. One has every right to refrain, especially if one thinks it's bad *chinuch* (education) to glorify certain behaviors. This is also true when it comes to TV shows, movies, video games, web sites and all other forms of media.

Of course, monitoring what one's children watch and read, it's important not to play "morality police" with others. If your tolerance level includes *Mary Poppins* but not *Harry Potter*, by all means let your kids read *Mary Poppins* and not *Harry Potter*. Just remember that somewhere there's someone else who doesn't approve of *Mary Poppins*, either. So treat *Harry Potter* readers as you would want to be treated.

Beauty and the Beast

Q. *In the movie Beauty and the Beast, the main character Belle is kept prisoner by a Beast whom everyone hates and fears, but she sees the good in him. What does Judaism say about seeing the good in other people?*

A. What I'm going to say may surprise you but I'm going to go with "hate and fear the beast." Let's look at the facts:

1. The Beast is holding Belle captive against her will. This is not something good people do. Seeing the good in him in such a situation is not admirable, it's called Stockholm Syndrome. Belle will require years of therapy.
2. I didn't see the live-action remake but I know that in the cartoon, the Beast was prone to lashing out in fits of anger, slashing things with his claws. In my opinion, caution is called for among such volatile people.
3. Finally, while I don't advocate judging people based on their appearances, the Beast is not a person; he's an animal in human clothes. You know who else is an animal in human clothes? The Wolfman as portrayed by Lon Chaney. Or the Big Bad Wolf dressed up in Grandma's clothes. Again, in any such situation, I'm going to exercise caution.

So, yes, I'm going to tell you to judge people favorably but at the outset I'm going to set some parameters. When a stranger pulls up and offers you a ride in his van, you do *not* "judge him favorably" and get in. That's a good way to get an episode of *Law & Order: SVU* based on your life. You exercise caution and get away.

As far as judging others favorably, let's start at the beginning: the Mishna in *Avos* (1:6) tells us, "Accept a teacher upon yourself, acquire a friend for yourself, and judge every person favorably." But what does it mean to judge everyone favorably? Let everyone in jail go free? No, clearly some people are guilty but until the facts are in, we should give them benefit of the doubt, similar to the secular legal principle of a presumption of innocence. This includes considering the possibility of improbable situations as in the following famous story:

A man worked for three entire years, at the end of which he asked for his wages only to be told by his employer that he had no cash. The worker asked for produce as payment, only to be told that there was none of that either. Whatever he asked for—livestock, real estate, utensils—the boss said he didn't have any. The man went home for the holidays dejected. After Succos, his employer showed up with the man's wages plus five donkeys carrying expensive gifts. After enjoying a banquet, the boss asked, "What did you think when I said I had no money?"

"I assumed you had invested it in a sudden opportunity," the man replied.

"And when I said I had no livestock?"

"I assumed you had rented them out."

"And when I said I had no produce?"

"I assumed you hadn't taken tithes yet."

And so on for all the other things the boss had claimed not to have. When this exchange was finished, the boss exclaimed, "Everything is exactly as you said! As you judged me favorably, so may God judge you favorably!" (Talmud, Shabbos 127b)

This presumption of innocence is commensurate with a person's actions and the reputation he has earned. For example, if you see your rabbi (or any observant Jew) coming out of a McDonald's, it's appropriate to assume that he only went in to use the restroom. If you see him driving on Shabbos, you should assume that there's a medical emergency. But if you have a Jewish neighbor who doesn't keep kosher or Shabbos, there's no reason to assume anything beyond the apparent.

Which brings us back to going too far in this matter, as with a potentially dangerous Beast. Rabban Gamliel once hosted a stranger in his home. He set the guest up with a bed on the roof but he removed the ladder. (People in those days used the roof for all sorts of things so this was not unusual.) In the middle of the night, the guest tried to rob the house but the ladder was gone, so he fell to the ground.

"You didn't judge me favorably!" the man complained.

"Judging others favorably doesn't mean being a patsy," Rabban Gamliel replied (loosely translated). (*Derech Eretz Rabbah* 5)

Don't get me wrong—it's extremely important to judge favorably. Seeing the good in others is a sign of the good in ourse Menashe ben Yisroel, *Nishmas Chaim*). People are punished for sus innocent people of wrongdoing (Talmud, *Shabbos* 97a) and the way we judge others is how we ourselves will be judged (*Shmiras HaLashon*). Seeing others positively is definitely a characteristic we should cultivate within ourselves but within healthy parameters. In other words, *stay out of the van.*

Life on Other Planets

Q. What does Judaism say about life on other planets?

A. It may not surprise you that people think a lot about the afterlife. Is there Heaven? Hell? Reincarnation? Eternal nothingness? I once heard a rabbi say, "Everyone wants to know where they're going next; how come nobody wonders about where they were before they got here?"

Similarly, people think a lot about the creation of the universe. Some people are obsessed with reconciling the literal Biblical accounts with the current scientific theories of the Big Bang and evolution.

All this makes for an interesting diversion but, ultimately, it's unimportant. None of it affects our obligations in the here and now.

The topic of life on other planets is in the same category. Does Judaism have what to say on the subject? Certainly. Does it matter? Not a whole lot, no. So a caveat before we begin: whatever Judaism has to say on the subject, however I present it, and whether you agree or disagree, it makes no difference. It's an interesting thought experiment, nothing more.

That having been said, it should come as no shock to us that there may be forms of intelligence aside from humanity. There's certainly precedent for it. First of all, there are angels, referenced throughout the Bible. Angels may not have free will (or, more specifically, they have limited free will) but they are intelligent and self-aware. Not only that, Maimonides attributes intelligence to the spheres in which the various heavenly bodies were once believed to be set. This does not appear to an allegory; it would seem that Maimonides considers the spheres to be a form of spiritual intelligence comparable to angels. Such an approach explains literally verses that describe the universe as praising God, such Psalms 19:2 ("The heavens declare the glory of God…").

If we can consider the possibility that the skies themselves may be intelligent in a way we do not fully understand, it is certainly a much smaller leap to the idea that there may be life recognizable as such on other planets. There are a number of allusions in both the Jewish Bible and the Talmud that support the idea.

A personal favorite, which I've had occasion to cite in the past, is from the famous song of the prophetess Deborah (Judges chapter 5). The key verse for our purposes is 5:23, which states, "'Cursed be Meroz,' said the angel of God. 'Curse bitterly the inhabitants thereof because they did not come to the aid of God, to help God against the mighty!'" Rashi on this verse cites the Talmudic opinion that Meroz is the name of a distant star. That Meroz is a star makes sense in context as verse 20 states that "They fought from Heaven; the stars in their orbits fought against Sisera." Nevertheless, Meroz is said to have inhabitants. Even if the intention of the verse is like the other Talmudic opinion (that Meroz is the name of a city), we see that Rashi and the Talmudic sources he cites are not opposed to the idea of life on other worlds.

Other verses also suggest this possibility. Among these are Psalms 145:13, "Your Kingdom is a Kingdom of all worlds…," and *Shir HaShirim* 6:8, which refers to "worlds without number." (The former verse is familiar from Ashrei, recited in prayer thrice daily, as the verse *malchuscha malchus kol olamim….*) Similarly, the Talmud refers to God supervising "18,000 worlds" (*Avodah Zarah* 3b). Arguably, if God's Kingdom encompasses so many worlds and He goes to the effort of supervising them, there very well could be something there to rule and supervise!

Of course, if there is life on other worlds, we have no idea what it would be like. On this, the primary sources are silent. Are they humanoid? Are they sentient? Do they possess free will? Did God give them a Book of Law as He did us? We have no way of knowing for sure. There are different opinions based as much on logic and conjecture as on text. The *Sefer HaBris* by Rav Pinchas Horowitz (Poland, 18th-19th century) suggests quite convincingly that, just as sea life differs significantly from land-based life, we should expect any life found on other worlds to be very different from what we know on Earth.

In researching this topic, one name kept coming up: Rav Chasdai Crescas (Spain, 14th-15th century), author of a work called *Ohr Hashem*, which supports the possibility of life on other planets for reasons similar to those we have discussed. On the other hand, his contemporary, Rav Yosef Albo, author of *Sefer Ha'Ikkarim*, discounts the possibility on the basis that the universe was created for the sake of humanity. In his opinion, extraterrestrials that would never interact with mankind would have no purpose.

So who's right, Rav Crescas or Rav Albo? We have no way of knowing. But as we've said, at the end of the day it really doesn't matter. It's an interesting question to consider but whether or not there's life on Krypton, Ork or Melmac, we have our responsibilities down here on Earth.

Parallel Worlds

Q. Does such the concept of parallel worlds and alternate realities exist in Jewish thought?

A. Readers may be acquainted with the multiple-worlds model from comic books and television shows like *Sliders*. In real life, the many-worlds interpretation is an explanation of the quantum mechanics phenomenon in which different results exist in a superposition of states that collapse to a single result when observed. According to the many-worlds interpretation, all possible results actually do occur. We see just one of them; the other results occur among an infinite number of parallel universes.

This concept was popularized by Erwin Schrödinger's famous thought experiment involving a cat. In Schrödinger's scenario, a cat is imprisoned in a box with a vial of poison gas and a radioactive atom that has an equal chance of decaying or not. If it decays, the gas is released and the cat dies; if the atom doesn't decay, the gas remains in the vial and the cat lives. Mathematically speaking, the results are in a superposition of states and the cat is both dead and alive. (People misunderstand Schrödinger's point.

He wasn't trying to prove that the cat was actually both dead and alive until observed; he actually called the idea ridiculous. Not only have lay people taken Schrödinger's cat more literally than Schrödinger ever intended, many later physicists actually use the example in the literal sense, counter to Schrödinger's original point.)

So, if you're asking does Judaism support the idea of parallel worlds—a world where Abel killed Cain rather than the other way around, a world where Egyptian viceroy Joseph exacted revenge against his brothers, a world where Korach overthrew Moshe, etc.—then no. There's nothing that supports such a thing. (Not that there's anything that precludes it *per se*. To my knowledge, the subject is simply not addressed.) But there are other worlds in Judaism, and I don't mean just other planets. There are realities that exist in other planes entirely so that it would be impossible for us to travel there physically.

In our discussion of life on other planets (above), I wrote:

> Other verses also suggest this possibility. Among these are Psalms 145:13, "Your Kingdom is a Kingdom of all worlds...," and *Shir HaShirim* 6:8, which refers to "worlds without number." ... Similarly, the Talmud refers to God supervising "18,000 worlds" (*Avodah Zarah* 3b). Arguably, if God's Kingdom encompasses so many worlds and He goes to the effort of supervising them, there very well could be something there to rule and supervise!

There, I work under the assumption that "worlds" means "planets," though perhaps such is not the case. For example, let us consider Psalms 146:48, "Blessed be Hashem, the God of Israel, from world to world...." Rashi explains "from world to world" to mean "from this world to the Next World," so at least there it refers to different planes of existence rather than to planets.

So what are "this world" and "the Next World?" *Olam hazeh* (this world) is easy enough. Like the name says, it's this world: the world where we're born, where we live and where we die. It's the world where we grow up and go to school and get jobs and work until we retire. It's the world where we eat and drink and excrete and reproduce. It's the world where we have the opportunity to earn merits for our actions, but also the world where we run the risk of falling prey to our urges. You know. This world.

Olam Haba is trickier. The Sages of the Talmud contrast this world with *Olam Haba* but they don't define it. This term could refer either to a place or to a time, depending on whom you ask. The Rambam (Maimonides) is of the opinion that *Olam Haba* is a place—namely, where our souls go after we die. The Ramban (Nachmanides), on the other hand, believes that it refers to the state of the world after the future revival of the dead. For our purposes, we'll follow the position of Maimonides. (Most people translate *Olam Haba* as "the World to Come" but I prefer "the Next World." What can I say? It's an affectation.)

According to *Derech Hashem* ("The Way of God"), the classic work of Jewish metaphysics by Rabbi Moshe Chaim Luzzatto (AKA the Ramchal), God placed man on the crossroads with the ability to choose his own path. Mankind has therefore been imbued with free will in the form of his *yeitzer hara* (evil inclination) and *yeitzer hatov* (good inclination). Man is a synthesis of two opposite components: a physical body and a spiritual soul. The body pursues physical things, while the soul pursues the spiritual, with the result that the two parts of a person are in constant struggle. At the end of this struggle, one is rewarded according to the degree of perfection he has achieved.

The period of earning reward and the period of enjoying it differ in that the former is limited and the latter is unlimited. It is therefore appropriate that the experiences of the two periods are also different. When we are engaged in our struggle for perfection, it makes sense that our environment contains the elements that cause our conflicting urges to struggle. Therefore, in this world, physical and spiritual elements are in constant battle, and there's nothing to stop our physical urges from gaining the upper hand. In the Next World, however, the opposite is appropriate: when it is time to receive our reward, it is fitting that the spiritual side dominate and the physical is suppressed. This is why God created two worlds of different natures. We strive for perfection in this world (*olam hazeh*) and we enjoy our reward in the Next World (*Olam Haba*), each one designed for its intended purpose.

This reward, however, is only temporary. One's ultimate reward awaits in the reborn world following the aforementioned revival of the dead, when one's soul is reunited with his newly-purified body. In the period awaiting that revival, the body and soul must reside in appropriate locations. The body is returned to the ground as per Genesis 3:19 ("For dust you are and to dust you shall return") while the soul awaits reunification with the body in what is called the *olam ha-neshamos*, the "world of souls." Rambam, as we have said, identifies *Olam Haba* with the *olam haneshamos*; according to the Ramban, however, they would be different things. (*Derech Hashem* I, 3—I explore this more fully in *The God Book*.)

Not every soul is ready for *Olam Haba*; some people simply haven't earned it. But most of these souls can be cleansed of their misdeeds so that they can then be rewarded for their merits. This takes place in Gehinnom ("Hell"). This is another world you "can't get to from here," though getting into the details of Divine reward and punishment strays a little too far from our current topic.

Another world aside from our own is actually all around us. I refer to the spiritual world. We can perceive the physical world with our senses, including both terrestrial and celestial phenomena. The former includes such things as soil, water and air, while the latter includes the stars and planets. The spiritual world, however, cannot be detected with our senses or technology. Creations of the spiritual world are of two types: *neshamos* (souls) and *nivdalim* ("those set apart"). Souls are spiritual creations designed to be placed into bodies in order to perform certain tasks. *Nivdalim*, on the other hand, are independent spiritual creations, not designed to merge with bodies. These include both angels in their various types as well as numerous forces.

We are familiar with the physical realm because we live in it. The phenomena of the spiritual world, on the other hand, are outside of our experience, with the result that we lack the ability to discuss them properly. The only meaningful way we can express ideas on this subject is through the traditions that have been passed down to us. One of the basic concepts we have received is that everything physical has a spiritual counterpart. The physical and spiritual entities are somehow connected so that the physical item is like an extension of the spiritual thing into our world, like the branch of a tree. Additionally, every physical thing is under the supervision of an "angel" (which need not be a sentient being) whose job it is to maintain the object according to its nature. The physical world's existence is maintained by forces emanating from the spiritual world.

Since man is a physical being, our actions can only affect the physical world directly. However, since the physical and spiritual worlds are linked, our actions indirectly affect objects' counterparts in the spiritual world as well. God has set limits, however, to the amount that humanity can affect the spiritual world. (*Derech Hashem* I, 5—again, discussed in greater detail in *The God Book*.)

So are there other worlds just as real as our own but beyond our ability to perceive? Absolutely. But a world where Lincoln was never shot, where the British won the revolution or where Moshe led the Jews into Israel and built a Temple that was never destroyed? To my knowledge no Jewish source discusses or supports such an idea. If you're looking for that kind of thing, you'll have to stick to *Star Trek* and DC comics.

Robot Uprising

Q. Elon Musk warned the world that we had better get AI under control before robots take over the world. Is this a fear according to Jewish wisdom?

A. Judaism acknowledges that life comes in many forms, both physical and spiritual. The physical forms are pretty obvious—examples include trees, bumblebees, zebras, octopi, daffodils, paramecia and people. Spiritual life forms are not as apparent to us but they include angels and (for those of us who believe in them) demons. The Rambam tells us in *Yesodei HaTorah* ("Foundations of the Torah") 2:9 that even the heavenly spheres are alive in a way that we cannot understand. They possess a form of consciousness, hence various verses in Psalms that call upon the heavens to praise God.

The lines between different stages of life can get pretty blurry. The Arizal (Rabbi Isaac Luria, d. 1572) and his disciple Rabbi Chaim Vital (d. 1620) described how coral represents an intermediate stage between rocks and plants, and monkeys represent the intermediate stage between "dumb" animals and man. (It is interesting to note that the Kabbalists considered primates an evolutionary "link" centuries before Darwin.)

Different categories of life can resemble the categories on either side in different ways. For example, the Talmud (*Chagigah* 16a) discusses three ways in which humans resemble animals (a lower physical life form) and three ways in which we resemble angels (a spiritual life form). Like animals, we eat, excrete and reproduce. Like angels, we think, speak and walk erect. (The Talmud there also discusses three ways in which demons resemble humans and three ways in which they resemble angels. Personally, I fall into the "demon skeptic" camp but those who are interested in such things can go look it up.)

So we see that life comes in a lot of forms, not all of it physical, with a lot of gray areas of overlap. Is virtual life possible? Absolutely. The only real question is whether man is capable of creating life and consciousness. The answer to that is already in: Judaism says yes.

The Talmud in *Sanhedrin* (65b) says that humans have the potential to create worlds, including life. Using the Kabbalistic work *Sefer Yetzirah* (the Book of Creation), Rava made a man (presumably a golem). He sent this man to Rabbi Zeira, who questioned it, but Rava's creation lacked the power of speech. When the creature failed Rabbi Zeira's "Turing test," he realized that it was an artificial life form and told it to go back to the dust from which it was formed. (We are also told that Rav Chanina and Rav Oshiya would create a calf each week, which could be eaten just like a calf born through natural means.)

Rava's creation may have looked like a human being, and it may even have been sentient, but it still wasn't a human being. (If it was, Rabbi Zeira would probably not have told it to drop dead!) The Maharsha notes that such creations do not have souls; presumably, that part of creation is reserved for God alone. So man may be able to create artificial intelligence—and it may even be indistinguishable from natural intelligence—but that doesn't make it identical with natural life.

So am I worried about a robot uprising à la *The Terminator*, or some other form of AI takeover, as in *The Matrix*? Not really. We have pretty good forecasts for our end-of-the-world scenario—the Messianic era, the future revival of the dead, etc.—and being taken over by a giant computer or sentient holograms doesn't really fit into that scenario too neatly. True, there is the war of Gog and Magog, which may or may not happen depending on which path we take to reach our Messianic future. Could that war be between humans and artificial life forms? I imagine so but even that scenario is but a chapter in the story and not the tale's end.

So is a scenario like the one Musk warns about possible according to the Torah? I don't think anything rules it out. But looking at the state of the world in general and the Middle East in particular, a robot uprising is not even remotely the threat that most concerns me.

Moshiach and the Messianic Era

When's He Coming?

Q. When is Moshiach coming?

A. There's nothing like the easy ones!

Happily, I don't have to answer this question on my own because the Talmud discusses it in great detail. The subject is examined in tractate *Sanhedrin* on pages 97a-99a, with occasional tangents for related topics. Here, I will hit just a few of the high points but there is much more to be found in those pages.

On page 97a, a number of Sages share their opinions as to what the world will be like prior to Moshiach's arrival. Rav Yochanan says that Moshiach will come in a generation when Torah scholars are decreasing, the people are in despair, and afflictions just keep on coming without a break. R. Yehuda says that Moshiach will come in a generation when the study halls are used for promiscuity, people despise those who shun sin, and people's faces will resemble those of dogs (meaning that they are shameless). Rabbi Nehurai says that Moshiach will come in a generation when young people are insolent to their elders and those elders honor the young. Daughters disgrace their mothers, daughters-in-law humiliate their mothers-in-law, and sons feel no shame in front of their fathers.

Rabbi Yitzchak said that before Moshiach would come, the entire Roman Empire would convert to Christianity—an impressive statement given that Rabbi Yitzchak lived in the second century and died about 150 years before Emperor Constantine would realize his prediction!

The Sages say that Moshiach won't come until things are so bad that the people have despaired of redemption altogether.

Of course, many of these things have come to pass and Moshiach has not yet come because our sins delay his arrival. Alternately, God's attribute of strict justice (as opposed to His attribute of mercy) is delaying Moshiach's arrival. If this is the case, the Gemara asks, why should we even bother waiting for him? It answers that we wait for Moshiach because doing so earns us a reward as per Isaiah 30:18, "Happy are all those who wait for him."

The Sage known as Rav says that all the scheduled times for Moshiach to arrive have already passed; the only things that can bring him now are *teshuvah* (repentance) and performing *mitzvos*. His counterpart, Shmuel, says that the suffering the Jews endure in exile will be sufficient to do the job even if the Jews do not repent.

Rabbi Nosson expounds on Habakkuk 2:3: "The vision is reserved for the appointed time; it declares the end and does not lie. Though it tarries, wait for it because it will surely come and will not delay." This verse, he tells us, "penetrates and descends to the depths." That is to say, just as the extent of the depths are unknowable, so too the date of Moshiach's arrival is an impenetrable mystery. He then cites three opinions about the date of Moshiach's arrival—those of the Sages, Rabbi Simlai and Rabbi Akiva, all of whom based their positions on Biblical verses. They all have it wrong, Rabbi Nosson says. None of those verses are talking about Moshiach. Rather, he says, they foretell the durations of the Hasmonean dynasty, the Herodian dynasty, and Bar Kochba. The advent of Moshiach, however, is incalculable.

Rabbi Abba thinks that the time of Moshiach's arrival is obvious, based on Ezekiel 36:8, "But you mountains of Israel will shoot forth your branches and yield your fruit for My people Israel because they are coming soon." (This, of course, happened when the Jews returned with the founding of the modern-day State of Israel.)

Rabbi Yochanan said that if you see a generation beset by afflictions that are relentless like a river, you should expect that Moshiach is coming soon. This is based on verses in Isaiah chapter 59. Verse 19 says that "distress will come in like a flood, driven by the breath of God." Verse 20 continues, "And a redeemer will come to Zion...."

Rabbi Yochanan also said that Moshiach will only come either in a generation that is totally innocent or one that is totally guilty. "Totally innocent" is based on Isaiah 60:21, "Your people will all be righteous; they will inherit the land forever." "Totally guilty" is based on several verses, including Isaiah 48:11, in which God says, "I will do it for My Own sake."

Rabbi Yehoshua ben Levi pointed out an apparent contradiction in Isaiah 60:22. The verse says, "I will hasten (Moshiach's arrival) in its time." Which is it? Will He hasten it, meaning He will make it happen quickly, or will it happen in its assigned time? He reconciles the conflict as follows: if the Jews are worthy, God will hasten the redemption. If we are not, it will come about at the designated time.

Of course, there are those Talmudic authorities who discourage thinking at all about when Moshiach is coming. Whenever Rav Zeira saw people speculating as to the timing of Moshiach's arrival, he would ask them to desist because the mere act actually delays him. Rav Zeira based this on a dictum that three things only happen when people are not thinking about them: finding an object, a scorpion stinging and Moshiach arriving.

Rabbi Shmuel bar Nachmani actually cursed those who try to calculate the time of Moshiach's arrival. This is because such people end up causing a decrease in others' faith. They name a time and, when Moshiach doesn't adhere to their timetables, those who accepted the prediction assume he must never be coming.

Ultimately, it's up to us to bring Moshiach. Rabbi Yehoshua ben Levi asked Eliyahu HaNavi (the prophet Elijah) when Moshiach would arrive. Eliyahu said, "He's sitting at the city gate—go ask him yourself!" So Rabbi Yehoshua found Moshiach and asked him, "When are you coming?" "Today," Moshiach replied.

Rabbi Yehoshua was excited by this news but he was subsequently disappointed when Moshiach didn't show up as expected. He complained to Eliyahu, who explained that Rabbi Yehoshua had misunderstood Moshiach's meaning. What Moshiach meant was Psalms 95:7, "Today, if you will just listen to His voice!"

In short, if we want Moshiach to come, we should stop talking about it so much and actually do something about it!

The Messianic Era

Q. What will happen when Moshiach gets here?

A. Ah, a follow-up question! I love a good sequel as much as the next guy but with rare exception, they're usually not as satisfying as the original. Here, too, I'll answer the question but it may not be so satisfying if you're expecting an age of miracles. Which is a shame, because it should be extremely satisfying, with or without miracles.

Maimonides addresses this topic in the very last chapter of his *magnum opus*, the *Mishneh Torah*. In *Hilchos Melachim* (the Laws of Kings), chapter 12, he writes, "Don't think that any aspect of the world's nature will change in the messianic era or that there will be anything new in the work of creation. Rather, the world will continue as it always has" (12:1). That actually sounds pretty mundane. In the next *halacha*, the Rambam quotes the Talmud (*Brachos* 34b) that the only difference between the world as it currently is and the messianic era is the absence of our subjugation to the other nations. That part sounds rather significant!

The Rambam acknowledges verses like Isaiah 11:6, which states, "The wolf will dwell with the lamb and the leopard will lie down with the kid" but he explains that such things are metaphors for how Israel will finally dwell peacefully with her neighbors, who currently attack her like predators. He says that other such prophecies are likewise allegorical and, when the messianic era arrives, we will understand all the metaphors.

So let's look at what will occur:

First and foremost, the Beis HaMikdash (Temple) will be rebuilt. The prophet Ezekiel foretold this when he wrote, "I place My Sanctuary in their midst forever...The nations will know that I am God, Who sanctifies Israel, when My Sanctuary will be in their midst forever" (Ezekiel 37:26-28). The future third Temple is described in great detail starting in Ezekiel chapter 40.

Additionally, the exiled Jews around the world will be returned to the land of Israel. The Torah itself foretells this ("God will return your captives…He will gather you from among all the nations where God has scattered you…" Deuteronomy chapter 30). This promise is reiterated in Isaiah chapters 11 and 43, Jeremiah chapter 23, Ezekiel chapters 20, 36, and 39, and Amos chapter 9. This includes the ten "lost" Tribes (see Talmud, *Sanhedrin* 110b). [That the Moshiach is the one who will spearhead the rebuilding of the Temple and the ingathering of the exiles is codified in *Hilchos Melachim* 11:1.]

In the messianic era, good will triumph over evil. Zephaniah 3:13 tells us that "The remnant of Israel will do no wrong, they will speak no lies and a deceitful tongue will not be found in their mouth." Other chapters that describe the ascent of righteousness include Isaiah 60, Jeremiah 50, Ezekiel 37 and Malachi 3.

Not only that, the whole world will abandon idolatry and turn to the service of God. Isaiah 40:5 tells us that "The glory of God will be revealed; all flesh will see it together because the mouth of God has spoken." That other nations will join us in this service is evident from such verses as Zechariah 14:9, "God will reign over the entire earth. On that day God will be One and His Name One." Other sources for this include Isaiah chapters 2, 11 and 52, Jeremiah 31, Joel 3, Micah 4, Zephaniah 3 and Zechariah 9.

The promise of peace also appears throughout Tanach. Both Isaiah 2:4 and Michah 4:3 tell us that "…they will beat their swords into plowshares and their spears into pruning-hooks. Nation will not lift sword against nation, and they will not wage war any longer." Hosea 2 and Zechariah 9 also describe world peace, while the aforementioned metaphors of predator and prey dwelling together peacefully appear in Isaiah 11 and 65.

I'm not even getting into the revival of the dead, which is an event subsequent to and separate from the arrival of Moshiach (and perhaps a topic for another day).

Returning to the Rambam, he tells us that we don't await the messianic era in order to party, to be honored or to rule the world. We're not in it for any selfish motivation or temporal pleasure. Rather, we yearn to be able to serve God without the distraction of oppression so that we can get closer to Him (*Melachim* 12:4).

The details of how all these things will come about are unknown. All we have is the "big picture" that God revealed to the prophets, not an exhaustive play-by-play. We'll find out the details when they happen. The Rambam tells us we shouldn't be concerned with all the fanciful stories (which he considers metaphors) because they are not essential to our faith in the messianic era (*Melachim* 12:2).

The world will be a wonderful place with the Temple rebuilt, the Jews in Israel and the other nations not oppressing us. Maybe a lion won't literally eat straw like an ox (Isaiah 65:25), we won't literally fly on eagles' wings (Isaiah 40:31) and women won't literally give birth every day (Talmud, *Shabbos* 30b). But will an absence of such things really spoil your enjoyment of the Messianic era? Somehow I think it'll still be a pretty good deal!

Bacon in the Messianic Era

Q. *I heard that when Moshiach comes, bacon and pork will be kosher. Is this true?*

A. Long story short, no.

Now, short story long. I know exactly what you're talking about and I'll explain it. The first thing you need to know is that the Hebrew word for a pig is *chazir*; the second thing to know is that the word for "return" in Hebrew is *ChZR*. With this in mind, let us turn to a Medieval midrash that says, "Why is it called *chazir*? Because in the future, God will return it to Israel," i.e., it will become kosher.

"Aha!" I hear you exclaim. "You said that pig wouldn't become kosher but that source clearly says that it will!" Well, we're not finished yet.

Consider, if you will, Isaiah 11:6: "'The wolf will live together with the lamb; the leopard will lie down with the kid of goats." The Bible says that, so in Messianic times, it must be true that predator and prey will co-exist, right? I say no. But I'm not disagreeing with the prophet Isaiah, I merely adhere to the Rambam's understanding of the Messianic era.

In *Hilchos Melachim* 12:1, the Rambam tells us not to expect the nature of the world after Moshiach comes to be different from what we know today. He specifically mentions that verse from Isaiah and explains that it's a metaphor. What this and similar verses are expressing is that Israel will be able to dwell securely with formerly evil non-believers. (These evildoers are compared to predatory animals in verses like Jeremiah 5:6, "…a leopard will stalk their cities," *et al.*)

If the Rambam doesn't hesitate to classify actual Biblical prophecies as metaphorical, we certainly need not be concerned about not taking literally later-era midrashim of uncertain origin. The question is, what metaphor is that midrash trying to communicate?

There are many non-kosher animals but for some reason, the pig is the archetype of *treif*. Why is that? Well, in order for an animal to be kosher, it needs to have two kosher signs—it needs to chew its cud and have split hooves. The pig is one of only four animals that has one of the two signs of being kosher. The other three animals—like the camel—chew their cud but don't have split hooves. The pig is the only animal that has split hooves but doesn't chew its cud. Because of this, the pig is the rabbinic symbol of hypocrisy. It puts forth its split hoof as if to say, "Look at me! I'm kosher!" but in reality, its insides don't match its external presentation (*Bereishis Rabbah* 65:1).

The same midrash that calls the pig the symbol of hypocrisy also says that it symbolizes Rome (Edom, the spiritual descendants of Yaakov's brother Eisav). Eisav was rotten but he tricked his father, Yitzchak, into thinking he was righteous. Similarly, Rome touted all their public works but this was only a façade to mask their depravity. With this in mind, perhaps, "in the future, God will return the *chazir* to Israel" refers to the repentance of Edom and a reconciliation of the estranged brother nations.

The Rambam (*Hilchos Melachim* 11:3) says that the Torah and its laws are eternal—they will neither be added to nor subtracted from; I assume this includes the prohibition against eating pig. The Radvaz (2:828) is appalled at the thought of taking this midrash literally. Rabbeinu Bachaye interprets the midrash somewhat less charitably, saying that the "*chazir*" of Edom is that they will have judgment for their misdeeds returned (i.e., revisited) upon them.

There are certainly those who take this Midrash literally and look forward to eventually enjoying a thoroughly kosher authentic BLT. I, however, am strictly in the metaphor camp. Accordingly, I have resigned myself to the continuing use of veggie bacon even after the Moshiach arrives. Of course, as with all things relating to the messianic era, we'll find out for sure when we get there!

Tisha b'Av in the Messianic Era

Q. *I've heard that, after Moshiach comes, Tisha b'Av will become a day of joy and that the only holidays we will celebrate will be Purim and Chanukah. Is that true?*

A. That's a great question. In fact, that's two great questions! Let's discuss the first question: that after Moshiach comes, Tisha b'Av will become a day of joy.

In the book of Zechariah (8:19), the titular prophet says, "Thus says the Lord of Hosts: The fast of the fourth month (i.e., 17 Tammuz), the fast of the fifth month (9 Av), the fast of the seventh month (Tzom Gedaliah) and the fast of the tenth month (10 Teves) will be joy, celebration and holidays for the house of Judah, and they will love truth and peace." This verse is cited by the Rambam in his *Mishneh Torah.* In *Hilchos Taaniyos* (Laws of Fasts) 5:19, he writes that all the rabbinically instituted fasts will be abolished in messianic times and will be transformed into days of rejoicing and festivity as per the verse in Zechariah.

The subject under discussion when this topic arises is the prevalent practice not to read Eicha, the Biblical book of Lamentations, from a handwritten parchment on Tisha b'Av as we do when it comes to reading *Megillas Esther* on Purim. The Levush (Rabbi Mordecai Yoffe, a 16th-century kabbalist from Prague) writes that the reason we don't read Eicha from a scroll is that the scribes simply didn't transcribe this book very often. Writing a scroll is expensive, time-consuming and labor-intensive. The scribes' hesitancy to bother with this particular work is an expression of faith that such scrolls simply don't warrant the effort, as we anticipate Moshiach's imminent arrival and the transformation of Tisha b'Av from a day of mourning into one of rejoicing. (You will notice that we do bother transcribing *Megillas Esther* because, after Moshiach comes, we'll keep using those scrolls.)

Another source for Tisha b'Av turning into a day of joy in the messianic era is *Pesikta Rabbasi*, a ninth-century collection of aggadic midrashim. (There are two types of midrashim, halachic and aggadic, dealing with the legal and non-legal portions of the text, respectively.) According to the *Pesikta Rabbasi*, joy will only come on Tisha b'Av, again reflecting the idea that the nature of the day will be reversed from mourning to rejoicing. This may be based on the idea stated in the Talmud Yerushalmi (*Brachos* 2:4) that Moshiach will be born on Tisha b'Av.

It should be noted that Tisha b'Av is called a *moed* (holiday) in Eicha itself (1:15). This isn't just wordplay or homiletics—it has actual halachic ramifications! The *Shulchan Aruch* (*OC* 559:4) cites this verse as the reason we do not recite the *Tachanun* prayer on Tisha b'Av, just as we do not recite it on festive occasions.

So there's plenty of precedent for the idea that Tisha b'Av is already a partially-joyous occasion, a situation that will only intensify in the future.

Now, as far as Purim and Chanukah… honestly, I'm surprised that you included Chanukah! You're not wrong but the famous and oft-cited quote is only about Purim.

That Purim will be observed forever is explicit in the text of *Megillas Esther*: "these days of Purim will never cease among the Jews…" (9:28). It's the *Yalkut Shimoni* (another collection of midrashim) that teaches us that, in the messianic era, this will be to the exclusion of other holidays (*Remez* 944). It should be noted that Rabbi Elazar there expresses the opinion that Yom Kippur will also endure since the Torah calls it "an eternal statute" (Leviticus 16:34). This should not surprise us since "Yom Kippurim"—"day of atonements"—also means "a day like Purim!"

That the "except for Purim" includes Chanukah is an idea stated by Rav Moshe Feinstein, *ztz"l*, among others. Rav Moshe's grandson once expressed hope that he would never have occasion to use his new silver menorah on the basis that all holidays would be abolished when Moshiach comes. Rav Moshe clarified that "except for Purim" also includes Chanukah, as the two of them are the same kind of holiday (*Mesoras*

Moshe). As noted, other authorities express the same idea but it's nowhere near as widely known for Chanukah as it is for Purim.

It must also be pointed out that numerous authorities, such as the *Bnei Yissaschar*, refuse to take literally the idea that the Torah's holidays will ever be abolished. After all, how can the Moshiach's arrival cause us to suspend the observance of *mitzvos*? Rather, the intention is merely that the observance of the holidays that commemorate the Exodus and the giving of the Torah will pale in comparison to the everyday wonders of life in messianic times.

A similar conversation is held regarding Biblical books. The Rambam says that in the messianic era, all the books of Nach (the Prophets and the Writings) will be discarded except for the book of Esther (*Hilchos Megillah v'Chanukah* 2:18). Again, most authorities have trouble taking this at face value. As the *Lechem Mishneh* and other commentators explain, all the books of Nach have many deep lessons that we learn from them and it would be detrimental to jettison all those teachings. Rather, they understand it to mean that all the Biblical books will still be canon in messianic times but we won't have occasion to read them publicly as we do now. *Megillas Esther*, however, will always be read publicly.

Just as the consensus regarding eliminating Biblical books is not to take the Rambam's statement at its surface reading, perhaps it would be prudent not to take too literally the Midrash about abolishing holidays. The one obvious exception is Tisha b'Av itself. The idea that Tisha b'Av will ultimately be a day of joy seems to be long-reaching, well-founded, and intended to be taken literally. But as I always say regarding messianic matters, we'll find out for sure when we get there.

Will There Be Zombies?

Q. I want to convert to Judaism but I just can't imagine there being a human messiah, which I know is one of Maimonides' 13 Principles of Faith. When I come to the belief in the resurrection of the dead, the only thing I can imagine is zombies coming out of their graves. I feel I have a Jewish soul but I can't grasp these two concepts. What should I do?

A. You didn't tell me exactly what it is that you find hard to accept, so I'm going to make some assumptions. Are you picturing the Moshiach as some kind of magical demi-god? A lot of people have very fanciful ideas about the Moshiach and the messianic era but the Moshiach is just a person. A righteous person and a great leader, but a normal human being—nothing supernatural about him!

Information about Moshiach and the messianic era is scattered throughout the Bible. Much of it is in the book of Isaiah; chapter 11 is a good start. Read up and you'll see how down-to-earth it really is. The Sages of the Talmud tell us that there will be no difference between the messianic era and now except for one change: we'll no longer be persecuted. Yes, you'll find prophecies like "the lion will lay down with the lamb," but those are widely accepted as metaphors meaning that the mighty will no longer oppress the meek. So when people say things like, "When Moshiach comes, we'll go to our shuls which will then fly to Israel," I think they're just wrong. I think they're being overly literal with midrashim that are intended to be read allegorically.

As far as the resurrection of the dead, that's another area that most people don't really understand. First of all, it's not when Moshiach comes; it's some time subsequent to that—could be hundreds of years! Secondly, it's not everybody. Only some people will merit resurrection and, honestly, I think it's pretty egotistical for people to assume they make the cut. Personally, I think it will be the exception rather than the rule.

As with Moshiach, references to the resurrection of the dead are scattered throughout the Bible. One pretty explicit source is in the last chapter of Daniel. You say that you're "with the program" except for these two concepts. Since these two concepts are in the Bible, it creates a new issue: believing vs. disbelieving what's in the Bible. If you find my explanations, plus the fact that they're in the Bible compelling, great. If you still have a problem with these concepts, then you also have a third problem: accepting what's in Scripture.

As an aside, these things both have precedents in past events: Moshe led the Jews out of Egypt the way Moshiach is meant to redeem us from exile; a mass resurrection was witnessed by the prophet Ezekiel at the valley of the dry bones in chapter 37 of his book. If you can accept them in the past, why not in the future?

If you find it hard to believe that Biblical prophecies can come true nowadays, many have been fulfilled in modern times: The Jews returned to Israel as foretold (Isaiah 43); the land of Israel, which was desolate in the Jews' absence, has bloomed (Isaiah 41). Jerusalem has expanded to many times its original size (end of Ezekiel); nations like Amon, Moab and Edom are gone but Egypt remains, no longer the world power it once was (Jeremiah 46); etc., etc., etc. So many amazing things have already been fulfilled, I have no trouble expecting a few more. If you really just can't accept these ideas, perhaps look into being a Noachide. You have no obligation to convert and this way you'd be fulfilling what God wants from you as you are now.

Peace in the Middle East

Q. *At the end of his life, Yishmael did teshuvah. According to Jewish sources, will there ever be peace between Jews and Arabs?*

A. There's a lot to unpack here so let's start with Yishmael.

When Avraham and Sarah didn't have children, Sarah suggested that Avraham conceive with her handmaid, an Egyptian woman named Hagar. The offspring of this union was named Yishmael (see Genesis chapter 16). Later, Sarah gave birth to a son, Yitzchak. When she saw Yishmael "מצחק," she had Avraham expel him from the household. This pained Avraham to do but God told him to listen to Sarah because Yishmael had his own destiny to fulfill (Genesis 21).

Now, what exactly did Yishmael do wrong? מצחק in this verse is usually translated along the lines of "making fun" but the commentators express a number of opinions as to the specific nature of Yishmael's offense; I'll share just one. *Bereishis Rabbah* (53:11) records a three-way debate on this question in which Rabbi Akiva opines that Yishmael violated the three cardinal sins. Rabbi Akiva illustrates that this same Hebrew verb is used to refer to adultery (Genesis 39:17), idolatry (Exodus 32:6) and bloodshed (in II Samuel 2:14). The Tosefta objects to the possibility that such things might have been going on in Avraham's house but the fact that the Torah permits such a reading is telling.

We see that Yitzchak and Yishmael were ultimately reconciled from Genesis 25:9, in which we are told that "Yitzchak and Yishmael, (Avraham's) sons, buried him in the Machpeila cave...." Why is Yitzchak, the younger son, listed before Yishmael, the firstborn? Rashi on this verse cites the Midrash Rabbah that Yishmael repented and now deferred to Yitzchak as their father's primary heir (see also *Bava Basra* 16b).

So, whatever problems we may have with Yishmael's descendants, it doesn't go back to his expulsion because Yitzchak and Yishmael settled their differences in their lifetime.

Of course, even in Biblical times we had our problems with our uncle Yishmael's descendants. Consider Isaiah chapter 21, "The harsh prophecy regarding Arabia" (starting in verse 13), which begins, "In the forest of Arabia you lodged, on the roads of your cousins...." Who are our cousins in Arabia? The Arab nations, who are the descendants of Yishmael. (This predates the founding of Islam by many centuries. Remember, not all Arabs are Muslims and not all Muslims are Arabs!) The Midrash Tanchuma, cited by Rashi to varying degrees on Genesis 21:17 and Isaiah 21:14, explains the event leading to this "harsh prophecy." When the Jews were exiled by Nebuchadnezzar, the refugees expected their cousins to have mercy on them and to provide them with bread and water. Instead, they fed them salted fish and gave them skins filled with air. When the Jews thirstily inhaled this air, their stomachs burst and they died.

Nevertheless, we see that Yishmael was considered an acceptable Jewish name in the Biblical and Talmudic periods. Aside from Avraham's son, we see other Bible figures named Yishmael in Tanach—Yishmael ben Nesanyahu (Jeremiah 40, *et al.*), Yishmael ben Pashchur (Ezra 10), Yishmael ben Atzeil (I Chronicles 8), Zevadyahu ben Yishmael (II Chronicles 19) and Yishmael ben Yehochanan (II Chronicles 23)—all Jewish! Plus there's the famous Rabbi Yishmael, whose accounting of Torah-study methodologies is recited every day as part of the morning service. Clearly, Yishmael was not always an unthinkable Jewish name, probably because our differences with the original Yishmael were ancient history.

So, will we ever be reconciled with our Arab cousins as our ancestor Yitzchak was reconciled with his brother Yishmael? I expect so, though there's not a lot that addresses this directly.

The aforementioned *Bava Basra* 16b illustrates that, while Yitzchak was reconciled with his brother Yishmael, Yaakov was not similarly reconciled with his brother Eisav, despite the Torah's account of a civil reunion. (Just as Yishmael is the biological and/or spiritual ancestor of the Arabs and the Muslims, respectively, Eisav—also known as Edom—is the biological and/or spiritual forebear of the Romans and, ostensibly, the Christian faiths.) Our messianic prophecies focus more on our eventual reconciliation with Edom than with Yishmael. For example, Obadiah 1:21 tells us that "saviors will ascend the mountain of Zion to judge the mountain of Eisav and the kingdom will be God's."

In fact, I only found one reference to the fate of Yishmael's descendants in messianic times. *Pirkei d'Rabbi Eliezer* (chapter 28) describes Avraham praying at the "covenant between the parts" (Genesis 15) that his descendants not be enslaved by four kingdoms: Edom, Persia, Babylonia and Yishmael. (It cites a verse referring to each of these empires that connects it to the verse in Genesis.) When discussing Yishmael, it says "upon whom the son of David (i.e., the Moshiach) will sprout." So here we have an oblique reference to the Moshiach overcoming the Arab nations; I have found literally nothing else.

Not that we need anything because the point of the messianic era isn't conquest, it's peace. Generally speaking we are told such things as "they will beat their swords into plowshares and their spears into pruninghooks; nation will not raise sword against nation and they will not practice war any longer" (Isaiah 2:4) and "on that day, Hashem will be One and His Name, One" (i.e., everyone will recognize God and worship Him—Zechariah 14:9).

So what will happen to Yishmael at the end of days? Presumably the same thing that will happen to everyone else. As we recite in the High Holidays prayers, "Then everyone (i.e., Jews and non-Jews) will form a cohesive unit to perform Your will with pure sincerity."

Jesus as Messiah

Q. *Why don't Jews accept Jesus as the messiah? Who was he according to Jewish texts?*

A. I always hesitate to answer questions like this in a public forum because I don't want to be misconstrued (or misrepresented) as "picking a fight" with our Christian neighbors. That's not at all what I'm doing when I answer such questions. Obviously, there are huge theological differences between our religions; if there weren't, we'd all be the same religion! So, I will explain why we Jews believe what we believe but this is just for the edification of Jews, or for others who care to know why we differ in these points. Jews don't proselytize so I have no interest in trying to convince Christians that they're wrong or that they should come around to our way of thinking.

I actually get asked this question, or variations of it, all the time from students in parochial schools and college comparative religion classes. Sometimes the students have trouble grasping that Jesus simply isn't a figure in Judaism at all and that the New Testament books of their Bible carry no significance for us. When they don't understand that, I ask them about the significance of Mohammed and the Quran in their religion. When they invariably tell me that there is none, I say, "Same thing."

So there's the answer to part 2 of your question. Who was Jesus according to Jewish texts? It's basically a non-issue because Jesus isn't a figure in Judaism.

There are some who will tell you that the Talmud talks about Jesus here and there but it's not really quite so clear that it does. There are two individuals who are popularly associated with Jesus: one was named ben Stada and the other was named ben Pandira. It's not 100% clear whether ben Stada and ben Pandira were the same person or two separate people and it's even less clear that either of them is supposed to be Jesus. The "evidence" that people like to cite in support of the theory is actually pretty flimsy and easily refuted. For example, the Talmud says that ben Stada's father was Pappos ben Yehuda. Pappos ben Yehuda lived about 100 years after Jesus is supposed to have lived. That being the case, ben Stada couldn't be Jesus. (If you accept the Talmud's hypothesis that ben Stada is also ben Pandira, that alone would be enough to knock the latter out of consideration, as well.) While the Talmud does record occasional debates with "*minim*" (early Christians who were actually apostate Jews), the Sages were probably more concerned with Zoroastrianism, which posed an existential threat, than they were with Christianity, which was still a relatively minor cult (in the original, technical sense of the word).

As far as why we don't accept Jesus as the messiah, it's simple enough: he doesn't fulfill the Biblical prophecies regarding what the Moshiach is supposed to accomplish, while the prophecies that they claim he did fulfill aren't actually prophecies at all.

The Bible tells us that, among other things, the messiah will rebuild the destroyed Temple, gather the dispersed exiles and return them to Israel, and unite the world in an era of peace. None of those things has yet happened. (Rebuilding the Temple would have been particularly tricky since it was still standing in Jesus' lifetime and would not be destroyed until about 35 years after his death.) Rambam, in detailing the laws of the Moshiach (*Hilchos Melachim* 11:4) explains that if a person we think might be the messiah dies without accomplishing these tasks, then we know he wasn't the one. The idea that the messiah might accomplish these things in a "second coming" is without Biblical support.

Conversely, the things that people say he fulfilled aren't really messianic prophecies. For example, the fact that Jesus was born in Bethlehem is irrelevant. Aside from the fact that lots of people are born in Bethlehem, that's not a messianic requirement. Rather, the messiah must be descended from King David; it's David who was born in Bethlehem.

Similarly, riding into Jerusalem on a donkey is neither an uncommon occurrence nor necessarily a messianic prophecy. While there are certainly those who understand it that way, others feel that the prophet Zechariah was describing Judah Maccabee (an interpretation I favor because Zechariah focuses heavily on the Hasmonean dynasty). Even those who consider it to be a messianic reference consider it only one potential scenario (*Sanhedrin* 98a).

The claim of a virgin birth actually works against the case for Jesus being the messiah. First of all, Isaiah 7:14 isn't a messianic prophecy at all (and even if it were, the word *alma* means "young woman," not a virgin). But aside from that, the messiah absolutely must be a direct patrilineal (i.e., father to son) descendant of Kings David and Solomon—that's requirement #1. If a person didn't have a human father, he couldn't be a patrilineal descendant of anyone.

There are many other such examples (not breaking a bone, suffering servant, original sin, etc.) but I don't intend to go through them one by one. The bottom line is that Jews don't accept Jesus as the messiah because he didn't do the things that Moshiach is supposed to do, while the things we're told that he did fulfill are not messianic prerequisites. (Again, I stress that my purpose is only to explain why Jews don't believe in Jesus. I am absolutely not trying to enter into a debate with Christians in order to persuade them.)

There is one relevant source about Jesus that I'd like to mention. Remember that, historically, the world was polytheistic and only the Jews were monotheists. Now, most of the world is monotheistic. The Rambam (*Melachim* 11:4 again) says that while we clearly don't agree with Christianity and Islam, Jesus and Mohammed served to turn huge swaths of the world's population towards monotheism, paving the way for the ultimate coming of Moshiach. So while we may not agree with Jesus as the end goal of the messianic process—honestly, he's completely irrelevant for Jews—we do understand him as an important step towards the messianic era for much of mankind.

NEW! Was Isaiah 53 Concealed Because It "Proves" That Jesus Was the Messiah?

Q. *Can you please tell me why Isaiah 53 was removed from the Hebrew Bible?*

A. It wasn't. We have Isaiah 53 in our Bibles, we just don't understand it the same way that some Christian religions might, i.e., as a messianic prophecy.

Isaiah 53 is what at least some Christian faiths refer to as "the suffering servant," and they take this chapter as a foretelling of Jesus. Jewish tradition disagrees with this. We don't see it as a messianic prophecy at all, let alone

one referring to Jesus.

The reason we don't see the chapter as a messianic prophecy is that, in the Jewish Bible, you'll find the messiah is referred to as a "servant" exactly zero times. (The prophet Ezekiel occasionally uses the phrase "My servant David" to refer to the Moshiach, as in 34:23 for example. Moshiach is a descendant of King David and it is David who is being referred to as God's servant.) Throughout the book of Isaiah, however, he repeatedly refers to the nation of Israel as the servant. This can be seen in the chapters leading up to Isaiah 53, such as Isaiah 41:8-9, 44:1-2, 45:4, 48:20, 49:3, all of which overtly call the nation of Israel the servant. Accordingly, this chapter would be speaking of punishments that would ultimately befall the nation.

Consider, if you will, Isaiah 53:4, in which we are told that the servant "bore our illnesses and carried our pains, yet we considered him as if plagued, smitten by God and oppressed." Now take a look at Jeremiah 30:17: "I will bring healing to you and I will cure you of your wounds, says Hashem, because they called you an outcast...." Thematically, they are very similar—*someone* has been injured and shunned. The similarity is because they're discussing the same event. But the chapter in Jeremiah spells out exactly who is being discussed. A few verses earlier, in Jeremiah 30:10, he addresses this prophecy to its recipient, saying "fear not, My servant Jacob, says Hashem, and do not be dismayed, Israel...." The victim of the injury and shunning is still the servant but here the servant is clarified as the nation of Israel.

Q. What I mean is that, previously, the chapter was read in the synagogues but it was decided by the Rabbis to stop reading it during the haftarah. It is about our Messiah, surely the most important person in all Scripture. What is the reason to remove it from the haftarah?

A. Your question is based on misinformation, erroneous assumptions and perhaps some outright lies that you may have read online. The charge is that we Jews "hid" this chapter because it represents a "slam dunk" for Christian theology. Of course, this is ridiculous.

There are 380 chapters in the books of the Prophets, about 75 of which are read as part of the synagogue service. Are the other 300+ chapters "hidden?" Of course not! This chapter is as published, translated and commented upon as any other. People are encouraged to pick up their Bibles; if they don't, that doesn't make the chapter hidden!

Isaiah 53 was never removed from the *haftaros* because Isaiah 53 was never a *haftarah* to begin with. The claim that it had previously been a *haftarah* is a mere assumption based on the fact that portions of Isaiah 52 and 54 are read as *haftaros*. These are part of the "seven weeks of consolation" that follow Tisha b'Av. The *haftaros* read on the seven weeks of consolation are: (1) Isaiah 40:1-26; (2) Isaiah 49:14-51:3; (3) Isaiah 54:11-55:5; (4) Isaiah 51:12-52:12; (5) Isaiah 54:1-10; (6) Isaiah 60:1-22; and (7) Isaiah 61:10-63:9. These *haftaros* skip around from Isaiah 40-63, skipping Isaiah 53, yes, but also chapters 42-48 and 55-59. You know why these chapters are skipped? Because they don't contain words of consolation! They simply don't fit the theme of the season's *haftaros*.

Compare this with the Dead Sea Scroll document 4Q176, also known as 4QTanhumin ("Tanhumin" meaning "consolations" in Hebrew). This document contains Isaiah 40:1-5, Isaiah 41:8-9, Isaiah 49:7, 13-17; Isaiah 43:1-2; Isaiah 43:4-6; Isaiah 51:22-23; and Isaiah 52:1-3, 54:4-10. Also no Isaiah 53! Is this proof of another "cover-up?" Clearly not, as these documents predate the dawn of Christianity by several hundred years! And yet Isaiah 53 and other chapters are once again omitted because they simply don't fit the theme.

You claim that Isaiah 53 is "about our Messiah…." As I mentioned in my first reply, Judaism does not understand that chapter to be a messianic prophecy. Even if it were, that would not be a reason to include or exclude it from the *haftaros*, which are based on thematic relevance to the week's Torah reading or, as in this instance, holidays.

The fact that Christians might understand a Bible chapter differently from Jews would not be a reason for us to discard it from our liturgy if it ever were a *haftarah*. To support that assertion, I refer you to Isaiah 9:5 (or 6, depending on the Bible version consulted): "For unto us a child has been born, a son given to us, and the authority is upon his shoulder, and the wondrous adviser, the mighty God, the everlasting Father, called his name 'the prince of peace.'" Christians understand this verse as a messianic prophecy, while Jews understand it to be referring to the birth of King Hezekiah (who had already been born, so it's not even a prophecy). Despite the fact that this verse is important in Christian theology and we understand it very differently, this verse *is* read in the *haftarah*. Similarly, if Isaiah 53 ever had been in, its significance in another religion would be immaterial to our liturgy.

Troubling Questions

Is God "Abusive?"

Q. Sometimes we see a fire-and-brimstone God and sometimes a softer God. Isn't a relationship where the other person is sometimes abusive and sometimes nice still an abusive relationship?

A. I agree with half your premise: if a spouse or parent (or anyone else) is nice 50% of the time and abusive 50% of the time, it is indeed an abusive relationship. But I have to disagree with the assumption that God is ever "abusive" to us. God's inherent goodness is a basic tenet of Judaism, as expressed in such verses as Psalms 92:16 ("...God is upright; He is my Rock and there is no injustice in Him"), II Chronicles 19:7 ("...with Hashem our God there is no unfairness, favoritism or corruption"), Deuteronomy 32:4 ("He is a faithful God; there is no injustice in Him"), *et al.*

Sure, sometimes God can be strict with us, but that's not the same as being abusive. It's like a parent who disciplines a child. When the child gets out of line, the parent may have to respond with a time-out, grounding, or even corporal punishment. (I'm not a fan of spanking *per se* but if a child runs into the street, a swift "*potch*" may be called for in order to discourage such impulsive behavior. Such "tough love" is completely for the child's protection.)

Someone once objected to an article I wrote in which I compared the way God disciplines us to the way we're supposed to discipline our children. "I'm not a child and I don't need to be disciplined," he wrote.

First of all, such an attitude is supremely arrogant; a human child is a lot closer intellectually to a human adult than a person of any age is to God! A child also thinks that he should be able to do whatever he wants without consequences but a parent knows that doing certain things could have a negative impact on a child physically, emotionally or ethically. For this reason, we punish them if they eat too much candy, visit age-inappropriate web sites or shoplift. Similarly, God knows that certain things are bad for us spiritually and He dissuades us accordingly.

Second of all, it's not even my simile—it's Moshe Rabbeinu's! In Deuteronomy 8:5 he says, "…just as a man chastises his son, so Hashem your God chastises you." This sentiment is echoed by King Solomon: Proverbs 3:12 says, "God chastises the one He loves, just as a father does to a son in whom he delights."

That being the case, it's not abusive to punish us in an attempt to direct us back onto the straight-and-narrow. If anything, not being strict when we need it might be considered neglectful parenting! Proverbs 13:24 tells us that "One who spares his rod hates his son; one who loves him disciplines him when necessary." What would you say if your neighbors permitted their kids to run wild at all hours of the day and night without any parental intervention? You'd call Child Services! Once again, God applies the same standard to us as we should apply to our smaller, less-developed humans. Not stepping in would be the irresponsible thing!

There can be many reasons why God permits unpleasant things to occur to us. These include (but are not limited to): to test us so that we know what we are capable of; to punish us for our misdeeds; to keep us from dangerous situations; to motivate us to examine our deeds and change our ways. The entire Book of Job is an examination of the question of why righteous people suffer, a phenomenon not even Moses could fully comprehend (Talmud, *Brachos* 7a, based on Exodus 33:13). Nevertheless, King Solomon tells us that it is a joyous occasion when God punishes a righteous person in order to correct his ways (see Rashi and other commentaries on Proverbs 21:15).

We may not always intuit the reasons for our trials but we should always be confident that, whatever the reason, they are for our ultimate good, as per Deuteronomy 8:16, "…that He might afflict you and test you, which would be for your own benefit in the future."

Fearing God

Q. *It seems a little scary to fear God. How am I supposed to have a good relationship with a Being of Whom I'm terrified?*

A. This is not an uncommon question. The problem here boils down to one of linguistics. I'll illustrate.

In my capacity as an editor, I have long imposed a moratorium on the adjective "awesome." The original meaning of "awesome" was "extremely impressive or daunting; inspiring great admiration, apprehension, or fear." The power of God, for example, is awesome. One might say that the majesty of the Grand Canyon is awesome, though I, personally, would prefer "awe-inspiring." If you say that your sandwich is "awesome," that tells me nothing about the sandwich, though it does tell me that you have an incredibly low threshold for awe. Through overuse, the word has gotten watered down, so if anyone wrote an article that an event was awesome and everyone had an awesome time, I would send it back so that they could use adjectives that actually tell me something.

Similarly, you're working under the assumption that "fear of God" means to be in terror of God. It doesn't. This assumes that the translation of *yirah* is properly "fear" and that the meaning of "fear" when the Bible was translated hundreds of years ago was the same as it is today. As with "awesome," a lot of water has gone under that bridge over the years and the way we read it may not reflect the intention of what was written. When I write about this obligation, I prefer to translate *yirah* as "reverence" rather than "fear."

The mitzvah to "fear" (i.e., revere) God is conceptually similar to another mitzvah: the obligation to "fear" our parents (Leviticus 19:3). Do you really think that we're meant to be in terror when our parents enter the room? That we should cower under the kitchen table? Clearly not. Rather, the intention is that we defer to them. This means things like we don't contradict our parents or sit in their designated places.

Before we are commanded to "fear" (revere) God, we are commanded to love Him (Deuteronomy 6:5). This mitzvah requires us to familiarize ourselves with God and His works. If we get to know Him, we won't be able to help but love Him. This love will then arouse us to tell others all about Him.

Later (Deuteronomy 10:20), we are commanded to "fear" (revere) God. The *Sefer HaChinuch* explains this mitzvah as follows: The best thing for us to do is to perform *mitzvos* from a love of God. An awareness that He loves us and gave us the Torah in order to benefit us should be all that's necessary to motivate us to do His will. Nevertheless, human nature being what it is, sometimes a carrot isn't enough. Sometimes we need a stick. Because of this reality, a healthy "fear" can be an effective deterrent to wrongdoing. Having this "fear" of God is intended to help keep us from straying off the proper path.

Let's use the police as a metaphor. Assuming that we are not actively committing or concealing a crime, most of us can walk down the street and pass a cop on the beat without experiencing the rapid heartbeat, sweating or trembling that one might experience upon passing a street gang or a vicious dog.[6] Sometimes, we actively seek out the police, such as to report a crime. Children's television may have taught us "The policeman is your friend" but if we see a police cruiser, we're going to slow our cars down or not roll through that changing traffic light. This isn't because most of us are terrified of the police (certain exceptions notwithstanding), it's because seeing them reminds us that our misdeeds can have consequences. This causes us to act with extra caution.

That's what "fear" of God is for. We're supposed to get to know Him and to love Him. And if humans were perfect, that would be all we need. But humans aren't perfect. Therefore, we sometimes need to see the

---

6. A lot has happened since this was originally written and I recognize that it might no longer jibe with some readers' impressions of the police. One might mentally edit the analogy by replacing the police with other authority figures, such as rabbis, doctors or high school principals, though I don't think they convey the same shared experience of slowing down simply because we see a police cruiser. I must, however, acknowledge the painful reality that there are communities that are scared of the police, and rightfully so.

police car to remind us to slow down and to stop at the light. Terror is not required, nor is it desirable.

Honoring Bad Parents

Q. *The Torah tells us to honor our parents but what is one to do when they're not good parents? If a child is neglected or even hated by his mother, how is he to honor her?*

A. It's an unfortunate reality that there are some bad parents out there. Some are well-meaning but ineffective. Others may be neglectful, negligent, or outright abusive. However, the Torah's definition of honor is pretty narrow. The Torah does not require us to love our parents, or even to like our parents; it only requires that we respect them. We owe them this much for providing the gift of life even if their parenting skills are otherwise wanting.

I'll give you a non-parent example. Let's say for the sake of argument that I had some major issues with a sitting president. Be that as it may, when I meet him, I wouldn't scream at him about the economy or his foreign policy. I would speak to him respectfully because that's what the office deserves regardless of what I may think of the person who holds that office. The same is true with parents.

The Torah requires that we not contradict our parents. We may not sit in their designated spots. If they ask us to do something, we do it. If we must disagree or refuse a request, we must do so politely, without raising our voices. These are ways in which we respect our parents; they are things that can be done even if a parent is aloof or not a particularly pleasant individual. We are not required to shower our parents with kisses and affection.

There are some nations that may never marry into the Jewish people because of the way they treated us. These include Ammon and Moav but, surprisingly, not Egypt. Regarding Egypt, the Torah says, "you shalt not reject an Egyptian because you were a stranger in his land" (Deuteronomy 23:8). Egypt's crimes against the Jews, with the slavery and the oppression, were far greater than those of Ammon and Moav but, unlike Ammon and

Moav, we owe Egypt a debt of gratitude for taking us in during the time of Joseph. Things later went awry, but that doesn't erase the good that they did for us. Similarly, when a parent ignores or mistreats a child, it cuts deeper than the same misdeed would when perpetrated by someone else. Nevertheless, it doesn't change the fact that they also have done good for us, by giving us life if nothing else.

It should be noted that there are times when we may, or even must, disagree with our parents. For example, one is not obligated to marry a suitor that their parent prefers, nor is one required to live where their parents prefer they live. If one's parent wants him to violate the Torah (say, "Drive me to bingo Friday night" or "Here, eat this BLT I made you"), one is obligated to decline. This is because, while we must listen to our parents, both we and our parents must listen to God. (Sergeants outrank privates but privates, sergeants, captains and colonels all must listen to the Commander-in-Chief.) Refusal must be polite, however, never raising one's voice and certainly not a hand.

Honoring a parent is a difficult mitzvah, even when the parent and the child have a good relationship. It's all the more complicated when relations are strained. God knows how hard it can be, but He wouldn't ask it of us if it couldn't be done. For this reason, the Torah promises rich spiritual rewards for the performance of this mitzvah, as per Exodus 20:11, "Honor your father and mother so that your days may be long upon the land that Hashem your God gives to you."

Sacrificing Children

Q. *When learning about akeidas Yitzchak (the binding of Isaac), my daughter asked me what I would do if God asked me to sacrifice her like He asked Avraham to sacrifice Yitzchak. How do you respond to such a question?*

A. I'm going to say that, should God command such a thing of you, you should not do it. That's not to say that Avraham was wrong for acting as he did. Quite the opposite—we see that he was right since God praises and rewards him! It's just that you're not Avraham. When God spoke to Avraham, it was prophecy. I promise you that I'm not trying to sound glib but if you ever think that God is speaking to you, you're having a psychotic break. We'll come back to that part soon.

For starters, God wouldn't ask us to perform human sacrifice. He didn't even really ask it of Avraham as it was a test! (All He asked Avraham to do was to "bring Isaac up as a sacrifice," which Avraham actually accomplished.) This was a test because, among other reasons, it's a known fact that God hates human sacrifice in general and child sacrifice in particular. We see this in many places. For example, Molech is singled out from other forms of idolatry as being particularly heinous because it involved child sacrifice, or at the very least child endangerment. See also II Kings chapter 3. There, the king of Moav saw that he was being defeated in battle. He tried to break through to attack the king of Edom, but he was unable, so he made the bold move of sacrificing his son. The human sacrifice had the effect of arousing God's anger, which is generally the opposite intention one has when offering a sacrifice. It's also unclear whether the Judge Yiftach (Jephthah) actually sacrificed his daughter in Judges chapter 11 or merely sanctified her so that she never married but, either way, he is criticized by the Sages and, despite his military prowess, is not remembered fondly because of it. So, when God asked it of Avraham, it was a pretty good test. If He asked it of you, you'd have the precedent of *akeidas Yitzchak* to know what to expect.

The bigger issue is that Avraham was a prophet. God spoke to him and there was no doubt about the matter. If you think that God is speaking to you—by which I mean directly and audibly—again, I do not mean to be glib, but you should go to the ER and check yourself in because something is seriously wrong.

I know that, despite my insistence that I'm not trying to be funny, some people will think that I'm making light of mental illness. I promise you that I'm not. Imagine a co-worker saying to you over coffee, in all sincerity, that God appeared to them and gave them personal instructions. This represents a serious break from reality even from the perspective of those (like me) who believe in the Bible and the prophets. Let's explore why that is.

Even in Biblical times, God never just appeared to random people with messages. The gift of prophecy was something that people had to work hard to achieve. There were even schools where one could study for prophecy, without any guarantee that he would ever receive it. So, even in the time of Avraham, Moshe or David, a lay person's claim to have received a prophecy would have been dubious to say the least. This is all the more so now that prophecy has ceased.

Let's discuss how, why and when prophecy ceased. First, one must accept that, in Biblical times, there was an incredible drive for idolatry that we cannot understand. It was comparable to the sex drive that we understand all too well. In Talmud *Sanhedrin* (102b), King Menashe, an infamous idolator, appeared to Rav Ashi in a dream and informed him, "If you had lived in my day, you'd have picked up the hem of your garment to run after idolatry." With this context in mind, the Talmud in *Sanhedrin* (64a) describes how the Men of the Great Assembly bargained with Heaven to remove the temptation for idolatry. It didn't disappear altogether but they got it under a reasonable amount of control. (They also tried to conquer the sexual urge but they quickly discovered that we need that to propagate the species.)

Until this time, there had been two opposing forces: the lure of idolatry and the prophets whom God sent to combat it. With the overpowering temptation to worship idols gone, it was no longer a level playing field, so prophecy had to go, too. (See *Seder Olam Rabbah* 30 and the commentary of the Gra there.) The last prophets were Chaggai, Zachariah and Malachi, who were members of the Great Assembly. After that, there was no more overt prophecy, though there was (and is) still Divine inspiration. The Talmud in *Bava Basra* (12b) tells us that the only ones who speak with prophecy nowadays are children and people lacking mental competence (meaning that they occasionally utter truths they logically shouldn't know). So, as suspect as a lay person claiming to be a prophet would have been in Biblical times, such a claim would be completely untenable now.

So, I say that you should ignore any such commands that you may imagine you receive because (1) God hates human sacrifice. Counter-intuitive orders may have been a good test for Avraham but it's only a test if you don't know what to expect; (2) Even in Biblical times, rank-and-file people like you and me did not receive random prophecies; and (3) Prophecy is currently gone so that no one is receiving messages directly from God like Avraham did.

This is not to say that God doesn't speak to us; He absolutely does but it's not so overt. He speaks to us through the things that happen in our lives. If your car breaks down and your washing machine overflows and your smoke detector battery dies on Shabbos causing it to chirp all night long, there's a message in there. (I don't know what that message is; it's up to you to unravel it.) But there are certain things He does tell us unambiguously: these are in the Torah. They include not offer sacrifices outside the Temple and not to murder. Those are two good reasons to set your daughter's mind at rest right now. Yes, God could tell prophets to violate Torah law (Elijah sacrificing on Mount Carmel, for example) but we need not concern ourselves with such things because we're not prophets and, nowadays, neither is anybody else.

Financial Inequity Toward Non-Jews

Q. *The halacha that we don't have to return lost money to a non-Jew has always bothered me. Maybe I could see it making sense in a society where non-Jews are anti-Semitic but does it also apply when non-Jews treat us nicely?*

A. There is a concept called reciprocity. What this means is that the parties in question extend equal courtesies to one another. For example, there isn't one US driver's license. Rather, all fifty states issue their own licenses based on different criteria. Nevertheless, the fact that I have a New York State driver's license doesn't limit me to driving in New York. This is because the states have reciprocity in this matter. People with New York licenses can drive in Seattle, Juneau, Memphis and Tallahassee, while licensed drivers who live in those cities can drive in New York (as well as in one another). Now imagine if New York suddenly announced, "We expect you other states to continue honoring our licenses but we're not going to honor yours anymore." I imagine that such an announcement would not go over very well with the other 49 states and they probably wouldn't agree to it. This is because doing so would make them patsies.[7] The same concept applies in *mitzvos*.

Jew have 613 *mitzvos*. Non-Jews are subject to the seven universal laws that were commanded to all mankind through Noah after the flood. Now, really, these are seven categories so there are more than seven individual laws; there are more like thirty. But no matter how you slice it, Jews have *wayyyyy* more *mitzvos* than non-Jews. This means that a small percentage of *mitzvos* apply to both Jews and non-Jews while a large percentage apply to Jews alone.

When *mitzvos* apply to both Jews and non-Jews, the concept of reciprocity applies. Jews are not allowed to kidnap non-Jews and non-Jews are not allowed to kidnap Jews. Non-Jews are not allowed to steal from Jews and Jews are not allowed to steal from non-Jews. It's a two-way street.

But what about when *mitzvos* apply to Jews alone? Let's take the prohibition against charging interest as an example. (This is the area where people typically voice objections to what they perceive to be inequity.) The Torah separately prohibits both lending with interest and borrowing with interest. But these *mitzvos* very clearly apply only to Jews. Regarding loans between Jews, Leviticus 25:36 says, "Take no interest or profit from him; fear God so that your brother may live with you." The words "your brother" specify that this only applies to Jews. If that weren't explicit enough, Deuteronomy 23:20-21 says, "You shall not lend with interest to your brother—not money, food or anything else that could be lent with interest. You may lend to an outsider with interest but to your brother you may not lend with interest."

Some people mistakenly think it's unfair that Jews can't lend to other Jews with interest but they can lend to non-Jews with interest but in fact it's very fair. This is because Jews can neither borrow nor lend to other Jews with interest but they can both borrow from and lend to non-Jews with interest. So if Moishe lends to Patrick, Moishe can charge Patrick interest, and if Patrick lends to Moishe, Patrick can charge Moishe interest. The relationship between Moishe and Patrick is fair and equitable; neither one has the upper hand. What would be unfair is if only one party could charge

---

7. Patsy—a person who is easily taken advantage of.

interest of the other. If Jews didn't charge interest to non-Jews but were charged interest by them, then we'd be patsies.

Now, when you talk about not returning lost property to non-Jews, that's an area in which the concept of reciprocity does not apply because non-Jews are not obligated to return lost property that they find. Jews are obligated to return found objects to their owners but, once again, the Torah limits this responsibility to other Jews. Deuteronomy 22:3 says, "so shall you do with every lost item of your brother, which he has lost and you have found."

This provides the conceptual reason not to return lost property to non-Jews: because they're not obligated to return it to Jews. If it's a one-way street, you're a patsy. But the *halacha* in actual practice has many more shades of gray than that.

The *Shulchan Aruch* (*Choshen Mishpat* 266:1) describes this law as follows:

> The lost property of an idolator is permitted (to be kept) since the Torah specifies "the lost property of your brother" (Deut. 22:3). One who returns it violates a prohibition because he strengthens the position of sinners. If one returns it in order to make a *kiddush Hashem* (a sanctification of God's Name), so that they will glorify Israel and know that they are people of faith, then it is praiseworthy to do so. In a place where (keeping the lost property would be) a *chillul Hashem* (a desecration of God's Name), it is forbidden to keep his lost property and he is obligated to return it. And in every situation, one is required to bring in (i.e., safeguard) their property as one does the property of Jews, in order to promote peaceful relations.

Now you will notice that I translated the piece above to say "idolators" rather than "non-Jews." That's because (a) it actually says "idolators" and (b) *Be'er HaGolah* on this *halacha* says that the piece of Talmud from which it is derived (*Sanhedrin* 76b) only refers to the non-Jews of the time, who were literal idolators. It does not apply to modern non-Jews, who recognize God (albeit differently than we do) rather than idols of wood and stone. When it comes to modern non-Jews, the *Be'er HaGolah* says, it is appropriate to return lost property.

So the idea that one shouldn't return lost property to non-Jews really only applies to idolators because doing so strengthens their position, which is detrimental to our own. To make a sanctification of God's Name, returning lost property to non-Jews is praiseworthy and to avoid making a desecration of God's Name, doing so is mandatory. While one could infer the answer, this doesn't directly address your question about times and places in which the non-Jews treat the Jews nicely. For this, let us turn to, of all places, the book of Psalms.

Psalms 15:5 says, "He has never lent his money with interest...." The Radak there comments as follows:

> ... David (the author of Psalms) ... only prohibits what the Torah prohibits, and the Torah only prohibits (lending with interest) when it comes to Jews. It is permitted in the case of non-Jews, as it says, "You may lend to an outsider with interest" (Deut. 23:21). This is not the case with robbery, theft, causing a loss[8] and oppressing someone; it is prohibited to oppress, rob or steal even from a non-Jew. Interest, however, which is given with his knowledge and consent, is permitted. A Jew is obligated to show kindness to his fellow Jew, and lending without interest is a form of kindness and a favor. Sometimes this is an even greater favor than a gift because people often hesitate to accept a gift more than they would a loan. This is not the case between Jews and non-Jews. We are not obligated to extend kindness or to lend them money for free because, generally speaking, they hate Jews. But if a non-Jew treats a Jew with kindness and favor, the Jew is obligated to return the kindness and do him favors in return.

---

8. The Radak here uses the word *aveidah*, which could be understood to mean a lost object, but since that does not reflect the basic *halacha*, I have chosen not to translate it that way.

So the bar for returning lost objects to non-Jews is incredibly low—the non-Jew not being an idolator is sufficient for that. Living in a time and place where non-Jews get along with Jews and treat them neighborly is sufficient reason even to forgo charging interest. So we're not required by the Torah to do these things in all times and places because of the lack of reciprocity but when such behavior is appropriate, it is permitted, praiseworthy or even obligatory to go beyond the baseline set by the Torah.

Lying

Q. *I know that George Washington once said, "I cannot tell a lie." Is that the Jewish approach or is lying justified sometimes?*

A. As the story goes, young George Washington once chopped down a cherry tree with his hatchet. When his father confronted him and asked who did it, George responded with "I cannot tell a lie" and confessed to the deed. This legend is an invention—it never happened! Nevertheless, it still contains an important lesson. How so? I'll explain with a story:

The Chofetz Chaim was once called upon to serve as a character witness in a court case. When asked the Chofetz Chaim's qualifications, the lawyer proceeded to relate stories of the rabbi's great piety. Those familiar with such "rebbe stories" know that they tend to be a little over-the-top. Accordingly, the judge asked the lawyer, "You don't really believe all that, do you?"

"No," the lawyer replied, "but they don't tell such stories about you and me."

Now I don't know if this courtroom drama ever actually occurred—and I know George Washington never chopped down a cherry tree—but the accuracy of such histories is immaterial. The Chofetz Chaim had a reputation for piety and George Washington had a reputation for honesty. This is why stories such as these "have legs."

As far as the position of honesty in Judaism, I can say without fear of contradiction that it is one of the most highly treasured values.

The Sages demonstrated the value of truth through some clever wordplay. In Hebrew, truth is *emes*; falsehood is *sheker*. *Emes* is spelled *alef mem sav* and *sheker* is spelled *shin kuf reish*. The letters of *emes* are the first letter (*alef*), the middle letter (*mem*) and the last (*sav*), demonstrating that truth is all-encompassing; it runs the gamut from A to Z. The letters of *sheker* are three consecutive letters at the end of the alphabet, illustrating that falsehood is marginalized.

Not only that, the letters that make up *emes* all have two legs or a solid base; if they were three-dimensional, they could stand. The letters that make up *sheker* all have one leg or a point for their base; if they were solid, they would tip over. This demonstrates that the truth can stand on its own but falsehood, if not propped up, collapses.

So much for the clever wordplay. Let's look at some nitty gritty:

- The Torah (Exodus 23:7) tells us, "Distance yourself from falsehood."
- Jeremiah 10:10 says, "Hashem, God, is truth." (We echo this sentiment by attaching the word *emes* to the words "Hashem, your God" at the end of the recitation of *Shema*).
- The Talmud (*Shabbos* 55a) reports that "the seal of God is truth."
- The Talmud (*Sotah* 42a) also lists liars among those who will not merit to greet God's Presence.

Here's an example of how far one must carry truth. Let's say that there are three lenders; we'll call them Abraham, Isaac and Jacob. And they all have the same borrower; we'll call him Moe.

Let's say that Moe borrowed $1,000 each from Abraham, Isaac and Jacob, and he didn't repay any of them. There are no witnesses and no paperwork. If Abraham, Isaac or Jacob takes Moe to *beis din* (the Jewish court), it's one man's word against the other's. The burden of proof is on the one trying to collect and, in such a situation, it's unlikely that any of the litigants would be able to recover their money.

Now let's say that Abraham takes Moe to court and claims that Moe borrowed $3,000 from him alone; Isaac and Jacob appear as witnesses substantiating his claim. In this manner, Abraham can easily collect $3,000 from Moe, recover his $1,000 and repay Isaac and Jacob the money they borrowed as well.

This is completely prohibited. One is not permitted to lie even to reach a just outcome (Talmud, *Shevuos* 31a).

Nevertheless, there are situations in which it is, in fact, permitted to lie—and we learn this from God Himself!

When God told Avraham and Sarah that they would have a child (in Genesis chapter 18), Sarah laughed, saying that she and her husband were too old. When God related Sarah's words to Avraham, He only mentioned that Sarah said that she was old. God selectively edited Sarah's words to prevent Avraham from being embarrassed and getting upset at Sarah. We learn from this that a "white lie" is permitted to promote *shalom bayis* (peace in the home—Talmud, *Yevamos* 65b).

This was also the *modus operandi* of Aaron, brother of Moshe. *Avos d'Rabbi Nosson* (chapter 12) details how Aaron would make peace between feuding friends. He would approach each party separately and tell them that the other person was sorry and wanted to make up. Aaron was so beloved because of this that the nation mourned his passing even more than they did that of Moshe, their great leader! (See Rashi on Numbers 20:29 and Deuteronomy 34:8.)

There are other situations in which one might tell a white lie. These include concealing one's own accomplishments for the sake of humility, protecting others from embarrassment, and saving people from trouble or inconvenience. Nevertheless, there are parameters. For example, one should try to avoid uttering an outright untruth; it is preferable to tell a "half-truth" (as God did when He merely omitted half of Sarah's statement). Similarly, one should only use this tactic when absolutely necessary. (There are other permitted scenarios and other parameters for their usage. This is not the place for an exhaustive overview of all the laws.)

So we see that truth is extremely important, so much so that one cannot lie in court even to reach a just verdict. Nevertheless, white lies that make peace and hurt no one are permitted. I think that even Presidents George Washington (who could not tell a lie) and "Honest Abe" Lincoln would be okay with that.

Opinion Shopping

Q. Is there a way to feel out a rabbi's opinion on something before committing to following their psak?

A. You've probably heard that one is not permitted to "shop around" for a *psak* (ruling) that one likes; rather, one should have a rav whose positions one follows consistently. But what's the source for this?

Let us turn to tractate *Pesachim*, page 52b. There, we are told that if one brought sabbatical-year produce from Israel to elsewhere, it is to be burned in that other place. We are then given a dissenting opinion from Rabbi Shimon ben Elazar that one must return to Israel and burn it there.

The Gemara then shares an incident in which Rav Safra brought barrels of sabbatical-year wine from Israel to another land. He asked his traveling companions, Rav Huna and Rav Kahana, how their teacher Rav Avahu ruled on this matter—leniently like the first opinion or stringently like Rabbi Shimon ben Elazar. Rav Kahana said that Rav Avahu ruled stringently like Rabbi Shimon ben Elazar, while Rav Huna said that Rav Avahu ruled leniently like the first opinion. Rav Safra decided to rely on Rav Huna's more lenient opinion, saying that Rav Huna is known to be meticulous about what he learns from his teacher. Rav Yoseif, however, disagreed with Rav Safra "shopping" for opinions in this way. He applied to Rav Safra the verse from Hoshea (4:12), "My nation asks advice of its wood, and its staff gives it to them." The word *maklo* (its staff) is understood as referring to one who is *meikil* (lenient), i.e., to people who gladly accept any lenient ruling they hear.

We don't need to defend Rav Avahu from Rav Yoseif's criticism; Rav Avahu was qualified to rule on matters of *halacha* and, as noted, the lenient opinion was expressed by Rav Huna, who was known to be meticulous in reporting the words of his teacher. The question does apply to the rest of us, who are not qualified to rule in matters of Jewish law. When presented with differing opinions, do we automatically leap straight for the lenient one? If so, that would certainly qualify for Rav Yoseif's disapproval, as expressed through this Biblical verse.

Elsewhere, we discussed the Talmudic dictum that one who always follows the lenient position is considered wicked, while one who always follows the stringent position is considered a fool (*Chullin* 43b-44a). Rather, one should make an intellectually honest investigation of a matter and follow whatever is the objective outcome. For our purposes that means having a rav and following that person's opinion consistently.

To give a real-life example, I am a big fan of the Halachic Organ Donor Society. A person can elect to have organs removed after the irreversible cessation of autonomous breathing, as confirmed by brain-stem death, or only after the irreversible cessation of heartbeat. My HODS card has the box checked for irreversible cessation of heartbeat (which is the more stringent position). This may limit the number of organs that might be used but it reflects the opinion of the halachic authority I consulted on the matter. Many authorities—probably most—agree that the irreversible cessation of autonomous breathing (i.e., the more lenient position) constitutes the moment of death. So I must act according to the *psak* that I received but I don't want others to follow me blindly. Everyone should investigate such matters with their own rabbi and not simply copy what others do, no matter how good-looking we might be.

That doesn't mean that a person can only have one rav. It is possible to have people that one consults on particular areas of expertise, such as matters of family purity. I have experts whom I consult on funereal matters and conversion issues. This is not because I expect these people to give me more lenient rulings, it's because they are experts in the intricacies of various areas of law.

Everyone is encouraged to find a rav whose approach speaks to them. If one is more inclined towards leniencies or stringencies, it's fine to accept upon oneself a rav whose rulings are in line with one's own tendencies. (It must be reiterated that, despite general tendencies towards lenient or strict, every ruling must be made in its own merits and not simply because it's lenient or strict.) It's also perfectly legitimate to have more than one rav and to consult with different authorities on different areas of *halacha* but that should be done because of the authority's expertise and not because it's a foregone conclusion that a certain person will necessarily tell you what you want to hear. However, if an authority is merely known to lean to the side of leniency, it's okay to ask him because his answer to your particular question might surprise you by being stringent. In all cases, though, once a question has been asked and an answer has been given, it is not permitted to seek a more lenient "second opinion."

Finally, to answer the question you actually asked, you could "feel out" a rabbi's opinion on a question by saying, "I'm not asking you to *poskin* but, hypothetically speaking, what would you say if…?" But to ask a rabbi his opinion, then ask another rabbi his opinion—even if one isn't asking them to *poskin per se*—would still seem to be the "leniency shopping" criticized by the prophet Hoshea.

Marrying a Rapist and Selling a Daughter

Q. *I heard that the Torah says that a woman must marry her rapist and that a father can sell his daughter into slavery? How can we possibly accept such horrible ideas in the modern world?*

A. It is true that not everything in the Torah is in line with the "modern sensibilities" of every time and culture. (Gay marriage is a perfect example.) However, people cast more aspersions than are called for, largely because they don't fully understand the parameters of the Torah's cases.

The idea that the victim of a rape must marry her attacker is one of the most misunderstood things in the Torah—and not without reason! In our day and age, it's virtually inconceivable that a woman would want to marry her rapist. Such, however, was not necessarily the case throughout history. There have been many eras and cultures where a woman who had been raped would have severely limited marriage options—and with marriage came a better chance for survival. (Also, the rape didn't have to be an attack by a stranger. Even nowadays, women are "date raped" by boyfriends or significant others, and they may choose to stay with them despite the trauma.) I have had to clarify this mitzvah many times over the years because people's assumptions about it are just plain wrong. It's all based on a faulty understanding of Deuteronomy chapter 22.

In the Torah's scenario, the man has abused the girl. He is the criminal and she is innocent of any wrongdoing. But as noted, in certain times and places this might severely limit the girl's marriage prospects. Accordingly, if the girl so desires, the attacker must marry her and he can never divorce her. The girl, on the other hand, is under no obligation to marry him. The rapist forfeits his choice in the matter through his actions; the victim retains her freedom to choose. (The mistaken idea that a girl has no choice in whom she marries is wrong on many levels. For example, if such were the case, all a rejected suitor would have to do is rape the object of his affections and she would be obligated to marry him. Happily, such is not the case.)

It is equally misunderstood that the Torah permits a man to "sell" his daughter into "slavery" (Exodus 21). Actually, that's not it at all. If a man becomes impoverished, what he can do is to betroth his daughter to a man as a bride, either for that man or for that man's son. What this does is give the girl a chance at a better life. The girl cannot be treated any differently from a wife that was married by any other means (21:9-10) and if the man (or his son) does not marry her, he must release her from her end of the arrangement (21:8). This is all explicit in the text—people just don't take the time to understand what the text means!

Before you get upset thinking that the Torah advocates child brides, let me disabuse you of that notion. First, it helps to know the following (but it's kind of technical so feel free to skip to the next paragraph): Marriage in Jewish law takes place in two stages. The first is called *eirusin*, which we translate as betrothal. This is more than engagement: a girl who is betrothed is considered married even though the wedding has not been consummated. If a couple calls it quits after *eirusin*, the woman requires a *get* (a bill of divorce) and she cannot marry a *kohein* because she's a divorcee, even though she may still be a virgin.

The girl in our case was betrothed as a minor. In some cases, she has the right to refuse the match until she reaches the age of majority; this is called *mi'un* (refusal). Here's what's truly exceptional: the girl can dissolve the union unilaterally, without a *get*, and she is not considered a divorcee. This is the only case in Judaism in which a marriage can be annulled altogether, making it as if the *eirusin* never even occurred. (There are limits to the situations in which *mi'un* could be used, such as when the girl was married off by her family after her father's death and a few other scenarios. It may not completely satisfy objections based on modern sensibilities but introducing the concept, on top of some other facts about this scenario, helps to show that what's going on here isn't what most people assume. In reality, things are far more nuanced.)

So, yes, there are things in the Torah that we must struggle to understand. But many of the things that people assume are misogynistic or otherwise "politically incorrect" are the result of not fully understanding what's going on. Often, the strange-appearing behavior is actually for the woman's benefit, as in obligating the rapist to marry his victim only if she so desires. In many cases, learning the full story answers objections before they even arise.

The Sotah

Q: *The mitzvah of sotah has always bothered me because only the woman is shamed, while there's no such shaming for the man who is suspected. I'm also troubled that the Torah gives a husband power to suspect his wife but not the other way around. How can we accept such inequity?*

A. People often have issues with the case of the *sotah*—the woman suspected of adultery in Numbers chapter 5. They envision the woman being dragged to the Temple by a jealous husband, her mouth held open while they force feed her the "bitter waters," and then she explodes. So much of this is wrong. First of all, the husband wasn't randomly jealous. He suspected his wife of impropriety and warned her against being secluded with a particular man. She then violated this warning by being secluded with that man, creating a situation of mistrust. Nevertheless, she was not compelled to undergo the *sotah* process. She could choose to do so in order to prove her innocence (or if she thought she could "beat the rap"), but she could also opt out, which would be tantamount to pleading "no contest." A woman was only compelled to drink the water once the document containing the Name of God was erased, close to the end of the process. If she was guilty, she wouldn't explode on the spot, she would waste away over the course of a year or two, depending on her merits—and, according to the Talmud, the adulterer would also die, wherever he was.

Please note what the woman drank: it was just some water with a little dust sprinkled on it. It wasn't poison. Despite the name, it wasn't even bitter! If the woman died as a consequence of the ceremony, it was a supernatural punishment. And there was a supernatural reward if she was innocent and falsely suspected—she was guaranteed to conceive. This is the only place where God promises to supernaturally judge court cases Himself. If one believes in the divinity of the Torah, how can one complain about the punishment, as it comes directly from God? If one doesn't believe in the divinity of the Torah, there's no punishment to complain about! She just drinks the water and goes home—nothing would ever happen as a consequence.

Was the woman shamed by having to go through the process? Yes, but this was not completely unfair. After all, even if she was innocent of adultery, she was still guilty of being secluded with the man about whom her husband had had suspicions.

So why wasn't the suspected adulterer forced to undergo a process similar to that of the woman? Simple enough: a husband can warn his wife about seclusion with men about whom he has suspicions, but he has no authority to warn those men about their behavior. He can take his wife to the Temple and divorce her if she refuses but even if he knows who the man is and is able to find him, there's no reason the suspected adulterer would agree to accompany him. It's simply impractical to expect the suspected adulterer to get on board with this process, while the woman has motivation to participate. But, as noted, if the couple is guilty, the adulterer would also suffer the punishment.

You are correct that a married man wouldn't be guilty of adultery for having relations with an unmarried woman. That's because polygamy was permitted; it's not adultery in *halacha* if the woman is unmarried. (After all, she could marry this man!) The question is, why was polygamy permitted? This was for practical reasons, which were actually for the woman's benefit! Let's say that Israel went to war against Aram and 100,000 Jewish soldiers were killed. This would create a huge *shidduch* crisis and many women would be unable to find mates. The option of polygamy reduced this concern. Similarly, the Talmud Yerushalmi (*Yevamos* 4:12) describes how, during a famine, Rabbi Tarfon (who was a *kohein*) married 300 women strictly in order to enable them to eat *terumah* (which was only permitted to *kohanim* and their dependents).

It should be noted the Torah specifically prohibits a man from taking on additional wives if it would reduce an existing wife's standard of living. Of course, polygamy has since been banned but even when it was permitted, it was never the preferred arrangement.

It might interest you to know that the *sotah* process was discontinued altogether when adultery became rampant and the husbands were as guilty as the wives they were accusing. Equity was actually more important than you think!

Finally, if you look at the mitzvah of *sotah* in context, it was actually a very good thing for the woman! Imagine a woman suspected of adultery by her husband in a Middle Eastern culture of 3,500 years ago. I don't know much about Hittite or Jebusite jurisprudence but I would imagine it would not be too far-fetched to assume that there were cultures where "honor killings" or other forms of vigilante justice would have been meted out. This mitzvah actually gave the irate husband something to do about it, and the necessary trip to Jerusalem provided a cooling-down period in which he might drop the charges altogether. So it may seem pretty horrific when viewed through 21st-century Western goggles but our goggles are not the only ones that there have ever been.

Pulling the Plug

Q. Does Judaism permit taking a patient off of life support?

A. This is a sensitive topic and I address it with two caveats. The first is that issues such as this are far above my pay grade. Accordingly, while I am striving to impart information, I am definitely not attempting to rule in any matter of law. If anyone ever has a question of practical application in this area, he should contact a recognized Torah authority. (This is beyond the usual level of "ask your local Orthodox rabbi.")

The second caveat is that there are no doubt readers who have had occasion to address such end-of-life issues. Some of these readers may have acted counter to what I will soon say is Jewish law. No one is judging you. Having a terminally-ill loved one is a terribly difficult situation and no two cases are exactly alike. As the Mishna in *Pirkei Avos* (2:5) says, we are not to judge another person until we have been in his or her place.

That having been said, the Jewish philosophy on life support is predicated on the belief that all life is sacred and is to be protected at virtually any cost. If a person will die from fasting on Yom Kippur, not only may he eat, he is required to do so. Similarly, in a life-threatening situation, one must violate Shabbos to call an ambulance or take someone to the hospital. Any mitzvah must be violated to preserve human life except for murder, incest/adultery, and idolatry.

Also integral in Jewish law's outlook on this topic is the fact that Judaism has no concept of "quality of life." All human life is equally sacred. An adult is not more entitled to life than an infant. An adolescent is not more deserving of life than a senior citizen. All of us—male or female, wise or foolish, able-bodied or infirm—everyone has an equal claim to survival.

This includes the terminally ill.

The Talmud (*Shabbos* 151b) tells us that one who closes the eyes of a dying person, hastening death by mere moments, is a full-fledged murderer. One who performs an act of euthanasia on a dying person could be executed for murder, the same as one who kills a healthy person (*Mishneh Torah Hilchos Rotzeiach* 2:7).

The idea that we don't evaluate a person's "quality of life" is a very good thing in that it keeps us from drawing lines between those we think have a reason to live and those we might deem to have no cause to keep on breathing. Our position is that everyone has a reason to live. We may not always understand another person's "quality of life" but God does and He has told us to preserve life. This can be challenging, however, when dealing with end-of-life issues. If someone is in a coma or in pain, our emotions may tell us otherwise. But God does not want us to start picking and choosing who we, in our limited wisdom, think deserving of life. Our job is to preserve it.

On the other hand, we also have an obligation to alleviate suffering. This, as they say, is where things get interesting. We might do what we can to reduce a dying patient's pain, even though some treatments may be life-shortening. Or perhaps we refrain from forms of treatment that might extend the patient's life. (Remember: every case is different and a competent Torah authority must be consulted!)

When prolonging life and alleviating suffering clash, there are a number of factors involved in the decision-making process. Is the person going to die regardless of whether or not the treatment is administered? Is he or she undergoing great suffering? Do we know their wishes? (A living will is highly advisable to make one's wishes known!) These are some of the main factors in evaluating such a case.

Pain medications like morphine are often given to terminal patients in order to alleviate their suffering. However, in addition to lessening pain, such drugs may also cause them to pass away sooner. Despite this unfortunate side effect, such drugs should not be withheld in all cases. Jewish law permits these narcotics to be administered provided that the intention is strictly to relieve the patient's suffering and not to hasten his passing.

It must be noted that there is a difference between forgoing potentially life-extending treatments like surgery or chemotherapy and withholding food, water or oxygen. These things are considered to be staples of life and withholding them from the patient may be the functional equivalent of murder. (Imagine withholding food from an infant. Why should keeping it from someone on life support be any different?)

Lots of issues fall into this category. For example, is a DNR (a "do not resuscitate" order) permitted under Jewish law? What about a DNI ("do not intubate"—i.e., putting someone on a respirator)? The answers to these and other questions may vary from case to case. I cannot stress enough the need to contact someone well-versed in this area of Jewish law.

End-of-life issues are never easy. Trying to do what's best for the patient is difficult to assess as the course of action to end their suffering may not always jibe with the course of action to extend their life. As trying as the situation is, the Torah provides us with the tools we need to walk that tightrope, all based upon the underlying premise that the patient's life and well-being are just as valuable and important now as they ever were.

Permitted Rape?

Q. I heard recently that an Orthodox rabbi said that Israeli soldiers are allowed to rape women in war. Is this true? If it is, how could that be part of Judaism?

A. You're referring to something that the new candidate for chief rabbi of the IDF is reported to have said in the past. It's important to note that the IDF issued a statement clarifying that Rabbi Karim's comment was "the answer to a theoretical question and not in any way whatsoever a question of practical Jewish law. Rabbi Karim has never written, said or even thought that an IDF soldier is permitted to sexually assault a woman in war—anyone who interprets his words otherwise is completely mistaken."

The numerous articles I saw on the subject all included the IDF's clarification but buried it at the very end of the pieces. I don't know what this rabbi actually said or meant, so I won't conjecture, but I can explain what Jewish law believes:

Sexual assault is horrific, and the idea that it could even be theoretically permitted in the Torah is very troubling. Thankfully, in today's world, sexual assault is 100% forbidden by Jewish law. Unfortunately, in a very different era, thousands of years ago, the Torah permitted a way for a soldier at war to marry a woman in a city he conquered—against her will. As you will see, though, it went to great lengths to try to discourage this behavior.

The mitzvah called is *eishes yifas to'ar*—"woman of attractive form" (Deuteronomy 21:10-14). In this mitzvah, a soldier in a time of war was permitted to abduct a girl (from the enemy) to whom he was attracted. He was supposed to give her a mourning period (of one month) for being taken from her family. During this time, she would cry, shave her head and let her nails grow out. The idea was that—hopefully—all this would make her less attractive to him, with the result that he would get over that initial urge he felt (the kind of raping-and-pillaging urge that came with many ancient wars). Once again able to think clearly, he would then send her back home. If he was still interested in her at the end of the mourning period, the Torah did permit him to convert her and marry her, but it did not allow him to keep her as a servant, because even a captive from the enemy deserves human dignity.

Neither the Torah nor the rabbis specifically wanted this to ever take place. Rashi on Deuteronomy 21:11 cites the Talmud (*Kiddushin* 21b) that this mitzvah was only given to assuage a soldier's *yeitzer hara* (evil inclination) in the hopes that having a permissible course of action would keep him from acting worse impermissibly. Rashi further cites the Midrash Tanchuma, which makes note of the context of the *eishes yifas to'ar*, as follows:

> The mitzvah of *eishes yifas to'ar* (Deuteronomy 21:10-14) is followed by the law of a man with two wives. His first-born son is the child of his "hated" wife and he wants to give the portion of the first-born to the (younger) child of his "beloved" wife. [He may not do so, by the way. This is in Deuteronomy 21:15-17.] This is followed by the law of a *ben soreir u'moreh*—the "stubborn and rebellious son" (Deuteronomy 21:18-21).

The *ben soreir u'moreh* drinks alcohol and eats meat to excess, disobeys his parents in every way, and instead of listening to their rebuke, tells his parents what to do. He demands that they pay for his excessive lifestyle and when they don't, he steals. The parents then must present themselves before the *beis din* (Jewish court) and inform the judges of their son's iniquities. The Torah then instructs the court to sentence the boy to death.

The Tanchuma cited by Rashi explains the sequence of events: if one cannot control his passions, he may marry the *eishes yifas to'ar* but we don't recommend it. She will just end up being hated and the child of such a union will end up being a *ben soreir u'moreh*.

Now this is important: even though the law of a *ben soreir u'moreh* is in the Torah, the laws are so specific that the Talmud (*Sanhedrin* 71a) says that it was never carried out and never could be carried out; it is taught strictly for the lesson it imparts. If the Midrash says that the ultimate fate of an *eishes yifas to'ar* is to become a hated wife and later to bear a *ben soreir u'moreh*, and there never was a *ben soreir u'moreh*, it would not be too far a stretch to infer that there might never have been an *eishes yifas to'ar* either. (We can't say this definitively but if there were any, it certainly wasn't a common occurrence. We don't see any examples of it in all the wars described throughout Tanach.) [What about Maacah, mother of Avshalom? See the addendum following this entry.]

So why have this mitzvah at all? The rationale underlying this mitzvah is that soldiers are going to behave a certain way in times of war. If we give them a permissible means, there is a possibility they will show restraint. This mitzvah—like the laws of sacrifices, slavery, polygamy, and many others—serves as a "halfway house" to wean us as a society off of undesirable behaviors and into a higher moral order. It is a means to an end, not the end itself. If the soldiers take the good advice not to take an *eishes yifas to'ar* as a wife (though technically permitted), all the better.

But what about today? Is there any practical application of this law? Many *mitzvos* only apply under certain conditions—when the Temple is standing, when all twelve Tribes reside in the land, when there's a sovereign Jewish nation, etc. The laws of warfare detailed in Deuteronomy—including the mitzvah of the *eishes yifas to'ar*—generally fall into the category of things that are not practiced today. So *eishes yifas to'ar*—which was always discouraged, even in Biblical times—is not even a hypothetical option in modern warfare. It's prohibited in both theory and practice. (Some may wonder about the Messianic era, but those days are promised to be an era of peace—"they will beat their swords into plowshares... nation will not lift sword against nation, nor will they make war any more"—Isaiah 2:4—so I can't see a law about prisoners of war becoming relevant even with the return of the Temple and sovereignty.)

Addendum: Maacah, Mother of Avshalom

When preparing the response to the *eishes yifas to'ar*, I was asked to include that (a) *eishes yifas to'ar* leads to *ben soreir u'moreh*, and (b) that there never was a *ben soreir u'moreh*, therefore (c) there must never have been an *eishes yifas to'ar*. I said that, while the logic is sound, Chazal don't say that as they do about the *ben soreir u'moreh* so we can only propose it as a possibility, which is what we did. But what about Maacah, mother of Avshalom, whom the Midrash says was an *eishes yifas to'ar*? You will note that I only say there aren't any in Tanach, not that there aren't any in Midrash. That's a completely different story.

Midrashim (and *aggados*) are not always meant as literal history. Often (I believe usually), they are allegories, meant to illustrate moral lessons. Midrashim frequently contradict one another. For example, Midrash A says that Job was not a historical person; he was a fictional character created by Moshe in a parable. Midrash B tells how Pharaoh had three advisors, Jethro, Balaam, and Job, each of whom was repaid by God according to the advice they gave. If I accept Midrash A as literal (which I do), I can only accept Midrash B as allegorical.

So we have Midrashim that say (1) *eishes yifas to'ar* inevitably leads to *ben soreir u'moreh*; (2) there never was a *ben soreir u'moreh*; (3) Maacah was an *eishes yifas to'ar*. One cannot accept all three literally, as their conclusions contradict. I do not believe that the Midrash is making a literal biographical statement about Maacah. Rather, it is explaining how David (who was righteous) could raise a kid as rotten as Avshalom, who led an armed rebellion against him. Basically, this Midrash makes the same point that Rashi makes based upon the juxtaposition of topics, namely that a relationship based upon *eishes yifas to'ar* is a bad idea and will lead to a messed-up family dynamic with kids who act out based upon that.

One can certainly accept the Midrash about Maacah literally—it's certainly not as far-fetched as, say, Pharoah's daughter stretching her arm like Plastic Man. I have accounted for the possibility of taking it literally by saying that, even if *eishes yifas to'ar* did occur, it does not appear to have been common. But the Midrashic comment is not a historical account.

While we're at it, the Talmud (*Sanhedrin* 21a) says that David's daughter Tamar was the daughter of an *eishes yifas to'ar* but there are many other opinions as to the relationship between Amnon and Tamar. Were they full siblings, half-siblings, step-siblings…? Again, there are contradicting opinions so the statement that she was the daughter of an *eishes yifas to'ar* is not necessarily the historically-accurate position. (As an aside, the Gemara in that very same piece says that Jewish women have neither armpit hair nor pubic hair, though I'm pretty sure that Chazal knew they do. As always, one may take such statements as literally or as allegorically as one likes.)

Animal Sacrifices

Q: *I am troubled by the mitzvah of animal sacrifices. We are taught to pray for the third Beis HaMikdash. If these commandments were just for ancient time, why all the daily prayers for and reminders of those practices?*

A: The purpose of the sacrifices is not to inflict pain on an animal; that's an unfortunate consequence. Regarding nature, God told Adam two things: to subdue it (Genesis 1:28) but also to guard it (Genesis 2:15). We see that we are permitted to use nature but not to abuse it. Hurting an animal out of cruelty is absolutely prohibited (this possibly even includes hunting for sport). But for needs, like food, we are permitted to kill animals, as our needs supersede theirs. This is true not just for physical needs, but also for spiritual needs, such as sacrifices.

Let me try a different approach—and this may blow your mind a little but here it is! In *Moreh Nevuchim*, the Rambam says that the Beis HaMikdash (Temple) was *not* the ultimate form of service that Hashem desired! Think about it: there was only one Temple. People could not offer sacrifices anywhere else. People could not train to be *kohanim*—you had to be born a *kohein*. Even if you lived in Yerushalayim, you couldn't go to the Mikdash whenever you wanted—there were a dozen forms of *tumah* (ritual impurity) that would keep people from attending! (Marital relations, bodily emissions, corpses, certain dead vermin, etc.) If God wanted us to go to the Mikdash and to offer *korbanos* (sacrifices), He certainly made it challenging! Contrast this with shuls the way we have them now (and, by the way, shuls *did* exist in Bible times as well). Shuls are everywhere and we go to them all the time. *Halacha* minimizes going to the Beis HaMikdash and maximizes going to shul—clearly, going to shul is the thing God wants us to do more!

If this is the case, why did God command that the Beis HaMikdash be built at all? Why didn't He just tell us to build shuls wherever we might live? The answer, the Rambam explains, is that the Mikdash was kind of a "halfway house." The Jews were surrounded by cultures that had temples, priests and sacrifices—it was all they knew! If God had said, "Effectively immediately, sacrifices, incense and libations are replaced by reciting *Shemoneh Esrei* and reading the Torah," the people would not have been able to adjust. The Temple was designed to transition the Jews from the practices of an idolatrous society to the way we have davening now.

It seems your ultimate concern is if sacrifices will be practiced again when the Beis HaMikdash is rebuilt. Who knows? Will we still refrain from eating chicken with milk, which is a rabbinic law? I assume so, since there were also rabbinic laws in Temple times. Will Ashkenazim still refrain from eating *kitniyos* (legumes) on Pesach? I have no idea. For that matter, I have no idea whether Pesach will still be celebrated since there is an opinion that the holidays will be suspended in the time of the third Temple. So will the *sotah* process be restored when the Mikdash is rebuilt? Will there be slavery or polygamy? I have no clue. Similarly, there are different opinions as to the practice of animal sacrifices in the rebuilt Temple. All we know for sure is that the time of the third Beis HaMikdash will be an era of peace and universal recognition of one God, without oppression. Beyond that, the details remain to be seen.

Religious Wars

Q: *How can one justify the killing of entire nations (which seems similar to Islamic holy wars) and killing the children of foreign nations?*

A: This is an extremely challenging topic and I'm the first to admit that I struggle with it as well. It would be easy to shrug it off as the product of a less-civilized time, or to say "do not question the will of God!" but the reality is that we're encouraged to question things—"All that God has said, we will do and we will hear" (Exodus 24:7). We agree to observe the commandments even as we struggle to understand them. What I can tell you is that, as is the case with so many other *mitzvos*, the reality of the situation is far more nuanced than most people assume from a surface reading.

The Torah does not encourage (or permit) genocide. There were rules of combat the army had to observe—extending offers of peace among them. Even when they did go to war, they had to leave one side open as an escape route for their enemies. This is true even of the seven Canaanite nations. Even members of Amalek could renounce their nation's evil ways and be safe—we see an Amalekite convert in *sefer Shmuel* (the book of Samuel), plus the Gemara says that Haman had descendants who studied Torah in B'nei Brak. (Some say that Rabbi Akiva was one of them!)

But what about children, whom we would normally consider to be non-combatants? Practically speaking, they don't really have the opportunity to renounce their nation's ways, so how do we justify including them in this obligation? We don't. We know that there is collateral damage in war, whether it's carpet bombing in Vietnam or the siege on the Branch Davidian compound in Waco, but this is still a difficult concept for us. Since we don't know who is descended from Amalek anymore, we are relieved of the burden of having to carry out this commandment, leaving our conflicted feelings strictly in the realm of the hypothetical.

COVID-19

As I write this, the world is locked down because of the global coronavirus pandemic. While I pray that quarantine and social distancing will be a distant memory by the time this sees print, we are experiencing a societal game-changer. Accordingly, I am including some of the coronavirus-themed questions that I have received.

Navigating COVID-19 Through Halachic Precedent

Q. Is there anything in Jewish texts from past plagues that could help us navigate the coronavirus?

A. The Torah tells us (Exodus 21:19) that if one person injures another, the offender is responsible to pay the doctor's bill to heal him. The Talmud (*Brachos* 60) points out from this that we are supposed to utilize medical assistance rather than relying on prayer and faith alone.

However, consider the case of King Asa. Though he was a righteous king, we see that he is criticized because, when he fell ill, he put his trust in doctors alone, to the exclusion of God (II Chronicles 16).

The point is clear: we need both things. We need *emunah* (faith) but we also need *hishtadlus* (human effort). Accordingly, if we want to end a plague, we need to do our part. Some of our efforts may be spiritual in nature but Judaism doesn't believe in "thoughts and prayers" to the exclusion of action.

There was a plague in *parshas Korach* (Numbers 17), sparked by the rebellious nature of our ancestors in the wilderness. The Torah tells us that

Moshe's brother Aharon "put on the incense and atoned for the people; he stood between the dead and the living, and the plague was stopped" (verses 12-13).

Similarly, there was a plague in II Samuel 24, which stopped when it reached the threshing floor of a man named Aravna the Jebusite. From this, David knew that the threshing floor of Aravna was the site where the Temple was meant to be built.

It's obvious from these examples that spiritual things have the power to halt plagues but here's the wake-up call: you're not Aharon and I'm not David. We need physical methods in addition to the spiritual.

Rabbi Daniel Glatstein recently gave a brief *shiur* on Rebbe Akiva Eiger's directions to his followers during the 1830 cholera epidemic. Not surprisingly, Rabbi Eiger's advice included some spiritual components, such as to recite Psalms 91 (*Yosheiv b'seiser*) and 142 (A *maskil* of David), as well as *parshas haketores*, the section describing the incense service in the Temple. (*Parshas haketores* can be found in many *siddurim* as part of the preliminary morning service. The reason for its recitation in such an instance is because of the demonstrated power of the Temple incense to ward off plagues.)

But equally important, Rabbi Eiger advised his followers in more temporal matters as well. He advised them not to gather together, prohibiting more than 15 people in shul at a time. He advised that people stay warm, eat well and keep their homes clean of any filth. He told them to get sunlight and to change into clean clothes regularly.

There's one crucial piece of advice that others might have overlooked: he told them not to worry. This should not be discounted, as a person's state of mind can potentially make him more susceptible to illness.

I think this is a good model for us to follow. Absolutely accept a mitzvah upon yourself. Recite *Tehillim*. Pay extra attention when reciting *asher yatzar*, which is a prayer that acknowledges the role that God plays in keeping us healthy. Use your extra time at home to listen to some Torah classes online.

But don't be misled into thinking that these things magically make you immune. God has told us in the Torah that we're also to utilize doctors and we're held responsible for recklessly endangering ourselves and others. Therefore, follow local rules for social distancing. Wash your hands appropriately. Stay home and stop the spread.

And, to paraphrase Rebbe Akiva Eiger, don't freak out. We're all anxious. We're all stressed. Panic, however, won't do anybody any good.

Misplaced Piety

Q. We see people who insisted on davening with a minyan now catching and spreading this virus. What Jewish laws are people breaking when they act with such misplaced piety?

A. You're being generous by referring to it as "misplaced piety." The term you're actually looking for is *chasid shoteh*—a "pious idiot." The Mishna in *Sotah* (3:4) teaches us that a pious idiot, a subtle sinner, a holier-than-thou woman and self-flagellating Pharisees all ruin the world; in each of these cases, the reason is because of their superficial piety. Since we're leading up to the pious idiot, let's define these, starting from the latter:

Self-flagellating Pharisees are people who beat themselves to show others how pious and humble they are. An example would be one who lowers his gaze so as not to look at women even though doing so causes him to walk into walls.

A holier-than-thou woman is one who prays all the time but her actions don't match up with the façade that she presents.

An example of a subtle sinner is one who subtly influences a judge before the opposing litigant has arrived—such a person sins with "plausible deniability." (The Gemara provides a number of other examples.)

Which brings us to the pious idiot. The Gemara on this Mishna (on page 21b) defines a pious idiot as a man who sees a woman drowning but refuses to save her because doing so would be immodest. Tosfos on this Gemara gives another example, from the Talmud Yerushalmi: a man who sees a child drowning so he starts to take off his *tefillin*. While he's busy removing the *tefillin*, the child drowns.

The self-flagellating Pharisee is a danger to himself: he's so determined to show off his piety that he risks self-injury. The "pious idiot" is a danger to others. He's so concerned with his own personal piety that he's willing to let *you* drown! He may be acting sincerely but his actions are no less dangerous.

When it comes to "pious idiocy," the best real-life example I can think of is the notorious 2002 fire that occurred at a girls' school in Mecca, Saudi Arabia. Fifteen students died because the Committee for the Promotion of Virtue and the Prevention of Vice—AKA the "religious police"—wouldn't let the girls leave the school without the socially-accepted garb. (In Saudi Arabia, women appearing in public wear a long black cloak called an *abaya*.) Happily, the Saudi authorities took the incident seriously. Following a government inquiry into the tragedy, control of the girls' schools was moved from a religious agency to the Ministry of Education.

(I chose this example not to pick on our Muslim cousins, because I'm sure there are plenty of analogous examples involving Christians and Jews. I cited this incident only because it's a well-documented calamity that actually resulted from misplaced piety rather than a speculative case of what might happen.)

Which brings us to *minyanim* in the time of COVID-19. Happily, most of our religious authorities are aligning with the CDC and WHO in this matter but there are a few outliers. I saw, for example, one community leader who assured his followers that if they continue to daven with a *minyan* but are careful to refrain from talking in shul, that they would not contract the coronavirus. I don't know his source for this assertion but you'll forgive me if I choose to follow the majority.

Rav Hershel Schachter is one such authority who agrees with the medical (and halachic) consensus. The March 18-24 edition of the *Jewish Vues* cites Rabbi Schachter as saying, "The mitzvah to safeguard and preserve life overrides all *mitzvos haTorah*. It is not a *midas chassidus* to ignore *saconas nefoshos*. On the contrary, it is expressly and strictly forbidden. In the words of the Ba'alei haTosfos "*domov be-rosho*"; such an individual is culpable for any loss of life r"l (*Rachmana litzlan*) that ensues."

Translating the Hebrew phrases, "The obligation to safeguard and preserve life overrides all the commandments of the Torah. It is not a trait of piety to ignore mortal danger. On the contrary, it is expressly and strictly forbidden. In the words of the authors of Tosfos, "responsibility for his blood is on his own head"; such an individual is culpable for any loss of life—God preserve us—that ensues."

You asked what laws one might violate through reckless endangerment. Well, there you go!

Years ago, when I worked for NCSY, a teen complained to me that her father yelled at her because he had to take her to the hospital on a Friday night. He blamed her for causing him to have to "break Shabbos." I explained to her that such was not the case. Under normal circumstances, we don't drive on Shabbos. Under other circumstances—such as if someone needs to go to the hospital—we do drive. That's not "breaking" Shabbos, it's *keeping* Shabbos because this is what the *halacha* requires!

This is true in many areas. Normally, we blow shofar on Rosh Hashana—it's a mitzvah! But we don't when the first day of Rosh Hashana falls on Shabbos. Even though doing so is called for by the Torah, the Rabbis forbade it to preserve the sanctity of the Sabbath. In most years, we show our love for Hashem by blowing the shofar; in other years, we show our love by *not* blowing the shofar, even though we really want to.

That's what's going on here. Under normal circumstances, we gather in our shuls to pray. But these are not normal circumstances and desperate times call for desperate measures. As with blowing the shofar on Shabbos, the proper course of action here is to refrain. The more one wishes he could attend his normal minyan, the more he will be rewarded for not doing so.

Is This the End Times?

Q. Does Coronavirus mean we're in the end of days? People I know say this is the end and either Moshiach or the war of Gog and Magog is imminent.

A. This question made me shake my head a little because of the things people are telling you. First things first, calm down about COVID-19. Yes, it's serious, and yes, we should absolutely follow Center for Disease Control recommendations, but this isn't the thing that's going to take down the human race.

We've gotten a little spoiled because our modern hygiene has eradicated so much disease. We have soap, vaccines, antibiotics, hand sanitizer, disposable cups, and a thousand other things that keep us healthy in ways that previous generations never could have imagined. Back in the day, if a cut got infected, you could die. We pour peroxide on it and forget about it. People died from diarrhea. We drink Gatorade to replenish our electrolytes and go back to work.

We've had health crises before, of course. I don't know how old you are so I don't know what you remember first-hand but I remember the Ebola scare (2014), SARS (2002), the AIDS crisis (1985) and Legionnaires' Disease (1976)—all of them serious, and yes, there were fatalities, but none of them wiped out mankind, leaving behind a civilization of damned dirty apes. (Depending on your age, you may not even know what SARS or Legionnaires' Disease is. There's a good chance that twenty years from now, teens will be going, "What was COVID-19?")

Coronavirus isn't even that deadly as plagues go. It's pretty much only threatening to the elderly and people with compromised immune systems. This is certainly terrible but the overwhelming number of people who contract the virus recover. The average person is more likely to die in a fire than he or she is from COVID-19. Perhaps the lesson here is that we should be more zealous in checking our smoke detectors.

COVID-19, while undeniably terrible, is not a doomsday scenario for the human race. But what if it was going to wipe out a significant portion of humanity? Would *that* be a sign of the end times? Short answer: nope.

Remember what I said about us being fortunate to live in an era of vaccinations and antibiotics? Well, most of mankind wasn't so fortunate, and plagues were just another part of life. Biblically, we see plagues in Numbers chapter 17 (death toll 14,700) and in II Samuel 24 (death toll 70,000). These plagues were limited to the Jewish nation and represented significant portions of the population. Historically, the Black Plague in 1340 killed as many as 200 million—about a quarter of the world population! Any of these represents a much higher mortality rate than the coronavirus and yet none of them triggered the end times.

So what would be signs that the arrival of Moshiach is imminent? For that, we turn to the Talmudic tractate of *Sotah* (49b), where it presents the following scenarios:

> In the time preceding the arrival of Moshiach, people will be more impertinent and inflation will run rampant. Even though produce will be abundant, wine will be expensive. The government will turn to heresy but no one will be in a position to give rebuke about it. The meeting places (of the Sages) will become places of promiscuity, Galilee will be destroyed and the Golan will be desolate. The people from the border towns will travel from city to city seeking charity but no one will have pity on them. The wisdom of Torah scholars will be scoffed at and God-fearing people will be looked down upon. Truth will be ignored. Young people will have no respect for their elders, who will have to stand up for the young. Sons will disgrace their fathers, daughters will contend with their mothers, and daughters-in-law with their mothers-in-law. A person's enemies will be the members of his own family. The generation will act like a dog (with so-called "leaders" yielding to popular opinion) and sons will have no shame in front of their fathers.

Now, I'm not saying that Moshiach's arrival *isn't* imminent—after all, we do have a lot of those things in our generation!—I'm just saying that a plague isn't one of the signs we've been given.

Now, since you mentioned it, the war of "Gog and Magog" is one possible pre-Messianic scenario. (There's more than one way that Moshiach can come—the "easy way" and the "hard way." The war of Gog and Magog is the hard way.) This war is discussed by name in Ezekiel chapters 38-39, not by name in Isaiah chapter 18, and is obliquely referenced in Zechariah chapter 14. Counter to popular misconception, it is not a war between nations called Gog and Magog; it's a war provoked by a leader called Gog, who rules a nation referred to as Magog. (These are code words and not their actual names.) Gog and his allies will attack the Jewish exiles returning to Israel but God will ultimately direct His wrath upon the invaders. Gog will regroup his forces for a second attack, after which they will be destroyed. It's an unpleasant scenario that we wish to avoid but, again, a plague isn't part of it.

I'm not saying that COVID-19 isn't serious; it absolutely is. And I'm not stating definitively that Moshiach's arrival isn't imminent; for all I know, it might be. I'm just saying that the former isn't a sign of the latter. As far as declaring that the "end times" are upon us, let us remember that the Sages of the Talmud cursed those who would try to calculate the Moshiach's arrival (*Sanhedrin* 97b). The reason is that, should one's calculations prove faulty (which, historically, all such calculations to date have), people may not conclude that you made a mistake. Rather, they might conclude that your math was right and there must be no Moshiach. Accordingly, our appropriate course of action is not to try to figure out God's calendar, it's to have faith and to anticipate Moshiach's arrival in the proper time. To that end, the Gemara cites Isaiah 30:18, "Therefore Hashem will wait so that He might be gracious to you… happy are all who wait for Him."

Re-Opening the Country According to Jewish Ethics

Q. As the world considers opening back up again in the middle of a pandemic to stave off economic doom and mental health and domestic violence deaths, is there any wisdom we can turn to in Jewish ethics to decide what's the least bad way to proceed?

A. The situation you describe is similar to the famous "trolley problem," a philosophical no-win scenario posed in its modern form by Philippa Foot in 1967. (It had historical precedents.) The current form of the dilemma is as follows:

You're standing near the switch that controls some train tracks while a runaway trolley is heading towards five people who are tied to the tracks. You can pull the lever, which will redirect the trolley onto another track, where there's only one person bound to the track. Your options are to do nothing and five people die, or to pull the lever and only one person dies.

The consequentialist school of thought would favor pulling the lever, positing that the best course of action is the one that yields the greatest good, in this case a minimum loss of life. The deontological school of thought, however, would have you refrain from pulling the lever on the basis that one's actions are inherently ethical or unethical regardless of their outcome.

Judaism does indeed have similar dilemmas and I'd have to say that our approach more closely approximates the deontological approach.

There's a well-known Talmudic dictum that if someone tells you to kill a third party or that he will kill you, you have to give up your own life rather than murder the third party (*Pesachim* 25b). This is true even if sacrificing one innocent person's life can potentially save many people. The Talmud Yerushalmi (*Terumos* 8:4) discusses a situation in which a group of travelers is confronted by a gang of brigands. The criminals say, "Give us one of your group to kill or we'll kill all of you." They may not throw an innocent person to the metaphorical wolves even if it means that they'll all be killed.[9]

Now, you might think that saving life takes priority over absolutely everything. Usually, it does. We don't hesitate to eat non-kosher foods, to drive on Shabbos or to eat on Yom Kippur if necessary to save a life but there are exceptions. Consider, if you will, the case described in *Sanhedrin* 75a. A certain man was so overcome with lust for a certain woman that he became seriously ill. His doctors said that he would die if he didn't have sex with that woman. They asked the rabbis, who said that he should die rather than let her have relations with him. The doctors said that she should at least let him see her naked and the rabbis replied that he should die rather than let him see her naked. Finally, the doctors said that at the very least he should be permitted to talk to her in private from behind a fence in order to derive some small pleasure from her. The rabbis replied that he should die rather than let him talk to her from behind a fence.

You'll note that this fellow's health is not a reason this woman has

---

9. This is different from the case of Sheva ben Bichri in II Samuel 20. Sheva ben Bichri instigated a revolt against King David so the army tracked him down. They were prepared to destroy the city that was giving him refuge, so the residents gave him up. That case has two important differences: (1) the army was demanding Sheva; the people didn't have to choose a victim and (2) Sheva was actually guilty of a capital offense.

to allow herself to be treated like a prostitute. You'll also notice that his situation changed quite a bit. There's a long way from "he'll die if he doesn't sleep with her" to "let him talk to her from behind a fence." Perhaps he wasn't in as imminent danger as they first said! They appear to have overstated the danger in the hopes of justifying the action they wanted to take.

There's also a difference between taking action and remaining passive, a point that is made in several different contexts throughout the Talmud (*Eiruvin* 100a, *et al.*). Tosfos on *Sanhedrin* 74b (*s.v. v'ha Esther*) apply this to our case in which one must allow himself to be killed rather than kill another. That, they tell us, is only the case when one is forced to take action. But what about acting passively? For example, let's say that a thug threatens to kill a person if he doesn't allow that criminal to pick him up and throw him on top of an infant. That may be terrible but one need not sacrifice his life rather than comply because it entails no action on his part. When coerced to do something actively, the logic is "who says that your life is more important than the other guy's?" When coerced to do something passively, the logic is "who says that the other guy's life is more important than yours?"

Finally, there's the question of how much danger one must assume in order to save others. If another person is drowning, I don't have to save him if it means that I'll certainly drown doing so. But what if the odds are 4 to 1 that I'll drown? What about 10 to 1? What about 100 to 1? What's the point at which I'm obligated to take a risk in order to save another? The *Mishnah Brurah* (329:19) rules that, while we need not endanger our own lives to save others, we must also be careful to make honest evaluations and not skew the results to get ourselves off the hook. (Leviticus 19:16 says, "Do not stand by when another is endangered; I am Hashem." Why does the verse conclude "I am Hashem?" Because if we claim to have refrained due to personal danger, He knows whether or not such was truly the case.)

There is a certain logic in getting back to work because the collapse of the global economy affects everyone. As Spock puts it in the *Star Trek* franchise, "The needs of the many outweigh the needs of the few." But when I see protestors holding signs saying, "Let the weak die," it disgusts me. Such signs make it clear that their motivations are selfish and reprehensible, not a difficult choice between two no-win scenarios. Those are people who are not objectively evaluating the situation. If they don't get their way, they'll say, "At least let us talk to her from behind a fence."

Ruling on this issue is far above my paygrade but it seems to me that the proper course of action is to continue the quarantine until it's medically justifiable to go out. The certain threat of death to the elderly and immunocompromised trumps the financial impact and potential threats to others. (And let's be honest, even young and healthy people can and have died from COVID-19, so there's a potential threat to everyone's life!) But most of all, we don't save ourselves by throwing others under the bus—or in this case, the trolley.

Wearing a Mask and Social Distancing

Q. What is the Torah perspective on wearing a mask and social distancing?

A. That you should do it.

Afterword

by Allison Josephs
Founder and Director, Jew in the City

In 2005, after working in the world of Jewish outreach for several years, I had a realization: less knowledgeable and observant Jews would have no reason to explore Jewish texts or observance because they have major hang-ups with both the traditional understanding of Judaism as well as its most devout adherents, i.e., Orthodox Jews.

I was raised with these hang-ups, despite being a proud Conservative Jew. My introduction to an Orthodox Judaism that I could conceive of for myself began with meeting Orthodox Jews who were nothing like the old-fashioned, closed-minded people I expected them to be. Instead, in my late teens, I encountered thinking, kind, educated, open-minded people whose Jewish practice enhanced their lives as opposed to being bothersome, empty restrictions.

My discovery of a Judaism that could offer wisdom in challenging times, was bold enough to confront difficulties in the Torah, and attached deep meaning to ancient rituals was the second step in my being ready to start a journey to observance

These are two ingredients I used to build Jew in the City, an organization I founded in 2007 with the mission of reversing negative associations of religious Jews by putting forth an approach based on kindness, tolerance, sincerity, and critical thinking and making engaging and meaningful Orthodox Judaism known and accessible.

We present our readers and viewers with examples of Orthodox Jews that shatter their negative associations about them, and we offer them a Torah that is inspiring and relevant. We don't shy away from asking or answering tough questions. In fact, we encourage them.

At the beginning of our website's launch, I was asking and answering the tough questions myself. Our organization was new and small, and I hadn't learned how to fundraise yet. As Jew in the City began to grow, more people began sending in comments and questions, more content needed to be created. I tried to figure out how to replicate my style, which was clearly resonating with many. My standards were high and I wasn't sure what to do.

Then I met a man named Rabbi Jack Abramowitz. It was 2013 and I was taking a tour of the OU and NCSY offices. After a brief meeting, Rabbi Abramowitz sent me a couple of his books and several of his pamphlets on hard-to-understand Jewish concepts, and I was blown away.

Here was an educator, who had a similar way of making *mitzvos* relatable to today's generation. His style wasn't exactly like what was on the site at the time, but it was wonderfully engaging and down to earth and, most importantly, could take some of the most challenging topics in the Torah and Jewish law and explain them in a way that personally helped even me.

We did not have too much funding to speak of, but my feeling has always been "if you don't try, it's a definite 'no,' if you do try, it's a possible 'yes.'" So I called Rabbi Abramowitz and told him that I was sure he would never consider such a thing, but would he join our team as a volunteer, to bring our readers his incredible insights and talents, and without missing a beat, he accepted.

I have seen Rabbi Abramowitz, a true Torah scholar (as well as a comic book aficionado and onetime CrossFit fanatic!), take the time to engage in lengthy discussions with Jews who have some of the most difficult issues with the Torah and help them finally come to peace with them. Some of those exchanges made it into this book, many of them did not. Rabbi Abramowitz gives a fellow Jew troubled by politically incorrect passages or theologically challenging concepts just as much time one-on-one as he does for an article or a book that can reach the masses. His talent and knowledge are matched only by his generosity of spirit and patience.

To this day, if I encounter a difficulty in the text or a challenging halachic topic I had not heard of before, Rabbi Abramowitz is one of the first people I turn to, and more often than not, he has a satisfying reading of the text, a deeper way to understand the halacha. Not every single question out there has an answer that we can grasp, but if the answer is out there, Rabbi Abramowitz likely will have it.

He has been a tremendous resource not only to our organization and our millions of readers, but to me personally. *Klal Yisrael* must have done something very right to have merited a leader like Rabbi Abramowitz in our generation.

Allison Josephs
New York, NY
Elul 5780

Made in the USA
Coppell, TX
23 April 2021